MICROSOFT ACCESS 2000

EDWARD G. MARTIN

CHARLES S. PARKER

CHARLES E. KEE

This manual contains numerous features that help you master the material quickly and reinforce your learning:

- *A Note about the Manual's Organization.* The topics in this manual are presented in three units, beginning with basic and moving to advanced skills. Within each unit, the topics have been divided into mastery sets, which are sequential by independent tutorials, allowing you or your instructor to skip sections or cover topics in a different order.

- *A Table of Contents.* A list of the manual's contents appears on the first page of the manual. Each unit starts with an outline, a list of learning objectives, and an overview that summarizes the skills you will learn.

- *Bold Key Terms.* Important terms appear in bold type as they are introduced. They are also conveniently listed at the end of each unit, with page references for further review.

- *Color as a Learning Tool.* In this manual, color has been used to help you work through each unit. Each step is numbered in green for easy identification. Within each step, text or commands that you should type appear in orange boxes. Single keys to be pressed are shown in yellow boxes. For example:

    1 Type WIN and press ↵

- *Step-by-Step Mouse Approach.* This manual stresses the mouse approach. Each action is numbered consecutively in green to make it easy to locate and follow. When appropriate, a mouse shortcut (toolbar icon) is shown at the left margin; a keyboard shortcut may be shown at the right, as follows:

    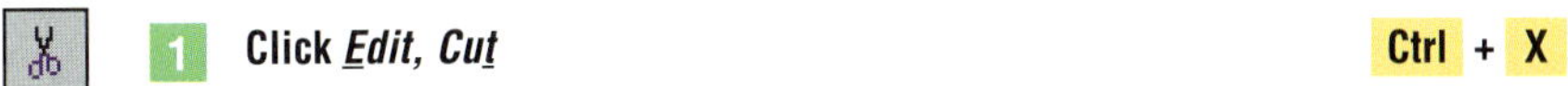

    1 Click *Edit, Cut*   Ctrl + X

As your skills increase, the "click this item" approach slowly gives way to a less-detailed list of goals and operations so that you do not mindlessly follow steps, but truly master software skills.

- *Screen Figures.* Full-color annotated screens provide overviews of operations that let you monitor your work as you progress through each mastery set.

- *Tips.* Each unit contains numerous short tips in bold type at strategic points to provide hints, warnings, or insights. Read these carefully.

- *Checkpoints.* At the end of each mastery set is a list of checkpoints, highlighted in red, which you can use to test your mastery of the material. Do not proceed further unless you can perform the checkpoint tasks.

- *Summary and Quiz.* At the end of each unit is a bulleted summary of the unit's content and a 30-question quiz with true/false, multiple-choice, and matching questions.

- *Exercises.* Each unit ends with two sets of written exercises ("Operations" and "Commands") and three guided hands-on computer applications that measure and reinforce mastery of the concepts and skills taught in the unit. The applications present problems relating to school, personal, and business use.

- *Mastery Cases.* The final page of each unit presents three unguided cases that allow you to demonstrate your personal mastery of the unit material.

- *End-of-Manual Material.* The manual also provides a comprehensive reference appendix that summarizes commands and provides alphabetical listings of critical operations, a glossary that defines all key terms (with page references), and an index to all important topics.

Ed Martin is a professor and department chair in the City University of New York. He teaches introductory and advanced microcomputer courses and has been a systems administrator, faculty trainer, and consultant. He has authored more than fifty titles on computer use, including Dryden's *Discovering Microsoft Office 97,* the *Mastering Today's Software Series,* and *PC Concepts.*

Charles Parker is the author of several successful computer textbooks, including the *Mastering Today's Software Series, PC Concepts,* and *Understanding Computers.* He has more than a decade of teaching experience in computers at both the undergraduate and graduate level and has worked as a consultant for several Fortune 500 companies.

Charles Kee is an Associate Professor teaching accounting and computer courses within the City University of New York. He is also a systems consultant and certified public accountant and has served as a Senior Financial Officer for a company traded on the NYSE. He has co-authored more than a dozen manuals in the Mastering Today's Software series.

The MTS authors along with the Dryden Press would like to thank the following reviewers for their thoughtful comments and technical advice on previous editions and preliminary drafts:

Elizabeth Boyd, Global Information Science Education; Clifford Burns, Sierra College; Betty Dalton, Tarrant County Junior College, Northeast Campus; George L. Elliott, Los Angeles City College; Michael Feiler, Merritt College; Keith Hendrick, Wallace State College; Jannett Jackson, Fresno City College; Deborah Morley, College of the Sequoias; Michael D. O'Conner, University of Montana; Susan M. Sanders, Western Michigan University; Jean Smelewicz, Quinsigamond Community College; Janice Wade, Pellissippi State Technical Community College.

1. Menu bar menus and toolbars are now personalized, displaying the commands that you use most often.

2. New Open and Save As dialog boxes help you to see more files at one time and access them fast.

3. Data entered are saved when you close a view window.

4. New Database Window that provides quicker access to wizards and views to creating and working with tables, queries, forms, reports, Web pages, and other objects.

5. New Web Page tools help you create three types of Web pages: Static HTML pages, Data access pages, and Server generated HTML pages. Static HTML pages are Web pages whose data do not change. Data access pages allows you to edit and work with data from either an Access database, Microsoft Explorer (version 5 or later), or a Microsoft SQL Server database. Server generated pages allows you to view only data from certain data sources.

6. Improved Office Assistant that provides help internally or through the World Wide Web.

Microsoft Access 2000

DATABASE MANAGEMENT

<table>
<tr><td colspan="3" align="center">OUTLINE</td></tr>
<tr>
<td valign="top">

OVERVIEW

MASTERY SET 1-1: GETTING
   STARTED
Starting Windows
Mouse and Keyboard
   Operations
Launching and Exiting Access

MASTERY SET 1-2: UNDERSTAND-
   ING THE ACCESS WINDOW
The Access Window
Menus and Toolbars
Creating a Database File
The Database Window

</td>
<td valign="top">

MASTERY SET 1-3: GETTING HELP
Using Access' Office Assistant
Using the Contents and Index Lists
Using the "What's This?" feature

MASTERY SET 1-4: CREATING A
   TABLE
Defining Fields
Default Values and Validation
   Options
Saving, Closing, and Opening a Table
Opening and Closing an Access Data-
   base File

</td>
<td valign="top">

MASTERY SET 1-5: ENTERING
   RECORDS
Entering Data into a Table
Entering Data into a Form

MASTERY SET 1-6: EXAMINING
   FIELD VALUES
Scrolling through Fields and Records
Locating Specific Field Data
Changing the Size and Order of Field
   Columns
Printing

UNIT REVIEW

</td>
</tr>
</table>

OBJECTIVES

After completing the mastery sets in this unit, you will be able to do any or all of the following:

1 Explain the general capabilities of a database management program.

2 Describe the procedures to launch and exit Microsoft Access.

3 Explain the various components of the Access screen.

4 Create a database file, table, and form.

5 Enter data into records.

6 Review data using keyboard and mouse.

7 View, locate and print data.

OVERVIEW

This unit presents the basic techniques for using Microsoft Access 2000, a well-known database management program. First, you learn how to launch and exit the program, interpret its screen, and access its features. You then learn how to create a database file and table to store and display data. Next, you enter data into records in a table and form, followed by learning viewing and printing techniques.

Units 1 and 2 of this manual discuss the use of Access as a file management system—working with one table at a time. Unit 3 explores the use of multiple tables in a true relational database application.

MASTERY SET 1-1: GETTING STARTED

A **database management system (DBMS)** enables you to organize data so that they can be easily stored, accessed, modified, and maintained. **Data** are essentially facts. They may include text, numbers, sounds, and objects (graphic images). A **database** is a collection of related data. Data within a database are arranged into *fields* and *records*. A **field** is single piece of data (for example, a customer name or logo). A **record** is a group of related fields—a customer's record may include fields for a customer's name, address, and telephone number. In Access, data are stored in a single table or in a collection of related tables. A **table** displays data in columnar (column and row) form. Each row represents a single record, and each column, a specific field. The intersection of a column and row is referred to as a *cell.* Figure DB1-1a summarizes the hierarchy of an application, and Figure DB1-1b displays an example of a table.

FIGURE DB1-1   ■   UNDERSTANDING THE DATA HIERARCHY

(a) The hierarchy categorizes data into levels of database, table, record, and field.
(b) A table presents data in rows (records) and columns (fields).

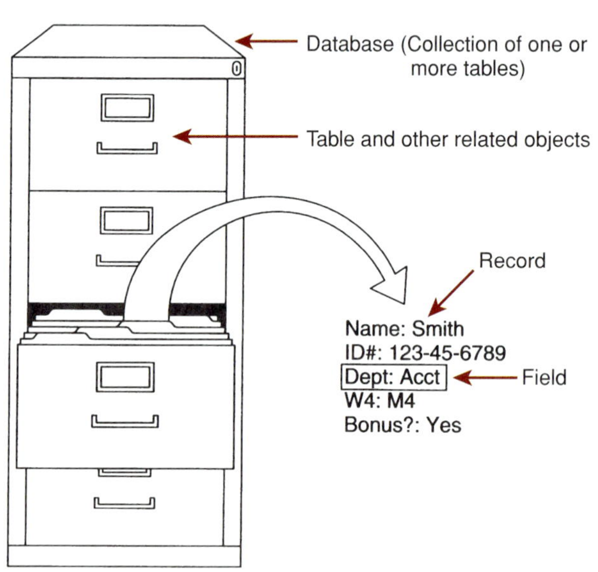

(a)

Customer List : Table

Customer Number	Last	First	City	State	Zip	Amount
067	Williams	DeVilla	Chicago	IL	60601	$965.42
101	Burstein	Jerome	San Jose	CA	95120	$230.45
111	Hill	Karen	Chicago	IL	60605	$456.78
176	West	Rita	Chicago	IL	60601	$965.42
389	Martin	Arthur	Flushing	NY	11367	$65.30
449	Kee	Charles	New York	NY	10003	$540.45
670	Parker	Charles	Santa Fe	NM	87051	$450.75
754	Martin	Edward	New York	NY	10001	$360.55
*						$0.00

Record: 1 of 8

(b)

The instructions presented here pertain to Access 2000 for Windows. Access is a program based on a *graphical user interface,* or *GUI* (pronounced "gooey"), which uses symbols *(icons)* and menus instead of typewritten commands to help you communicate with the computer. The GUI environment in which Access operates is called *Microsoft Windows.* Access is also a *What-You-See-Is-What-You-Get,* or *WYSIWYG* (pronounced "wizzy-wig"), database management program. This feature enables you to work in a screen that resembles your final printed page.

You can invoke Access's capabilities by mouse or keyboard. This manual presents mouse actions as the primary approach. When appropriate, shortcut keystrokes are shown in the right margin. When you operate Access, we highly recommend that you use the mouse to invoke commands. This approach is visually easier and often quicker than using the keyboard. Before you begin, be certain you have all the necessary tools: a hard disk or network that contains Windows and Access 2000 for Windows. Depending on your specific system, you may also need at least one formatted diskette on which to store the database files you create. (If you are going to save your work on your hard disk or network, you do not need the diskette.) This manual assumes that you are using Access from a hard-disk drive, although directions for networks are included.

STARTING WINDOWS

Before starting any Windows application, you must first start Windows. Whether you are using Windows 95, 98, or NT, in the Windows environment, you work in rectangular boxes called *windows.* A window may contain an application or a document, or it may request or provide information (in which case the window is called a *dialog box*). As you proceed through this unit, take note of the steps provided in each mastery set and follow them while sitting at your computer.

USING A HARD-DISK DRIVE.   This manual assumes that the Windows (95, 98, or NT) and Access programs are on your hard disk, which is identified as Drive C. To start Windows:

1 Turn on your system unit and your monitor's separate power switch, if necessary

Windows 95 or 98

Windows 95 or 98 should start automatically. A "Starting Windows" message may appear. If so, skip to Step 5.

2 If a screen appears asking you to "select the operating system to start," press the up or down arrow key to move the highlight to the desired Windows 95 or 98 option

3 If your system boots to another menu, go to Step 3 in the next section, "Using a Network"

Windows NT

2 If a screen appears asking you to "select the operating system to start," press the up or down arrow key to move the highlight to the Windows NT option

3 If a "Begin Logon" dialog box appears on your screen, press `Ctrl` + `Alt` + `Delete` to continue (hold down the `Ctrl` key, press and hold down the `Alt` key, press the `Delete` key and then release all three keys)

4 If a "C:\> prompt appears on your screen, type **WIN** and then press **↵** (this key may also be labeled "Enter" or "Return")

4 In the "Logon Information" dialog box that appears, type your *User Name,* press **Tab** , type your *password,* and then press **↵** (this key may also be labeled "Enter" or "Return")

> Note: Throughout this manual, text or typed commands are shown in an orange box.

5 If a "Welcome to Windows" dialog box appears, click the *Close* button or press **Esc**

You should now be at the Windows desktop as in Figure DB1-2. (The contents of your window may differ slightly from the figure.)

6 If appropriate for your lab, insert your diskette into Drive A (or B)

> Note: Your lab may use Drive B, the hard disk, or a storage area on your network server. Check with your instructor or lab manager for the proper drive and path identifier.

USING A NETWORK.   Access may be available to you through a local area network (LAN). In this case, Access is kept on the hard-disk drive of another computer that is shared by many users. To use Access, you must access the program from your own microcomputer. So many network configurations are in use today that it is impossible to know which one you are using. Check with your instructor for exact directions. In general, however, to start Windows,

1 Boot the network operating system (perhaps with your own diskette)

2 Type any command needed to display the network menu

FIGURE DB1-2 ■   THE WINDOWS SCREEN

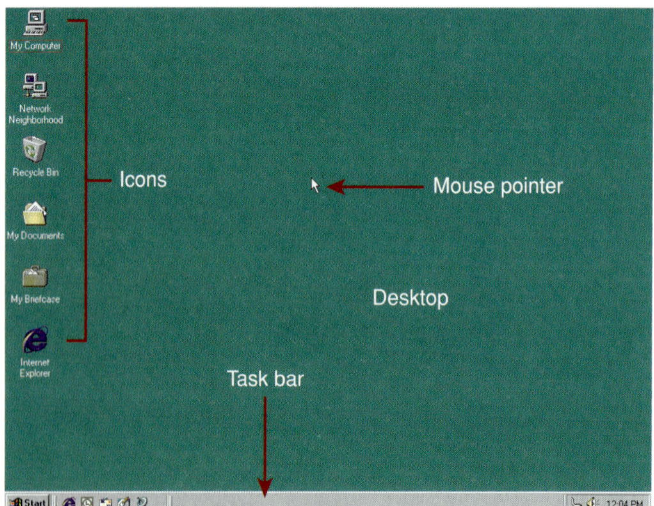

In many networks, this is done by typing **LAN** and pressing the *Enter* key.

3 | If appropriate for your lab, be sure your diskette is in Drive A (or B)

4 | Select (or type) the appropriate command on your screen to access Windows

MOUSE AND KEYBOARD OPERATIONS

Skip this section if you are already familiar with using a mouse and keyboard.

 **USING A MOUSE.**   A *mouse* is an input device that enables you to move a *mouse pointer* (graphical image) on your screen and select program features. Currently, the pointer appears as a small arrow. As you move your mouse on a flat surface, the mouse pointer moves on your screen in a similar fashion. In Access, the mouse pointer may appear in various forms, depending on its current use. *Pointing* means moving the mouse. To *point* your mouse:

 **1** | Carefully move your mouse on a flat desk surface or mouse pad (a small rubber pad) and notice the direction in which the mouse pointer moves on your screen. If you run out of space, simply lift your mouse and replace it. (The mouse pointer does not move if your mouse is lifted from the surface.)

 **2** | Point to the *Start* button in the taskbar—typically at the lower-left corner of the screen (use the tip of the arrow to point)

 **3** | Point to the *My Computer* icon (at the upper left of the desktop screen)

Clicking involves quickly pressing and releasing the left mouse button once. This action normally selects the item at which the mouse pointer is positioned. Try this:

 **4** | Click the *Start* button to access its menu

5 | Click anywhere in the desktop away from the menu to close the menu for now

Another basic mouse action is *double-clicking,* which involves quickly pressing and releasing the left mouse button twice. To practice double-clicking:

 **6** | Point to the *My Computer* icon and double-click it

Note: If a window does not appear, you may not be clicking quickly enough. Double-click the icon again. It may be helpful for you to hold the mouse stationary with one hand while double-clicking with the other—at least until you master this technique.

 **7** | Now click the "X" (Close) button at the upper right of the My Computer window

Many Windows applications also support a feature called *drag and drop,* which lets you use a mouse to move a selection (text or object) from one placc to another. This feature is illustrated later.

Table DB1-1 summarizes the common mouse actions.

TABLE DB1-1 ■ MOUSE ACTIONS

Mouse Actions	Description
Pointing	Moving the mouse (and thus the mouse pointer) to a desired item on the screen.
Clicking	Pressing and releasing the left mouse button.
Right-clicking	Pressing and releasing the right mouse button.
Dragging	Pressing and holding the left mouse button while pointing.
Dropping	Releasing the mouse button and thus the object pointed to after dragging.
Double-clicking	Rapidly clicking twice.
Shift-clicking	Pressing and holding the *Shift* key while clicking.
Ctrl-clicking	Pressing and holding the *Ctrl* key while clicking.

USING A KEYBOARD.   At times, you can access Windows features by keyboard. Keystrokes required to operate Access's menu system are discussed in the section "Menus and Toolbars" (later in this unit).

Most applications also provide special keystrokes called **shortcut keys.** Shortcut keys provide quick access to certain commands. Using shortcut keys requires that you press a key, either alone or in combination with the *Ctrl, Alt,* and/or *Shift* keys (a list of shortcut keys is in the appendix). For example, to open the Windows Start menu using its shortcut key:

1 Press **Ctrl** + **Esc** (hold down the **Ctrl** key while pressing the **Esc** key, and then release both keys)

To close the menu (or any menu) without selecting:

2 Press **Alt** to cancel the command

This manual presents its tutorials using the mouse approach. When appropriate, keyboard shortcuts are shown to the right of the step.

LAUNCHING AND EXITING ACCESS

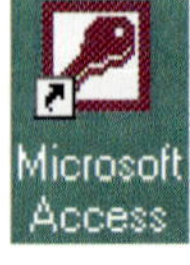

The procedure to start, or "launch," Access is the same as for any Windows application. You can double-click a desktop icon for Access 2000 (if it appears on your desktop—as shown in the margin) or locate Access's menu item as follows:

1 If you are using a diskette to save your work, insert it into the appropriate disk drive (if it is not already there)

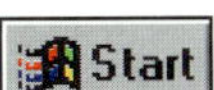

2 Click the *Start* button to access its menu

`Ctrl` + `Esc`

3 Point to the *Programs* item in the menu, as in Figure DB1-3

Note that the letter "P" in "Programs" is underlined. This indicates that you can press the *P* key if you want to select it. If the Access menu item appears in this list (as is usually the case), skip Step 3.

4 Point to the *MS Office* item in the next menu

If the Access program is located in a group other than MS Office, use the proper group in place of MS Office in Step 4.

To start Access using its menu item:

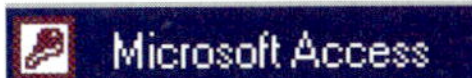

5 Click the *Microsoft Access* menu item, as in Figure DB1-3

An Access copyright screen may appear briefly but is quickly replaced by the Access window. In the center of the window is the Microsoft Access dialog box. This dialog box can be used to open an existing database or create a new one. For now, to remove it:

FIGURE DB1-3 ■ LAUNCHING ACCESS

To launch Access, click the *Start* button, point to *Programs,* and then click the *Microsoft Access* icon.

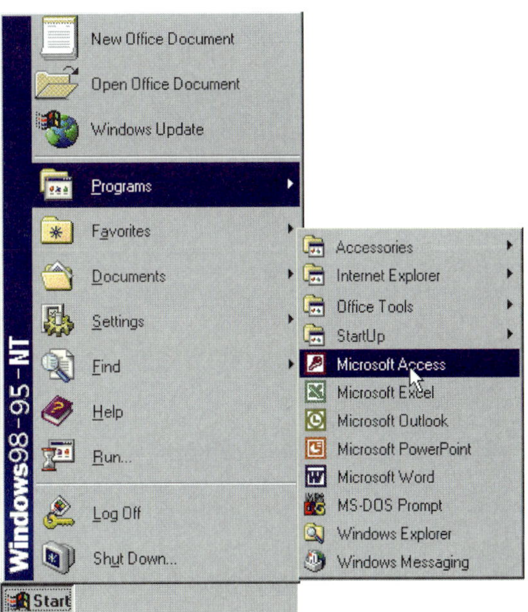

FIGURE DB1-4 ■ THE MICROSOFT ACCESS WINDOW

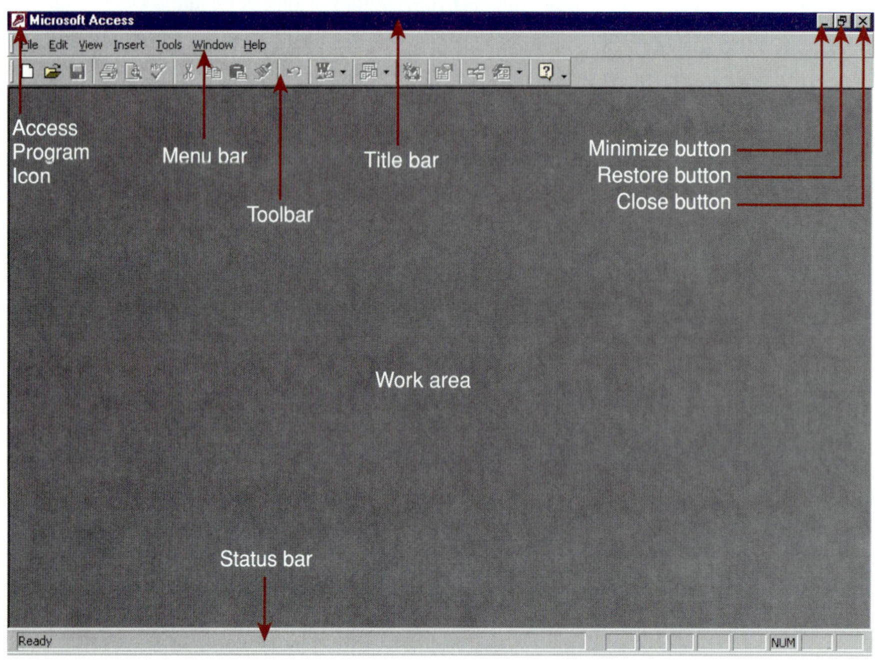

6 Click the *Cancel* button

Esc

7 If needed, click Access's Maximize button (near the top right corner of the window) to enlarge it to its maximum size

Alt + **Spacebar** , **X**

Your Access window should now resemble Figure DB1-4.

> **Note: When you want to leave Access, click its Close ("X") button at the extreme upper right of the window (or press *Alt + F, X*). You can then launch Access again to continue later.**

☑ CHECKPOINT

Answer these questions.
1. What is the purpose of the Windows *Start* button?
2. What is the difference between pointing and clicking?
3. What happens to the Access window when the "X" button at its top right corner is clicked?
4. What is a shortcut key?
5. What does "launch" mean?

MASTERY SET 1-2: UNDERSTANDING THE ACCESS WINDOW

You should now be looking at the Access window as in Figure DB1-4. If not, follow the start-up steps in the previous mastery set to launch Access now. This is the main program window that appears each time you launch the program.

THE ACCESS WINDOW

Access has only one application window. However, depending on your available memory, you can open many individual windows related to a database file within the Access window. The Access window has several standard Windows features as well as features unique to Access. Examine your screen as you read the following brief summary of these features and their operations.

TITLE BAR.   All windows have a title bar located across the top. The **title bar** identifies the name of the window with its icon and name, in this case, Microsoft Access. The title bar can also be used to resize, move, or close the window. These commands are available through the title bar's resizing and Close buttons (at the right end of the bar) or the window's control menu (click the Access program icon or right-click the title bar). See Figure DB1-4 for the location of these buttons.

MENU BAR.   Just below the title bar is Access's menu bar. This standard Windows feature provides mouse and keyboard access to the program's commands through pull-down menus. This will be demonstrated shortly.

TOOLBARS.   At least one toolbar is typically located below the menu bar. A **toolbar** provides quick access to commonly used features by mouse. Pointing to a toolbar item and waiting a moment will display its function in a small "tool tip" reference box. Clicking a toolbar item will invoke its command or open its drop-down menu.

WORK AREA.   All windows have an interior space called the *work area* or *workspace*. Windows that are related to a database file may be opened and used in this area.

STATUS BAR.   At the bottom of the Access window is a **status bar,** which displays messages regarding the operation in progress or a selected command (at the left) and toggle (on/off) switch indicators (at its right).

MENUS AND TOOLBARS

Access's features are accessible through its menu bar, shortcut keys, **shortcut menus** (context-specific menus), and toolbars. Access also automatically personalizes menus and toolbars as you use their commands. The following exercises demonstrate the operation of these command alternatives.

USING THE MENU BAR.   To select a command by mouse using the menu bar, simply click the menu bar item to access its pull-down menu, and then click the desired menu item. By keyboard, press the *Alt* key and the key for the underlined letter of the menu bar item, and then press the key for the underlined letter of the menu item. For example, to open the File menu:

1   **Click _File_**   Alt + F

> **Note:** When you open a menu from Access's menu bar, it displays only basic and recent commands that you have used. The menu will also display a "More" button (as shown in the margin) at the bottom of its list. You can click this button if you need to use a command not currently displayed. (Alternately, you can wait a few moments until the menu automatically expands to reveal the remainder of its commands and then click the desired item. Each item you use will appear on the menu the next time you open it. In this way, Access customizes the menus to reflect your personal use.

The upper portion of the File menu should appear as in Figure DB1-5. At this point, you can select a command from the menu by clicking it or pressing the key (using the appropriate underlined letter). You can also exit the pull-down menu without making any selection as follows:

2   **Click outside the menu**   Alt

FIGURE DB1-5 ■ USING THE MENU BAR

(a) Clicking a menu bar item or pressing _Alt_ plus its underlined letter will open its menu. To select from a menu, simply click the desired item or press the key for its underlined letter.
(b) Standard Windows menu indicators.

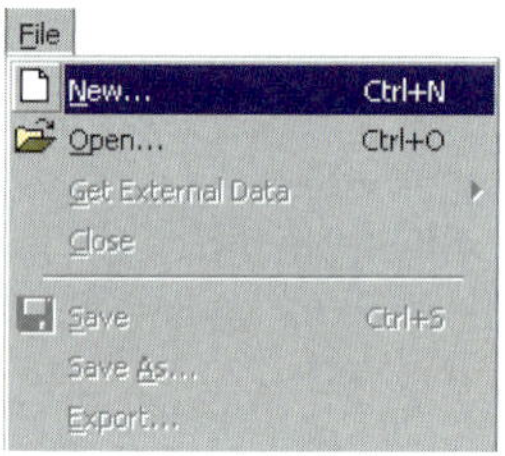

(a)

Menu Items with	Explanation
Ellipsis (...)	Opens to a dialog box or another window.
▶ at far right	Opens a submenu.
No notation	Invokes a command or other feature.
Keys at far right	Shortcut key (s) to invoke the menu item.
✓ to the left of item	A toggle (on/off) feature that has been activated.
Dimmed (or not visible) characters	A menu item not currently available.

(b)

FIGURE DB1-6 ■ **SHORTCUT MENU**

The toolbar shortcut menu.
Right-clicking certain areas
of the Access screen opens a
shortcut menu.

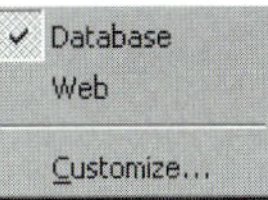

(After you complete the mouse method, you may want to try the keyboard method displayed to the right of the command.)

USING SHORTCUT MENUS.   Shortcut menus provide a quick way to access commands. Shortcut menus are location-specific. That is, different shortcut menus appear, depending on where you are pointing on the screen. To display a shortcut menu, right-click the item as follows:

1 **Right-click anywhere within the toolbar**

A shortcut menu should appear, similar to the one in Figure DB1-6. To select a shortcut menu item, click (using the left mouse button) the item, or press the key for its underlined letter. To exit the menu without selecting a choice:

2 **Click outside the menu**   **Alt**

UNDERSTANDING MENU INDICATORS.   Access uses standard Windows menu indicators in its menu system. These conventions apply to all types of menus. For example, in Figure DB1-5, the ellipsis (. . .) following the command *Open...* indicates that this item opens a dialog box. Table DB1-2 lists some of the standard Windows menu conventions.

USING A TOOLBAR.   As shown in Figure DB1-4, the Access toolbar appears directly below the menu bar. Access also offers a variety of task-specific toolbars that automatically appear when you invoke a command related to their operation. For example, the Print Preview toolbar appears when you display the print previewing screen. You can also turn task-specific toolbars on or off manually, using either the View menu or the Toolbar shortcut menu. See the appendix for a list of available task-specific toolbars. (You can also refer to Access's online help to learn how to create custom toolbars.)

Toolbars typically display only basic and recent toolbar buttons that you used. This is part of Access's personalized toolbar feature. If the toolbar you are using does not display its entire set of toolbar buttons, a *More Buttons* toolbar button will be displayed at its right-most end. You can click this button to access a set of the remaining toolbar buttons. As with the menu bar, each toolbar button you use in this manner will be added to the toolbar for future use.

To display a caption of a toolbar button's function (called a "tool tip"), point to it. Try this:

1 **Point to (do not click) the *Print* toolbar button and wait**

A small "tool tip" box appears beneath the button, identifying its function.

2 Point to another toolbar button, and wait for it to display its function

To invoke a command by toolbar button, simply click it. To select a feature from a toolbar drop-down box, click its  button, and then click the desired item from the list that appears. Try this:

3 Click the *Open* toolbar button   Ctrl + O

As expected, the Open dialog box appears. You will use this dialog box later to retrieve a saved workbook from a disk. For now, to close it:

4 Click the *Cancel* button   Esc

Toolbar drop-down boxes (toolbar icons that appear with a drop-down button) are discussed as needed.

USING WINDOW MANIPULATION COMMANDS.   Most windows can be resized, moved, or closed. Standard window resizing commands include the following:

- *Restore*—Reduces a window to less than its maximum size.
- *Minimize*—Reduces the Access application window to its task bar button and a database window to an icon resembling a small title bar.
- *Maximize*—Enlarges a window to its maximum size.

These commands are available through the window's control menu or command buttons. To open Access's control menu (or one related to a dialog box), you can click the program icon at the left side of the title bar, right-click the title bar itself, or press *Alt* + Spacebar. To open a database window's control menu, click its icon or press *Alt* + – (the minus key).

> Note: A database (or related) window's icon is located at the left side of the menu bar when the window is maximized or at the left side of its title bar when restored. Access's resizing and Close buttons are located at the right end of its title bar. A database (or related) window's resizing and Close buttons are located at the right end of the menu bar when maximized or at the right end of its title bar when restored.

CREATING A DATABASE FILE

Before you can use Access to store data, you must first create a database file. You can then store data in the database file within a table or a collection of tables. As described earlier, a table is a storage container that displays data in columnar (column and row) form. Each row represents a single record (a group of related fields), and each column, a specific field (a single piece of data). The intersection of a column and row is referred to as a *cell.*

You can edit table data directly, within the displayed table itself, or through a form (a display of a single record at a time). Data can be queried (located based on a set of criteria), analyzed, reorganized, presented in a report, or printed.

To create a database file named CUSTOMER:

1 Click *File* and then *New* to open its dialog box   Ctrl + N

FIGURE DB1-7 ■ THE NEW DIALOG BOX

(a) The *General* tab of the New dialog box currently contains a *Blank Database* icon and several other preformatted database icons.
(b) The *Databases* tab displays a variety of preformatted database files.

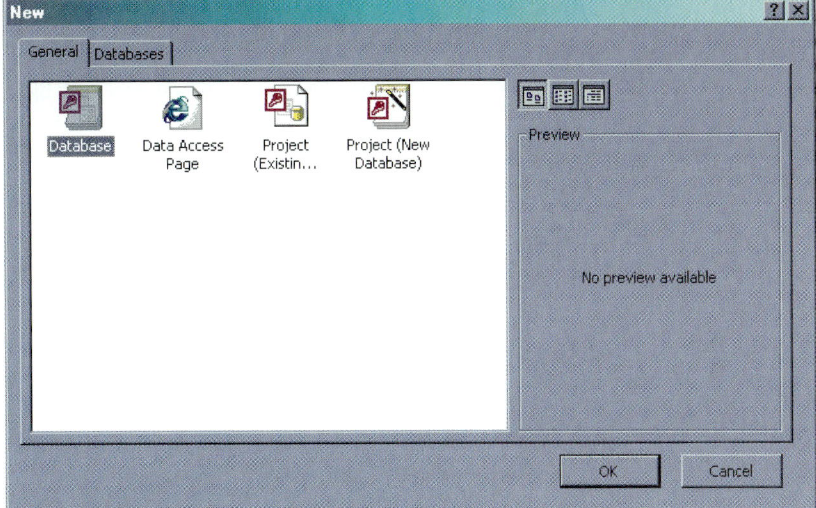

(a)

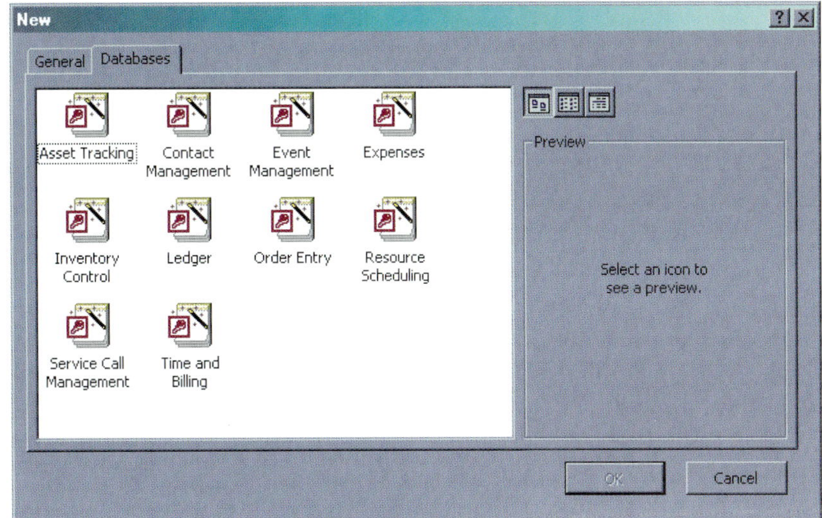

(b)

Your New dialog box should appear as in Figure DB1-7a. Note that it has two tabs: *General* and *Databases.* The *General* tab should currently display an icon entitled Database. The *Databases* tab contains a variety of task-specific databases, as displayed in Figure DB1-7b. You can use these prestructured databases to quickly store and manipulate data related to their titled function. You may want to try some of these databases on your own. For now:

2   Click the *Database* icon, and then click *OK*

If needed, perform Steps 3 and 4 to set the Save in default to the *3 1/2 Floppy (A:)* drive or the appropriate folder. If your *Save in* drop-down box already displays this, go to Step 5.

3 Click the ▼ button of the *Save in* box to see its drop-down list

💾 3½ Floppy (A:)   **4** Click the *3 1/2 Floppy (A:)* icon (or the drive or folder appropriate for your course)

5 If needed, press `Alt` + `N` or `Tab` to move to the *File name* text box

> **Tip:** As an alternative to Step 5, you can click the *File name* text box and then drag over its contents to select (highlight) it.

Note that the *File name* text box's contents are now highlighted. Although you can remove the highlight by pressing an arrow key or delete the contents by pressing the *Delete* key, typing will also delete the highlight. Try this:

6 Type **CUSTOMER** and then click the *Create* button

A Database window should appear, as shown in Figure DB1-8. Note that its title bar displays the database filename "CUSTOMER: Database." Your database file has now been created and is ready for data.

THE DATABASE WINDOW

Whenever you create or open a database file, the **Database window** appears in Access's work area. It acts as a graphical menu system for **objects**—items stored in

FIGURE DB1-8 ■ THE DATABASE WINDOW

The Database window can be used to create, open, or run objects stored in a database file. The List Box displays objects related to the object type button depressed, in this case, the Tables button.

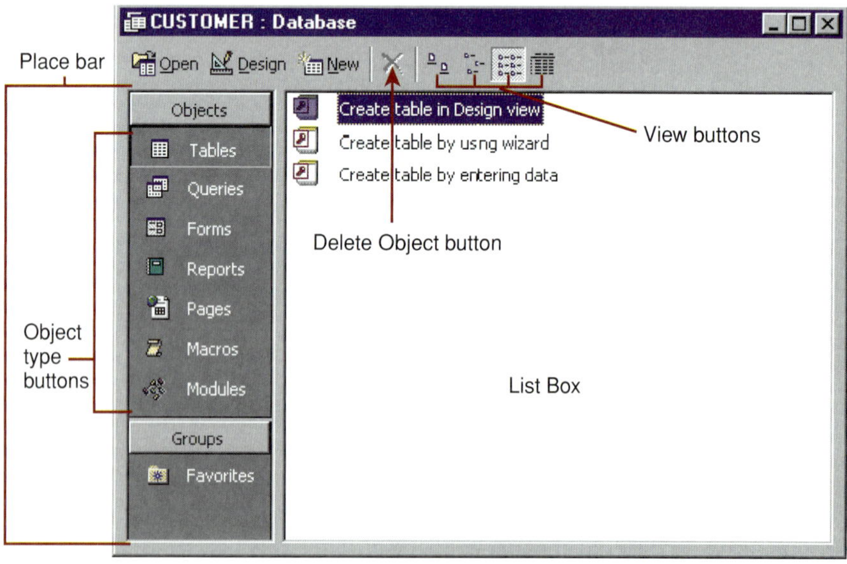

the database file. Objects include tables, queries, forms, reports, pages, macros, and modules.

OBJECTS.   In an Access database file, data are stored in a table or tables. *Tables* display database records in a grid-like format (spreadsheet). Each row displays a record, and each column, a field. This format allows you to examine or edit many records at once. You can also add records to, or remove them from, the table. A single database file can store multiple tables. You can develop tables to contain different types of information. For example, a retail business may have different tables that contain data for its customers, vendors, employees, and products.

A **query** is a search that lists records from a database based on criteria that you specify. A **form** is a screen that enables you to work with a single record at a time. You may also present data in a **report,** a more formal user-defined presentation of records. A *Page* or *Data Access Page* is a special type of Web page that allows you to view and work with data that are stored in an Access database. **Macros** are sets of commands that you can use to automate tasks. For example, you can create a macro that automates report printing when invoked. A **module** is a collection of programmed instructions that directs Access to perform actions on objects in a database.

NAVIGATING THE DATABASE WINDOW.   As in Figure DB1-8, the left side of the Database window displays a button for each object type. Clicking an object type button will display related icons in the window's list box. Several default icons also appear for each object type selected except for Macros and Modules. These icons can be used to help you create an object of the selected type. For example, when the *Tables object type* button is selected as in Figure DB1-8, three (3) icons appear in the list box to help you create a table. Soon you will create a table named Customer List. After you create it, its icon will appear within the Database window's list box when the *Tables* button is selected.

The Database Window also has a set of command buttons below its title bar. These buttons can be used to retrieve, display, or execute an object (*Open* button); edit an object (*Design* button); and create a new object (*New* button). There is also a *delete object* button and four view buttons that let you control the level of object detail displayed in the list box. By storing all the objects in one file, Access greatly simplifies database file management and backup.

For now, to exit Access:

1 Click *File* and then *Exit* (or click the Close button at the top right of the Access window's title bar)   **Alt** + **F4**

2 If needed, click *No*

☑ **CHECKPOINT**

Answer these questions and perform these tasks.
1.   Describe the parts of the Access window.
2.   Describe how to access a menu bar command by keyboard and mouse.
3.   What are data, and how can you store them in Access?
4.   Create a database file named DCHECK.
5.   Define the following objects: table, query, form, report, and page.

MASTERY SET 1-3: GETTING HELP

Access provides various methods for acquiring help, including an Office Assistant, Contents and Index lists, and a "What's This?" feature. The *Office Assistant* is an animated character that provides general and specific help in response to your questions. The Contents and Index lists allow you to select additional help screens. The "What's This?" feature allows you to access brief help notes ("captions") related to some component on the screen. You will look at each of these features in the next set of exercises.

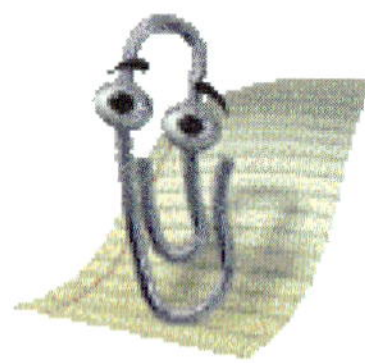

USING ACCESS'S OFFICE ASSISTANT

You can use Access's animated *Office Assistant* to access help whenever you need it. It is perhaps the most common method for viewing reference information. To activate the Assistant:

1 If needed, launch Access

 **2** Click *Help* and then *Microsoft Access Help*   **F1**
(or click the *Microsoft Access* toolbar button)

An Office Assistant dialog box and question area appear, usually at the lower right of the screen, as shown in Figure DB1-9a. A cartoon paper clip (called "Clippit") or one of eight other "assistants" may appear, depending on which cartoon image was installed

FIGURE DB1-9 ■ USING THE OFFICE ASSISTANT

(a) The Office Assistant appears when you invoke Access' help command.

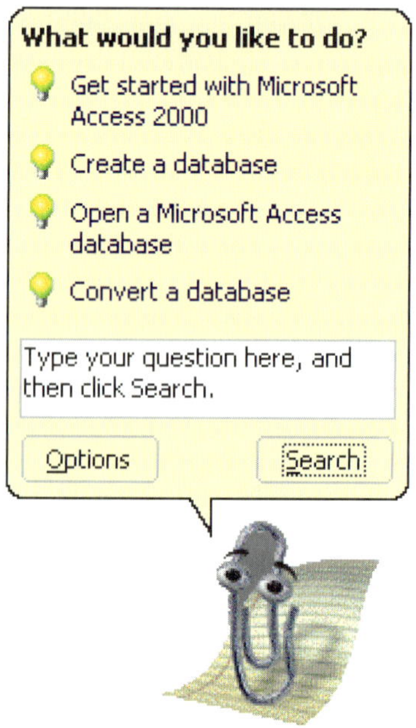

(a)

(b) The Microsoft Access Help window appears in the right side of your screen when opened.

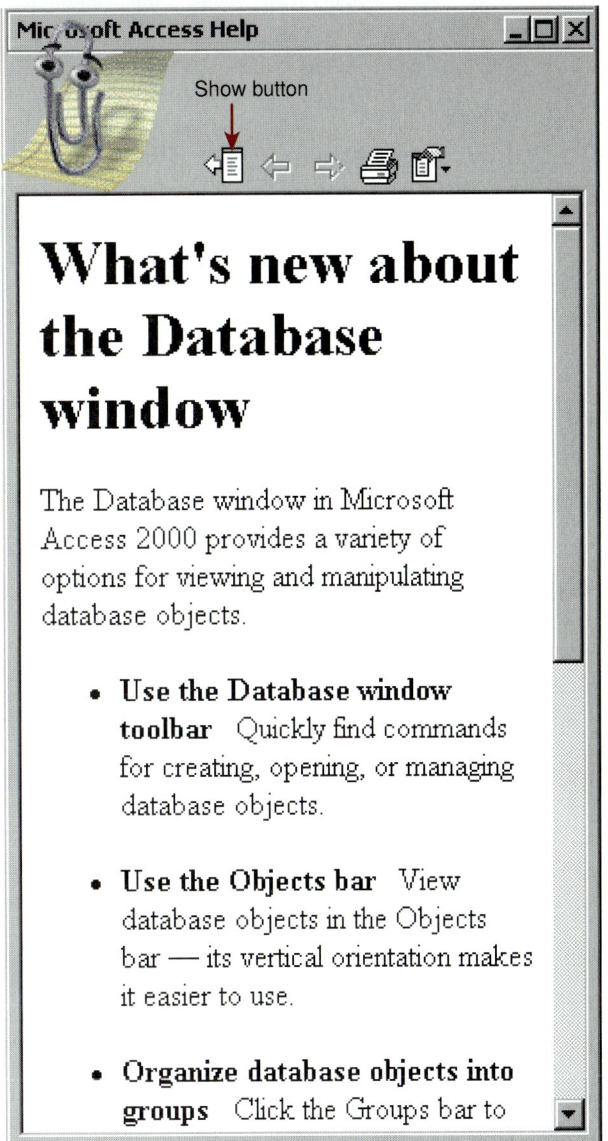

(b)

at a previous time. The **Office Assistant** allows you to pose questions as sentences or keywords and then presents customized responses to you. For example:

3 Type **Database window** and then click the *Search* button in the question area

The "assistant" displays some amusing animation as the Help program searches for related topics. In a short time, an option screen appears with appropriate search topics.

4 Click the *What's new about the Database window* option to select it

The help explanation appears in a window at the right of the screen, as shown in Figure DB1-9b. When you are finished reading the material:

 **5** Click the Help window's *Close* button to exit the window   **Esc**

 **6** Click *Help* on the menu bar and then click the *Hide the Office Assistant* option to close it (or, If you prefer, right-click the Assistant Image and then click *Hide*)

> **Tip: The Office Assistant can remain on the screen as you work, at times displaying amusing animations. In fact, the Assistant may appear from time to time, suggesting various courses of action based on your current task, even if you don't invoke it. At other times, a *lightbulb* may appear, which you can click for a help tip. You can always remove the Assistant from the current screen if you no longer want to see it.**

USING THE CONTENTS AND INDEX LISTS

Most of the time, the Office Assistant will be sufficient to answer your questions. However, once you open Access's Help window through the Office Assistant, you can also access a number of built-in references for every Access task. The *Contents list* is a set of introductory topics that provide overviews of most basic Access operations. The *Index list* contains almost every command that can be invoked in Access. To initiate these Help features:

1 Open the Help window (follow Steps 1 through 4 above)

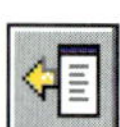 **2** In the Help window, click the *Show* button, and then the Help window's title bar (as shown in the left margin) to open the window to its full size, as shown in Figure DB1-10a

3 If needed, click the *Contents* tab located just below the Help window's title bar.

The Contents list presents a set of available topics in the left side of the window. You may simply scroll to, and then click, the desired topic and then click double-click the topic to view information about it at the right. You could then close the window when you're done. For now, however, leave the window open as you continue with the next exercise.

4 Click the *Index* tab

The *Index list* that appears (as shown in Figure DB1-10b) lets you search for help on a specific topic. For example, to search for help on Access's Database window:

5 Type **Database window** (in box #1 in the window) and then click the *Search* button

A list of related topics appears in box #3.

6 Scroll to, and click, one of the topics displayed in the list in box #3

An explanation of the topic appears at the right

 > **Tip: Once you have located a desired topic, you could click the *print* button (as shown in the left margin) to print a copy of the information for future reference.**

Now, to exit the Help window:

7 Click the *Hide* button (as in the left margin) to return the window to its default size

8 Close the Help window

USING THE "WHAT'S THIS?" FEATURE

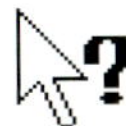

Access also provides a "What's This?" feature that you can use to access a Help caption—a brief explanatory note regarding any component of the Access screen. It is available through the Help menu, by pressing *Shift + F1,* or by clicking the "?" button (found in most dialog boxes to the left of the Close button). Try this to see how it works:

FIGURE DB1-10 ■ USING THE CONTENTS AND INDEX LISTS

(a) Clicking the *Show* button of the Help window will display the *Contents, Answer Wizard,* and *Index help* tabs.

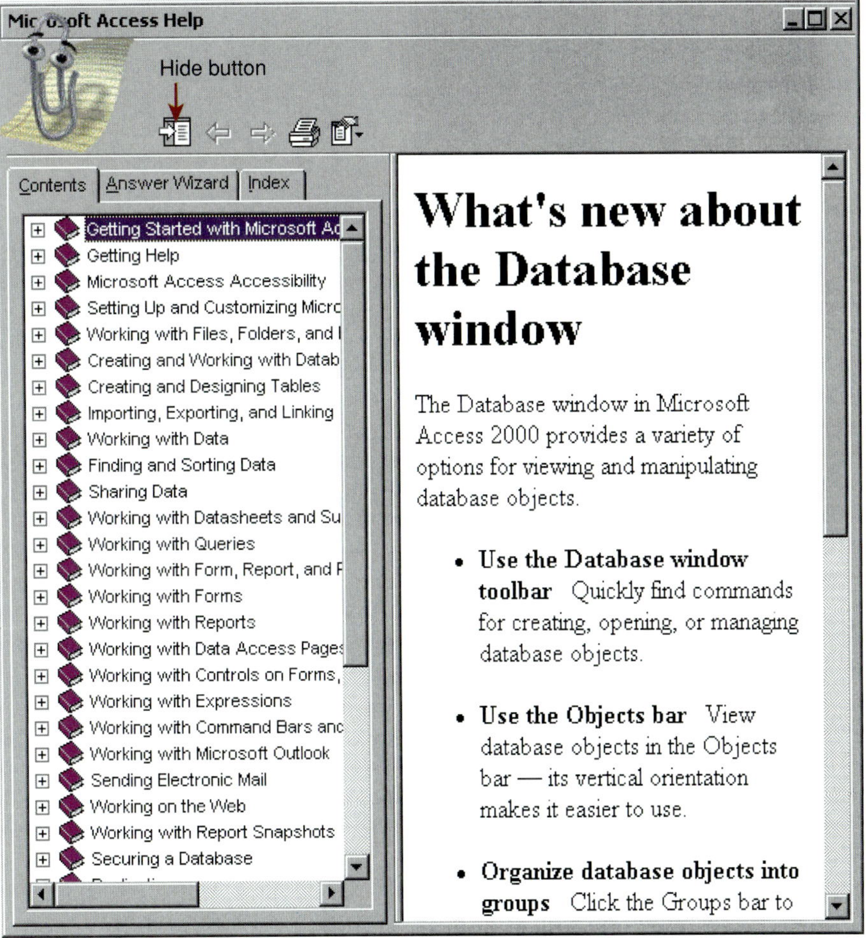

(a)

(continued)

(b) Access will provide help based on entering keywords in the *Index* tab.

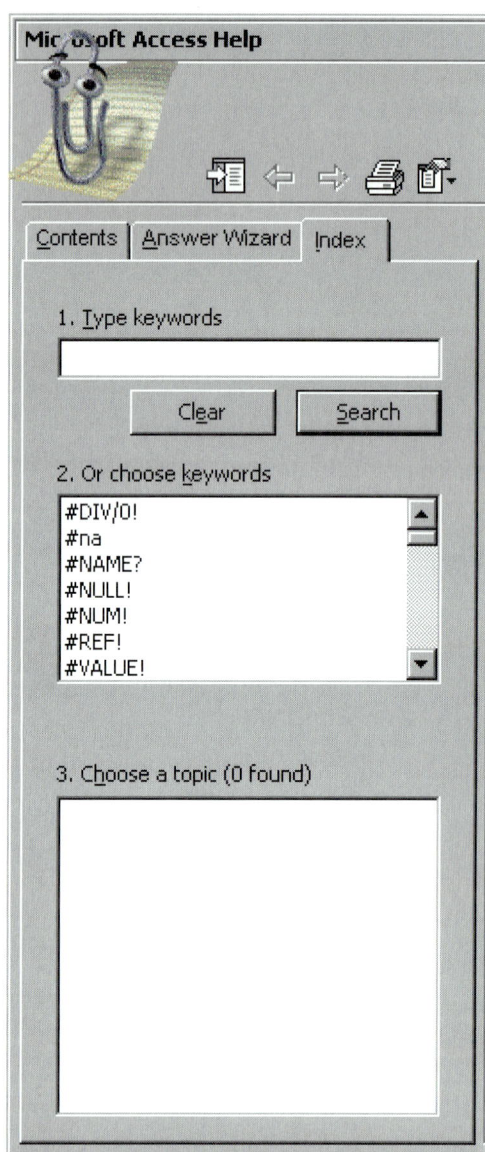

(b)

| 1 | Click *Help, What's This?* | Shift + F1 |

Note that the mouse pointer now includes a "?" symbol (as shown in the left margin). Once the "What's This?" feature is activated, you can then click any item to access its explanatory note.

| 2 | Click any toolbar button to display its help caption |

3 Click outside the help caption to remove it   **Esc**

4 If desired, click Access's *Close* button to exit the program

✓ CHECKPOINT

Answer these questions and perform these tasks.
1. Launch Access.
2. Use Access's Office Assistant to print information about how to create a database file.
3. How do you display and then hide the Contents and Index help features?
4. Use Access's "What's This?" help feature to get help on the parts of the toolbar.
5. Exit Access.

MASTERY SET 1-4: CREATING A TABLE

As you have learned, a table is used to store data in a database file. It displays data in columnar (column and row) form. In the following exercise, you will create a table named "Customer List." First, you learn how to define the table's fields. You then set a few field value options. Table saving, closing, and opening procedures are then reviewed.

1 Launch Access

You can open a saved database file using the Microsoft Access dialog box, the File menu, or the Open toolbar button. The latter two methods are demonstrated later. To use the Microsoft Access dialog box:

2 Click the *Open an existing file* option, *More Files,* and then *OK* for the Open dialog box

> Tip: As an alternative to Step 2, you can use the menu bar or toolbar to access the Open dialog box by clicking the *Cancel* button of the dialog box and then click *File, Open* or the Open toolbar button (see the margin).

 3½ Floppy (A:)

3 If needed, click the ▼ button of the *Look in* box, and then click *3 1/2 Floppy (A:)* (or the appropriate drive for your lab) to set the "Look in" drive

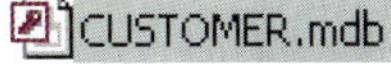 CUSTOMER.mdb

4 Click *CUSTOMER.mdb*

5 Click the *Open* button

> Tip: Instead of performing Steps 4 and 5, you can double-click the *CUSTOMER.mdb* icon to open it.

Your Database window should again resemble Figure DB1-8.

DEFINING FIELDS

As displayed in Figure DB1-8 and your screen, Access offers several ways to create a table.

You can create a table in Design view, by using a wizard (that contains a selection of preset tables), by entering data, or by using the *New* button. No matter which method you use, one of the first steps in creating any table is to define its fields. Remember, a *field* is single piece of data (for example, a customer name or logo). The process of defining a field involves assigning it a name and data type and then specifying its properties (characteristics). In the next exercise, you will create a table in Design view. Refer to the appendix or your online help if you want to use any of the other methods to create a table.

1 If needed, click the *Tables* object type button

2 Double-click the *Create table in Design view* icon in Database window's List box

Your Table Design window should appear as in Figure DB1-11. This window enables you to define the structure of a new table or modify the structure of an existing table. (A table's *structure* includes its field names and data type.)

The upper pane (section) of the Table Design window is where you define field names and the type of data the fields will hold. The lower pane's tabs let you set each field's **properties** (characteristics). The message area at the lower right of the window displays context-sensitive help. For example, currently, the insertion point appears in

FIGURE DB1-11 ■ THE TABLE WINDOW IN DESIGN VIEW

A Table window in Design view allows you to define the field structure of the table. The *F6* key switches between upper and lower panes.

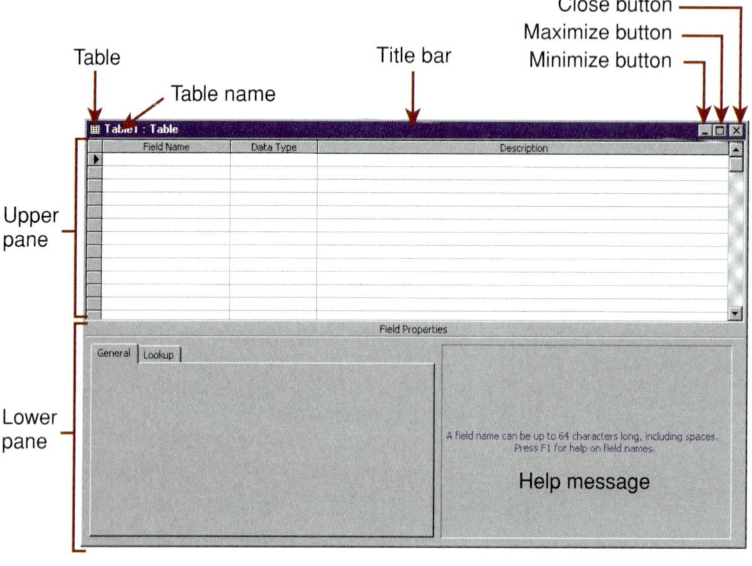

the first cell of the *Field Name* column. The help message displayed, as shown in Figure DB1-11, indicates that "A field name can be up to 64 characters long, including spaces." As you move to each area of this window, specific help messages appear to guide you.

ENTERING FIELD NAME, DATA TYPE, AND DESCRIPTION. A **field name** identifies the data that will be stored in the field. As you have learned and as the help message indicates, a field name can contain a maximum of 64 characters. Field names can contain letters, spaces, numerals, or underline symbols as well as many other special characters. Whereas spaces may be embedded in a field name (such as "GROSS PAY"), you cannot begin or end a field name with a space. In addition, do not use a bracket ([or]), an exclamation point (!), a period (.), or the "back quote" character (`) in a field name.

> **Tip: All Access objects follow these naming rules.**

A good field name reminds you of the data that is to be stored in that field. For example, an employee's total gross pay for the current pay period might be stored in a field named "GROSS," "GROSS PAY," or "CURRENT GROSS PAY." Most punctuation marks are legal in a field name, but they communicate little meaning. For example, "^~^#?{?t$" is a perfectly legal field name, but what does it tell you about its data? It is best to avoid using punctuation marks in field names unless you have a good reason to include them.

When you first see the Table Design window, the text *insertion point* (a vertical blinking line) should be in the first row of the *Field Name* column.

1 **Click the Table Design window's Maximize button (see Figure DB1-11 for its location)**   **Alt** + **-** , **X**

> **Tip: You need not work in a maximized window, but it is visually easier to do so.**

2 **If needed, click the first cell below the *Field Name* column label to move the insertion point there**

3 Type **Customer Number** and press **Tab** or **↵**

> **Tip: If you make a mistake, press Backspace to erase it. If you've already left the column, press the left arrow key to go back, and then reenter the field name. You may also use the *Insert* or *Delete* key to help correct errors.**

Customer Number appears in the *Field Name* column, and the data type Text now appears highlighted in the *Data Type* column. A ▼ button also appears to its right. You can now identify the type of field values (called **data type**) to be stored in this field. Access has already entered Text as the default data type, which is the correct type for this field. Text data consist of strings of characters that have no numeric value, such as a name, an address, a phone number, or a zip code.

Access offers ten data types (as listed in Table DB1-3). To accept the data type "Text" and move to the Description column:

4 Press **Tab** or **↵**

TABLE DB1-3 ■ DATA TYPES

Data Type	Description
Text	Contains 1 to 255 characters in any combination of letters, numbers, symbols, or other printable characters. Data in text fields have no numeric value.
Memo	Extended comments, usually sentences organized into paragraphs. Can contain up to 65,535 characters.
Number	Numeric data that can be used in mathematical calculations. Format choices consist of the following: Byte—Numbers from 0 to 255; no fractions Integer—Whole numbers from −32,768 to +32,767 Long integer—Whole numbers from −2,147,483,648 to +2,147,483,647 Single—Numbers from -3.4×1038 to $+3.4 \times 1038$ Double—Numbers from -1.79×10308 to $+1.79 \times 10308$
Date/Time	Dates (like 11/15/98) and time (like 11:45 am).
Currency	Monetary amounts. Same as number except that the currency symbol ($) is automatically inserted.
AutoNumber	A numeric value, beginning with 1 and incremented by 1 for each record you add to a database. AutoNumber fields cannot be edited.
Yes/No	Logical data containing yes/no, true/false, or on/off entries. Useful for data that can have only one of two values.
OLE Object	An object containing binary code, such as a graphic image.
Hyperlink	A hyperlink address. See the Unit 3 section, "Preparing Access Objects for the World Wide Web."
Lookup wizard	Displays a list of values from which the user can choose.

The insertion point is now in the *Description* column. This entry is optional. It should contain a descriptive line or phrase that describes the contents of the field. This line will be displayed later, during the data entry process, as a guide for you. For now:

5   Type   `An identification code unique to this customer`

SETTING A PRIMARY KEY.   A **primary key** is a field (or set of fields) that uniquely identifies each record in a table. Assigning a primary key will rearrange records in that order. It also prevents you from entering records with duplicate primary key data. Although it is not mandatory for this exercise, it is required in relational database operations (discussed in Unit 3) and is a useful tool.

Because the *Customer Number* field will contain a unique identifier for each record, it can be used as a primary key. To assign the *Customer Number* field as the primary key:

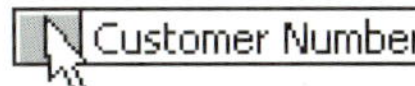

1 Click the row selector at the left of the field name Customer Number to identify this field

2 Click the *Primary Key* toolbar button to mark the selected field

A primary key icon now appears to the left of the *Customer Number* field name.

Note that any field can be assigned as a primary key using the above two steps provided that its data for each record is unique. A table may have only one primary key. However, the key may comprise of more than one field. To do this, click on the first row, then *Ctrl*-click on the next row.

SETTING FIELD SIZE.   Notice that the lower portion of the Table Design window contains an area where you can describe the properties of the field. One of those properties is already filled in—**Field Size.** The size of a text field—that is, the maximum number of characters allowed—is under your control. In Access, you can use up to 255 characters. To change the size of this field to 3:

1 Press **F6** or click after the "50" in the *Field Size* text box in the lower pane

2 Backspace over the default entry, then type **3** and press **↵**

For now, leave the other properties at their default settings. To enter the next field:

3 Click the *Field Name* cell in the second row of the upper pane to move the insertion point there

4 Type **Last** and press **↵**

5 Press **↵** again to keep the Data Type as Text

6 Type **Customer's last name** in the *Description* column

7 Press **F6** or click after the "50" in the *Field Size* text box in the lower pane

8 Backspace over the default entry; then type **15** and press **↵**

TURNING ON THE REQUIRED FEATURE.   Because in this example it would be pointless to create a record without a last name, you can instruct Access to "force" the user—whether it is yourself or a data entry clerk—to enter a last name for every record. This field property feature is called the **Required** feature. When the Required feature is activated, the field must contain data in order to create a record. (In practice, you can make any field a "required" field.) To turn on the Required feature:

1 Click after *No* in the *Required* box in the lower pane to move to its box   **↵** six times

Note that a  button appears. You can use it to switch to Yes, or you can simply delete the No and type **Yes.** To use the button:

2   Click the ▾ button in the *Required* box, and then click *Yes*   **Y** , ↵

This action prevents anyone from creating a record that has no last name. Now, use the data in Table DB1-4 to enter the next four field definitions:

3   Click the *Field Name* cell in the third row in the upper pane to move the insertion point there

4   Enter the data for the third field using the same techniques

5   Continue entering the next three field definitions (stop after you complete the Zip field)

Your upper pane should resemble Figure DB1-12 when you finish.

At this point, you can review the field properties of each entry by first moving to the desired field name in the upper pane. Try this to review your entry for City:

6   Click *City* in the *Field Name* column of the upper pane

Its Field Size in the lower pane should display 20.

TABLE DB1-4   ■   STRUCTURE FOR THE CUSTOMER TABLE

	Field Name	Data Type	Description	Field Properties
1	Customer Number	Text	An identification code unique to this customer	Field Size: 3
2	Last	Text	Customer's last name	Field Size: 15 Required: Yes
3	First	Text	Customer's first name	Field Size: 10
4	City	Text	Customer's city	Field Size: 20
5	State	Text	Customer's state	Field Size: 2
6	Zip	Text	Customer's five-digit zip code	Field Size: 5
7	Amount	Currency	Amount owed by customer	Default Value: 0 Validation Rule: <=5000 Validation Text: "You must enter an amount less than or equal to $5,000."

The first six fields are defined in the upper pane of the Table window. Note that the *Customer Number* field has been assigned as the primary key.

Primary key icon

	Field Name	Data Type	Description
	Customer Number	Text	An identification code unique to this customer
	Last	Text	Customer's last name
	First	Text	Customer's first name
	City	Text	Customer's city
	State	Text	Customer's state
▶	Zip	Text	Customer's five-digit zip code

7 Use the ↓ or ↑ key to move to each field name, check all entries for errors and correct them, and adjust as needed to match the data shown in Table DB1-4

DEFAULT VALUES AND VALIDATION OPTIONS

Default value and validation options are available for many data types. The **default value option** automatically places a defined value in a given field, which you can then accept or change. This technique eliminates redundant entries for such items as a city or state name. Validation options enable you to specify a rule to be used to verify the accuracy of data entered into a field. The **validation rule** can also be expressed as a formula (mathematical equation). The Amount field is used to demonstrate these field property options.

1 If needed, move to the *Field Name* cell below *Zip*

2 Type **Amount** in the *Field Name* column, and press ↵

3 Click the ▼ button of the *Data Type* box, and then click *Currency*

4 Press ↵ to move to the *Description* column

Note that the default value has been automatically set to "0" in the Field Property box (lower pane). Although you can set this value by entering a desired default value in its box, use the default setting for this exercise.

5 Type **Amount owed by customer**

The phrase you enter in the *Description* column will appear in the status bar as a prompt when you enter data into this field.

6 Click the *Validation Rule* box in the lower pane

Note that an ellipsis (…) button appears to the right of the box. Clicking this button will open a dialog box for entering your preferences. For now:

7 Type **<=5000** in the *Validation Rule* box

The formula entered in Step 7 restricts the value that can be entered in this field to an amount less than or equal to 5000.

8 Press ↵ to move to the *Validation Text* box

9 Type You must enter an amount less than or equal to $5,000.00.

The phrase you typed in Step 9 will appear in an error message if a value greater than 5000 is entered into this field.

> Tip: Whenever you place the insertion point in a Field Properties box (lower pane), you have two options:

(1) If an ellipsis (...) appears in the property's line, you can click the ellipsis to open a dialog box in which you can enter your preferences. (2) If a ▼ button appears in the property's line, you can click it and then click the desired value from a list of acceptable values.

OTHER FIELD PROPERTIES.   Access offers a variety of other field properties that you can set in the Table Design window. As you review them in Table DB1-5, keep in mind that different data types may have different field properties.

SAVING, CLOSING, AND OPENING A TABLE

Saving is a process of storing data in a file. In Access, data are automatically saved when they are entered into a table. However, a table's structure, when created or modified, needs to be saved. Up to now, you have not saved the structure of the table you created. To save the table structure in your CUSTOMER database file as Customer List, do the following:

1 Click *File* and then *Save* to display the Save As dialog box   Ctrl + S

Note that the Save As dialog box appears only when you invoke the Save command on an unsaved object or file. Once you save that object or file with a name, the Save command resaves the item under that original name. The Save As command, on the other hand, always opens the Save As dialog box.

2 Type Customer List and then click *OK*

(Remember, a table is an Access object, not a file. Saving it makes it part of your CUSTOMER database file.)

> Tip: If you had not assigned a primary key, a dialog box appears, warning you that "There is no primary key defined" and asking whether you want to create one. If you answered "Yes" to this question, Access would create an additional field named ID, with an AutoNumber data type, which would sequentially number each record you entered. This additional field would appear in the leftmost column of your table.

At this point, you can either close the Table Design window or switch the view for data entry. (Data entry is discussed in the next mastery set.) The **Close** command removes a window from Access's work area and frees up system memory. You should close a window when it is not in use.

TABLE DB1-5 ■ **FIELD PROPERTIES**

Field Properties	Description
Field Size	The maximum number of alphanumeric or numeric characters that can be entered in the field. For text fields, type a number between 1 and 255. For number fields, use the arrow to open a drop-down list and select from among byte, integer, long integer, single, and double.
Format Number	Display a number as a general number (1234.5678), currency ($1,234.56), fixed (1234.56), standard (1,234.56), percent (23.32%), or scientific notation (1.23E+03). Date fields can be displayed in the following formats: general date (12/25/98 7:19:34 AM), long date (Monday, December 25, 1998), medium date (25-December-98), short date (12/25/98), long time (7:19:34 AM), medium time (7:19 AM), and short time (7:19).
Input Mask	Automatically inserts literal characters into fields so that you do not have to type them. It can also restrict the characters that you are permitted to insert in any position in the field. For example, a mask for a telephone number could be (999) 000-0000. "9" in a field mask means that only a numeral can be entered in that position, but entry is not required. "0" in a field mask means that only a numeral can be entered in that position, and entry is required.
Caption	A descriptive word, phrase, or sentence that will be displayed instead of the field name when designing other Access objects.
Default Value	Provides a value for the field, which the user can accept or type over.
Validation Rule	User-specified limits on the type of data that can be entered. It can be set in terms of a mathematical formula. In validation rule expressions or formulas, the field name is enclosed in square brackets.
Validation Text	Provides a message displayed if the user attempts to enter a field value that violates a validation rule.
Required	A yes/no property. Yes means that you cannot create a record without entering valid data in that field. No means that you may create a record without entering data in that field.
Allow Zero Length	A yes/no property that applies to Text and Memo fields. Yes permits you to enter strings with a size of zero—two quotation marks with nothing between them. This is sometimes useful in linking files.
Indexed	Used when you expect to sort data by the field or you expect to search for values in that field. The indexed property has three possible settings: No, do not create an index. Yes, create an index and do not allow duplicate entries. Yes, create an index and allow duplicate entries.

 **3** Click *File, Close,* or click the Customer List: Table's *Close* button; if needed, click *Yes*   

Tip: If you invoke the Close command on an unsaved object or a modified object that was not resaved, Access will ask you whether you want to save.

The Customer List table icon now appears in the Table tab list. You can use this icon to open the table either in Design view or Datasheet view. **Design view** enables you to edit the table's structure. **Datasheet view** enables you to enter, edit, delete, and sort data in the table.

Try this to open the table in Design view:

4 Click the *Customer List* icon

5 Click the *Design* button

The Customer List: Table window appears again. At this point, you can edit the field structure. For now, to close it again:

6 Click *File, Close* or click the Customer List: Table's *Close* button   **Ctrl** + **F4**

Now, to open the table in Datasheet view:

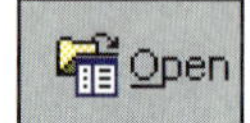

7 Click the *Customer List* icon

8 Click the *Open* button

Note that only a blank record appears because no data has been entered yet.

> Tip: Instead of performing Steps 7 and 8, you can double-click the *Customer List* icon to open it in Datasheet view.

You can also use the View menu to switch between Design and Datasheet view. Try this:

9 Click *View, Design View*

10 Click *View, Datasheet View* to switch back

11 Click *File, Close*, or click the Customer List: Table's *Close* button   **Ctrl** + **F4**

12 Click *File, Exit*, or click Access's *Close* button to exit   **Alt** + **F4**

The Save, Close, and Open commands for tables can be applied to any object in the Database window.

OPENING AND CLOSING AN ACCESS DATABASE FILE

Access offers you several ways to open a database file. Earlier, you used the Microsoft Access dialog box. You can also use the Open dialog box, or the File menu (if you've recently used the file). First, you will review opening a file using the Access dialog box and then practice opening a file using the other two methods.

1 Launch Access, and if necessary, insert your diskette into Drive A

The Microsoft Access dialog box should appear in the center of your screen with the Access window in the background.

> Tip: If you had recently used the file you wanted to open, it would be listed in the Microsoft Access dialog box. You could open the file by simply clicking its name and then the *OK* button instead of performing Steps 2 through 4.

2 Click the *Open an existing file* option and then *OK*

The Open dialog box should appear. If your *Look in* drop-down box does not display *3 1/2 Floppy (A:)* (or the appropriate drive/folder of your lab), perform Step 3 to change it.

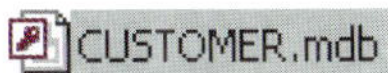 **3** Click the ▼ button of the *Look in* box for its list; if needed, use the scroll bar to locate *3 1/2 Floppy (A:)*, or the appropriate drive/folder, and click it

The Open dialog box should resemble Figure DB1-13. You can use this dialog box to perform a variety of file management operations. Some are identified in the figure. To open the CUSTOMER file:

 **4** Click the *CUSTOMER.mdb* icon

5 Click the *Open* button

> Tip: Instead of Steps 4 and 5, you can double-click the *CUSTOMER.mdb* icon or type the file's name in the *File name* box and then click *Open.*

The CUSTOMER: Database window appears in Access's work area.

 **6** Click the CUSTOMER: Database window's *Close* button, or click *File*, *Close*   

DB

FIGURE DB1-13 ■ THE OPEN DIALOG BOX

The Open dialog box can be used to open a saved database file. It can also be used to perform a variety of other file management operations.

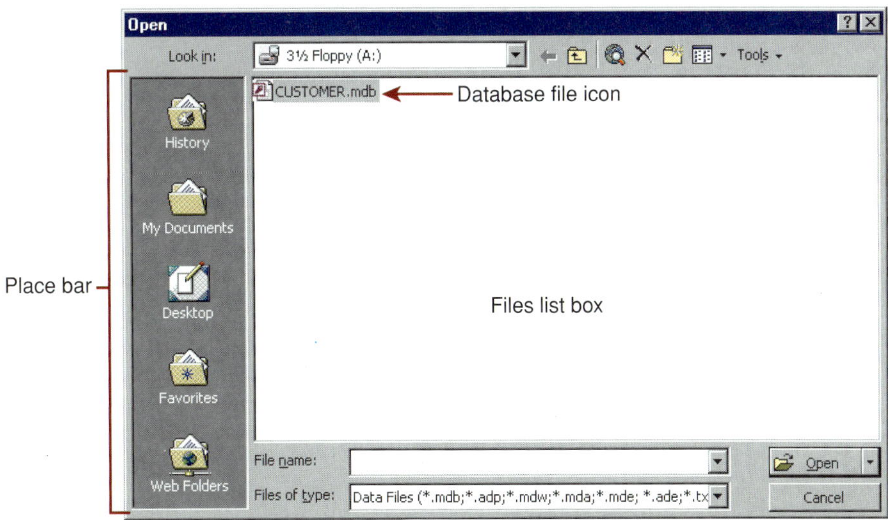

Note that when you close a database window, you close the file. When you close an object in a database, such as a table, you close only that object, not the database file.

Now, open the CUSTOMER file using the File menu:

7   Click *File*, *Open Database*   `Ctrl` + `O`

8   Click the *CUSTOMER.mdb* icon

9   Click the *Open* button

Again, the CUSTOMER: Database window appears. As with many Windows programs, the last few database files you've used can be opened directly from the File menu. Try this:

10   Click the CUSTOMER: Database window's *Close* button, or click *File*, *Close*   `Ctrl` + `F4`

11   Click *File*, *1 A:\CUSTOMER*

12   Exit Access

> **Note: Exiting Access also closes the database file. Diskettes should not be removed until the file in use is closed and the disk drive light is off on your system unit.**

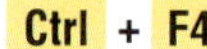 **CHECKPOINT**

Perform these tasks and answer these questions.
1. Launch Access, and open the DCHECK.mdb database file created in the Mastery Set 1-2's Checkpoint.
2. Create a new table named Students. Define these three fields: Name (Text, 15) (set as primary key), Test1 (Number), and Test2 (Number). Set the validation option for a maximum of 100 for each test.
3. Change the *Name* field's width to 20.
4. Save the table as Students and then close the table and the database file.
5. What is the difference between Design view and Datasheet view?

MASTERY SET 1-5: ENTERING RECORDS

Once you create a table in a database file, you can use it to enter (store) or edit data. As you enter the records in this mastery set, remember that a record is simply a collection of related data categorized into separate fields. For example, for each customer's record, you can enter data for the fields you previously created, such as Customer Number, Last, First, and so on.

1   If needed, launch Access

Now, open the CUSTOMER database file using the Microsoft Access dialog box:

2 If needed, click the *Open an existing file* option

3 Click *OK* for the Open dialog box

> Tip: Remember, instead of performing Steps 2 and 3, you can use the Open command of the File menu box by clicking the *Cancel* button (or pressing *Esc*) and then clicking *File*, *Open Database* (or pressing *Ctrl + O*).

4 If appropriate for your system, insert your data diskette

5 If necessary, click the *Look in* button for its list and then *3 1/2 Floppy (A:)* (or the appropriate folder) to set the default location

6 Click *CUSTOMER.mdb* in the list box, or click the *File name* text box and then type **CUSTOMER**

7 Click the *Open* button to open the database file

> Tip: Instead of performing Steps 6 and 7, you can also double-click *CUSTOMER* in the list box to open it.

8 If needed, click the *Tables* object type button in the Database window

9 Click the *Customer List* icon

10 Click the *Open* button

11 If needed, click the table window's Maximize button   **Alt + - , X**

Your Customer List: Table window should resemble Figure DB1-14a (if your screen is set to a lower resolution, it may display less information). Note that you are in Datasheet view. You are now ready to enter data into your Customer List table.

ENTERING DATA INTO A TABLE

This screen is really a blank table awaiting new data. The field names you created in the table design appear at the top of each column as identifying labels, one column for each field. Notice that the buttons on the toolbar have changed to match the current operation.

1 If needed, click the first cell in the *Customer Number* column to place the insertion point there

Note that when the insertion point is in a field, the description you typed while designing the table is displayed on the status bar. This provides you with a useful guide as to what data should be entered in each column.

2 Type **670** in the *Customer Number* column, and then press ↵

FIGURE DB1-14 ■ ENTERING RECORDS

(a) The Customer List: Table window maximized in the Access work area.
(b) The first record is entered.
(c) Three more records have been entered.
(d) The remaining two records have been entered.

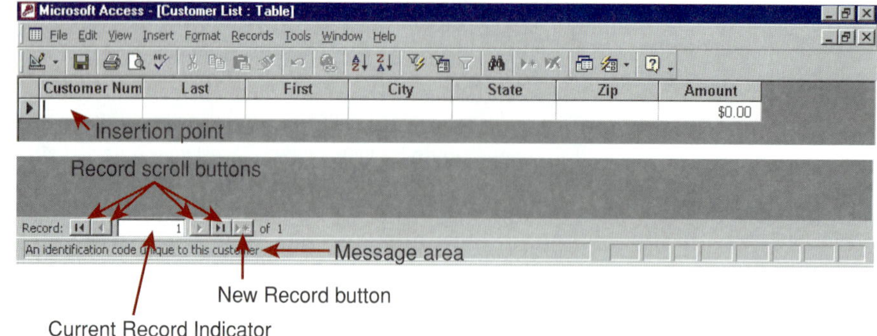

(a)

	Customer Num	Last	First	City	State	Zip	Amount
▶	670	Parker	Charles	Santa Fe	NM	87051	$450.75
✳							$0.00

(b)

	Customer Num	Last	First	City	State	Zip	Amount
	670	Parker	Charles	Santa Fe	NM	87051	$450.75
	101	Burstein	Jerome	San Jose	CA	95120	$230.45
	449	Kee	Charles	New York	NY	10003	$540.45
✎	754	Martin	Edward	New York	NY	10001	360.55
✳							$0.00

(c)

	Customer Num	Last	First	City	State	Zip	Amount
▶	101	Burstein	Jerome	San Jose	CA	95120	$230.45
	389	Martin	Arthur	Flushing	NY	11367	$65.30
	449	Kee	Charles	New York	NY	10003	$540.45
	670	Parker	Charles	Santa Fe	NM	87051	$450.75
	754	Martin	Edward	New York	NY	10001	$360.55
✳							$0.00

(d)

As you enter field values, you can use either the *Tab* or *Enter* keys to move to the next field. To move back a field, use the left arrow or *Shift + Tab* keys. If you make a mistake while typing, simply use the Backspace key to delete to the left, and then retype. (The *Delete* key will delete one character to the right.)

3 Type **Parker** in the *Last* column, and press ↵

4 Type **Charles** in the *First* column, and press ↵

5 Type **Santa Fe** in the *City* column, and press ↵

6 Type **NM** in the *State* column, and press ↵

7 Type **87051** in the *Zip* column, and press ↵

When entering data in the *Amount* column, don't forget to place the decimal point in its proper position. Also, do not enter a "$" character in front of the amount. Access will insert it automatically because the *Amount* column is already set for the currency data type.

8 Type **450.75** in the *Amount* column

Your screen should resemble Figure DB1-14b.

9 Press ↵ to move to the next row

When you move to another field, record (row) or a new one or close the table, Access automatically saves the data entered for the previous record. In this case, Customer Number 670's data was saved when you performed Step 9. Access Objects such as a table, on the other hand, require you to invoke the Save command (found in the File menu) to save or resave.

Access also always provides a new, blank row for the next record. Notice that the status bar at the bottom shows "Record 2 of 2," indicating that Access is currently pointing to the second record to be entered.

> Tip: To return to a previous row to correct an error in an entry, simply click the field value that you want to change. You can then backspace over or delete the error, correct the entry, and then press *Enter* (or point to the last record and click) to return to the current row.

10 Using the same technique as in Steps 1 through 9, and the data in Table DB1-6, enter Records 2 through 4 only

Your screen should resemble Figure DB1-14c. Although you could continue to enter records into the table using this method, you will now practice other ways to enter data.

TABLE DB1-6 ■ RECORDS FOR THE CUSTOMER LIST

Record No.	Customer Number	Last	First	City	State	Zip	Amount
1	670	Parker	Charles	Santa Fe	NM	87051	450.75
2	101	Burstein	Jerome	San Jose	CA	95120	230.45
3	449	Kee	Charles	New York	NY	10003	540.45
4	754	Martin	Edward	New York	NY	10001	360.55
5	389	Martin	Arthur	Flushing	NY	11367	65.30

Another way to enter records in your table is to use the **Data Entry** command. This command displays only a single record line in a table window for each new record entry. Try this technique to enter Record 5 from Table DB1-5:

11 Click *Records, Data Entry*

12 Enter the data for Record 5, and then press ↵ to save the data

To redisplay all records in the table:

13 Click *Records, Remove Filter/Sort*

The records now appear in customer number order (by primary key) as in Figure DB1-14d. Access will automatically present the data in primary key order unless you sort and save the table in a different order. Sorting is discussed in Unit 2.

14 Click *File, Save* to resave the table — Ctrl + S

15 Click *File, Close*, or click the Customer List: Table window's *Close* button — Ctrl + F4

The CUSTOMER: Database window should now appear maximized in Access' work area.

16 Exit Access to restore any default settings before you proceed to the next section

ENTERING DATA INTO A FORM

Data can also be entered into a table using a form. As described earlier, Form view lets you work with a single record at a time. You can use Access's Form Wizard to design forms using predesigned formats, or you can design one yourself from scratch. If all you need is a simple form that presents all the fields in a column, Access can provide it very quickly:

1 Launch Access, and open the CUSTOMER.mdb database file

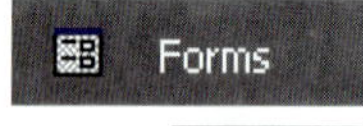

2 Click the *Forms* object type button in the CUSTOMER: Database window

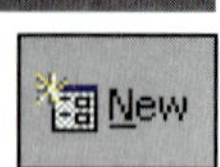

3 Click the *New* button to display the New Form dialog box

4 Click *AutoForm: Columnar*

5 Click the ▼ button in the box *Choose the table or query where the object's data comes from:*

6 Click *Customer List*

Your dialog box selection should resemble Figure DB1-15a. (Other Form options are discussed in Unit 3.)

FIGURE DB1-15 ■ CREATING A FORM

(a) The New Form dialog box can be used to create a form.
(b) The Form window.

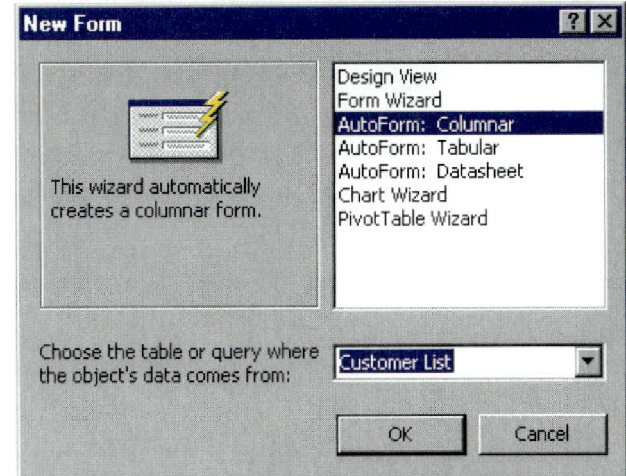

(a)

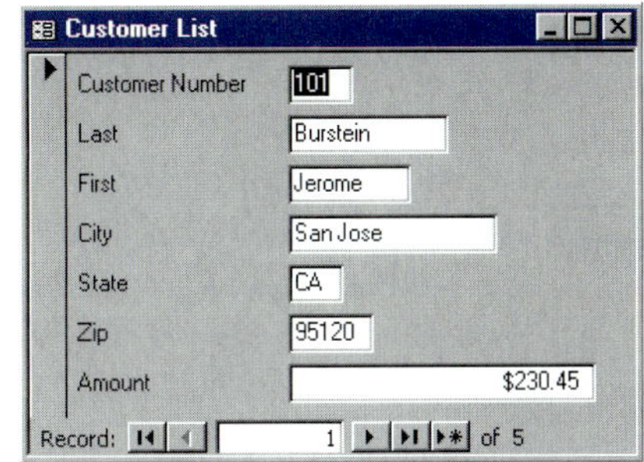

(b)

Now, to create a columnar form:

7 Click *OK*

Your Form window should appear as in Figure DB1-15b. Note that the first record of the database appears. To save the new object as Customer Form:

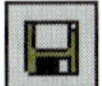 **8** Click *File, Save*   **Ctrl** + **S**

Note that when you invoke the Save command on an unsaved object or file, it opens the Save As dialog box so that you can name that item before saving. All other times, the Save command resaves an object or file under its original name. To open the Save As dialog box when an object or file has been saved previously, use the Save As command of the File menu.

As you type the first character in the next step, note that the highlighted (selected) text "Customer List" disappears from the text box. Typing over any selected text will delete it. You can also edit selected text by first using the left or right arrow keys to remove the highlight.

9 Type **Customer Form** in the *Form Name* text box and then press 

Your form's design has now been saved as Customer Form. To enter a new record's data:

10 Click *Insert, New Record* or the *Insert New Record* icon in the status bar of the Customer List form window (see the icon in the margin)

Using the information in Table DB1-7, enter Records 6 through 8 *only,* as follows:

11 Type 176 in the *Customer Number* box, and press ↵

12 Type West in the *Last* box, and press ↵

13 Type Rita in the *First* box, and press ↵

14 Type Chicago in the *City* box, and press ↵

15 Type IL in the *State* box, and press ↵

16 Type 60601 in the *Zip* box, and press ↵

17 Type 965.42 in the *Amount* box, and press ↵

As in a table, data that you enter in a form is saved when you move to the next record.

18 Repeat Steps 11 through 17 to enter the data for Records 7 and 8 from Table DB1-7

19 Click *File, Close* or click the Form window's *Close* button   **Ctrl** + **F4**

20 Exit Access

☑ **CHECKPOINT**

Perform these tasks.
1. Launch Access, open the DCHECK.mdb database file, and then open the Students table.

TABLE DB1-7 ■ ADDITIONAL RECORDS FOR THE CUSTOMER LIST

Record No.	Customer Number	Last	First	City	State	Zip	Amount
6	176	West	Rita	Chicago	IL	60601	965.42
7	067	Williams	DeVilla	Chicago	IL	60601	965.42
8	111	Hill	Karen	Chicago	IL	60605	456.78

2.   Enter the following records and then save the table:

Name	TEST1	TEST2
Smith	78	92
Jones	65	75
Green	84	88

3.   Close the Students table.
4.   Using the Students table as its source, create and save a columnar form named Students Form, and then enter the following three new records:

Name	TEST1	TEST2
Lee	100	88
Kim	70	93
Piper	40	75

When you have completed Steps 1 through 4, you should have six records in the Students form. You can also view all six records in the Student table.

5.   Try changing Green's TEST1 score to 125. Will Access let you do this? If not, change it back to 84 and then exit Access.

MASTERY SET 1-6: EXAMINING FIELD VALUES

Creating a database and entering field values are merely the preliminary steps to using Access. Once records exist, you can invoke a variety of commands to look at (view) the data within them. First, you learn how to scroll through fields and then records in both a table and a form. You then learn how to use the Find and Replace commands to locate specific data. After that, you learn how to change the size of field columns, change the order of fields, and use various printing techniques. Perform the following steps to prepare for the exercises in this mastery set:

1 If necessary, launch Access, and open the CUSTOMER.mdb database file

2 Open the Customer List table, and then maximize it (if needed, click the *Table* object type button, *Customer List* icon, and then the *Open* button)

SCROLLING THROUGH FIELDS AND RECORDS

Scrolling involves moving to a desired field or record to use or edit its data. You can scroll using either the keyboard or the mouse. Both techniques are discussed next.

SCROLLING FIELDS BY KEYBOARD.   A variety of shortcut keys can help you scroll to different fields quickly. As you experienced earlier, the right arrow, *Tab,* and *Enter* keys all move to the next field in a table. You can also go back a field by pressing the left arrow or *Shift + Tab* keys. The following keys move the selection highlight to different fields in your table quickly.

To scroll to the last field in a table:

1 Press **Ctrl** + **End**

Your selection highlight is now on $360.55. Be careful here: the next new character you type will erase the selected (highlighted) data. To edit the data in the selection:

2   **Press** **F2**

The insertion point now appears in the field. At this point, you can change part or all of the field's value. For now, to quickly go back to the first field of the first record:

3   **Press** ↵

4   **Press** **Ctrl** + **Home**

To move to the last field in Record 1:

5   **Press** **End**

To move to the first field in Record 1:

6   **Press** **Home**

See Table DB1-8 for a list of these shortcut keys (which can also be used in a form.)

SCROLLING FIELDS BY MOUSE.   To move to a desired field in a table by mouse, simply click the field. This also positions the insertion point for editing. If a desired field is not currently in view, you may need to use a scroll bar. (A scroll bar appears on the right wall and/or base of a window or list box when its content exceeds its display area.) For example, depending on the resolution setting of your screen, the Amount column data in the Customer List table may not be in the window's display

TABLE DB1-8   ■   **SCROLLING SHORTCUT KEYS**

Shortcut Keys	Function
→, ↵, or *Tab*	Moves to the next field.
←, *Shift* + *Tab*	Moves back a field.
Pg Dn or *Pg Up*	Moves down or up by one screen in a table. In a form, moves to the next record or back one record.
End	Moves to the end of the current record.
Home	Moves to the beginning of the current record.
Ctrl + *End*	Moves to the last field in the last record.
Ctrl + *Home*	Moves to the first field in the first record.

area. To move to Customer 754's Amount field, you may need to use the horizontal scroll bar at the base of the window. As shown in Figure DB1-16, a scroll bar has a scroll button at each end (with a triangular symbol) and a rectangular scroll box along its bar. If you do not need to use a scroll bar, simply click the desired item.

1 **If necessary, click the** ▶ **horizontal scroll bar button until the** *Amount* **column is in the viewing area**

Note that a scroll bar does not move the selection highlight or insertion point. It merely repositions a table or other object within the viewing area of a window. You must still click the desired item to move to it. For example, you can now move to $360.55:

2 **Click anywhere on** *$360.55*

The insertion point appears in the exact position that you clicked. To select (highlight) the contents of a field, try this:

3 **Point to the left margin of the field containing the Zip code** *10001* **until the screen pointer changes to a plus sign (see the margin image), and then click**

> **Tip: You can also drag across a field's contents to select it.**

4 **If necessary, click the** ◀ **scroll bar button until the** *Customer Number* **column is in view**

5 **Point to the left margin of the field containing the customer number** *670* **until the pointer changes to a plus sign, and then click**

> **Tip: These mouse field-scrolling techniques can also be applied to a form.**

SCROLLING RECORDS BY KEYBOARD.   To scroll one record at a time in a table, use the down or up arrow keys. The *Pg Dn* and *Pg Up* keys scroll one screen at a time in a table. Because each form screen displays a single record at a time, the *Pg Dn* and *Pg Up* keys scroll a record at a time in a form window.

1 **Press** `Ctrl` **+** `Home` **to move to the first field of the Record 1**

2 **Press** ↓ **four times to move to Record 5**

DB

Note that the record indicator at the bottom of the window displays Record 5 of 8.

3   Press ↑ twice to move to Record 3

4   Press Ctrl + Home to move back to the first field in Record 1

5   Click the Customer List: Table window's Minimize button   Alt + - , N

You have just minimized the Customer List: Table window (reduced it to an icon resembling its title bar.) Minimizing a window allows you to keep it available so that you can quickly access it when needed. Leave this table minimized for now as you practice record scrolling with a form.

6   Click the *Forms* object type button of the CUSTOMER: Database window

7   Click the *Customer Form* icon

8   Click the *Open* button

> **Tip: Instead of performing Steps 6 and 7, you can double-click the *Customer Form* icon to open it.**

The Customer Form window should appear on your screen. Your record indicator at the bottom of the window should now indicate that you are in Record 1 of 8. Note, too, that at least three buttons now appear on the taskbar, namely: CUSTOMER: Database, Customer List: Table, and Customer List (form). The *Customer List* taskbar button currently appears "pressed," indicating that it is the active window. You can switch to any of the other windows by simply clicking the appropriate taskbar button. For now:

9   Press Pg Dn three times to move to Record 4

10   Press Pg Up as needed to move to Record 2

11   Press Ctrl + End to move to the last field in the last record

12   Press Ctrl + Home to move to the first field in the first record

Leave this window open for use in the next section.

SCROLLING RECORDS BY MOUSE.   The scroll buttons at the base of the Form and Table windows can be used for scrolling to records by mouse. These scrolling buttons are identified in Figure DB1-17. Try this:

1   Click the ▶ record scroll button twice to move to Record 3

2   Click the ▶❘ record scroll button to move to the last record—8

3   Click the ❘◀ record scroll button to move to the first record

4   Close the Customer Form window

FIGURE DB1-17 ■ **SCROLLING RECORDS BY MOUSE**

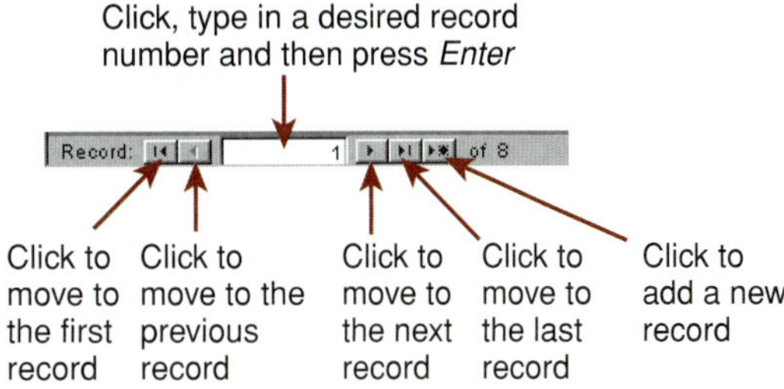

5 Click the Maximize button of the *Customer List: Table* icon

6 Repeat Steps 1 through 3

LOCATING SPECIFIC FIELD DATA

Find and Replace are two useful tools offered by Access. Although you could examine each record individually to search for desired data values, the **Find** command can help you quickly locate one or more specific field values within your data. In addition, the **Replace** command can be used to both locate and replace a specific field value (or values). When you perform a "find" or "replace" routine, it is important that the insertion point first be positioned in the field column in which the desired data are stored. This is because the default setting of the Find and Replace dialog boxes is to search the current field. (You can change this option.)

FINDING SPECIFIC FIELD DATA.   Try this exercise to find the State fields that contain the data "NY":

1 If needed, open the Customer List table and maximize it

2 Move to any record's data in the *State* field column—in this case, move to *IL*

3 Click *Edit,* (if needed ⌄), *Find*   Ctrl + F

The Find dialog box should appear as in Figure DB1-18a. In addition to the familiar features shared by other Access dialog boxes, this box enables you to enter the value for which you are searching. See Figure DB1-18a for a description of each Find dialog box component.

4 Type NY in the *Find What* box

5 Click the *Find Next* button

The selection highlight moves to the first field that contains "NY."

FIGURE DB1-18 ■ FIND AND REPLACE OPERATIONS

(a) The *Find* tab of the Find and Replace dialog box can be used to search for a string of text.
(b) The *Replace* tab of the Find and Replace dialog box can be used to search for and replace a string of text.

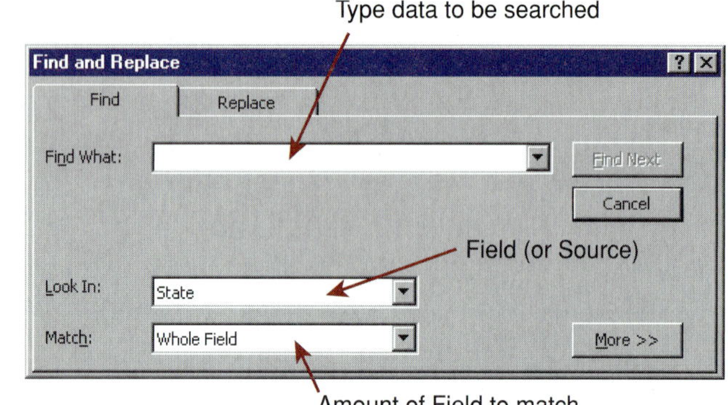

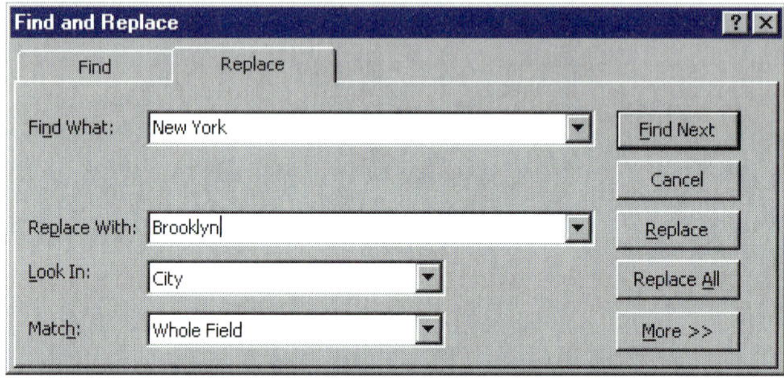

6 Click the *Find Next* button to move to the next occurrence of "NY"

7 Click the *Cancel* button of the dialog box

REPLACING SPECIFIC FIELD DATA.   To find and replace specific field data, use the Replace command (in the Edit menu). Try this to replace all City entries of "New York" with "Brooklyn":

1 Move to the *City* column (anywhere in the column)

2 Click *Edit,* (if needed ⌄), *Replace*   **Ctrl** + **H**

3 Type **New York** in the *Find What* box and then press **Tab**

4 Type **Brooklyn** in the *Replace With* box

Your dialog box should resemble Figure DB1-18b. To replace all occurrences:

5 Click the *Replace All* button

6 Click *Yes* when a message tells you that the Undo feature will not work after this operation

Both field columns are selected, as shown in Figure DB1-20a.

4 Point to either the *Last* or *First* column label

5 Drag and drop the selection to the left, just before the *Customer Number* column

The result of your reordering should resemble Figure DB1-20b.

6 Click any field cell to deselect

7 Click *File*, *Close*, *No* to close the table without saving the changes

Note that the change in column width will appear the next time the table is opened, but the change in the order of the columns will not.

8 Exit Access before continuing to the next section to reset to its default settings

Although it is not absolutely necessary to perform Step 7, it will ensure that your screens appear (especially window sizes) as those presented in the preceding sections.

PRINTING

Access's Print commands enable you to print a table, form, or other object on your screen (via Print Preview) or on paper (via Print).

PRINT PREVIEW. The **Print Preview** command allows you to see your table, form, or other object as it will appear when printed on paper. This gives you the chance to examine its appearance closely before printing. You can access the Print Preview command through the File menu or by clicking its toolbar button.

1 Launch Access, and open the CUSTOMER.mdb database file

2 Open the Customer List table, and then maximize it

3 Click *File*, (if needed ), *Print Preview*

Your screen should resemble Figure DB1-21. Note that your mouse pointer changes to a magnifying glass icon (as shown in the margin) when you point within the table. Clicking an item will enlarge or reduce its view. Try this:

4 Click the table to enlarge its view

5 Click it again to reduce it to its former size

Although you can print your form on paper from the Print Preview screen, do the following to exit this window for now:

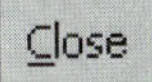

6 Click the *Close* toolbar button   **Esc**

PRINT. You can use the *Print* command to print a view on paper. Try this:

FIGURE DB1-21 ■ **THE PRINT PREVIEW WINDOW**

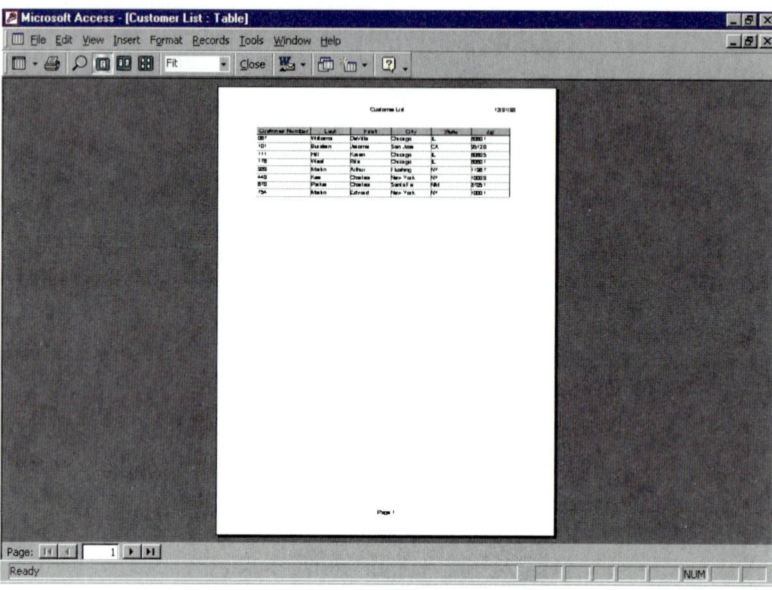

1 Turn on your printer, and be sure it is connected to your computer and ready to print

2 Click *File, Print* for its dialog box   `Ctrl` + `P`

As you can see in Figure DB1-22, the Print dialog box has options to change your printer or its properties (settings), specify the pages (the default is *All*), specify the number of copies (the default is 1), collate, or print to a file. Note that your printer may differ from the one displayed in the figure.

3 Click the *OK* button to print

Tip: Clicking the *Print* toolbar button will send the table directly to the printer without displaying the Print dialog box first. Whatever options were set in the last print operation will be used.

4 Close the *Customer List* table

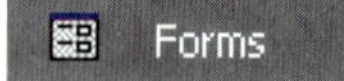

5 Click the *Forms* object type button 🔳

6 Double-click the *Customer Form* icon to open it

7 If desired, click the Customer Form window's Restore button to resize it to its default size   `Alt` + `-` , `R`

8 Click *File, Print*   `Ctrl` + `P`

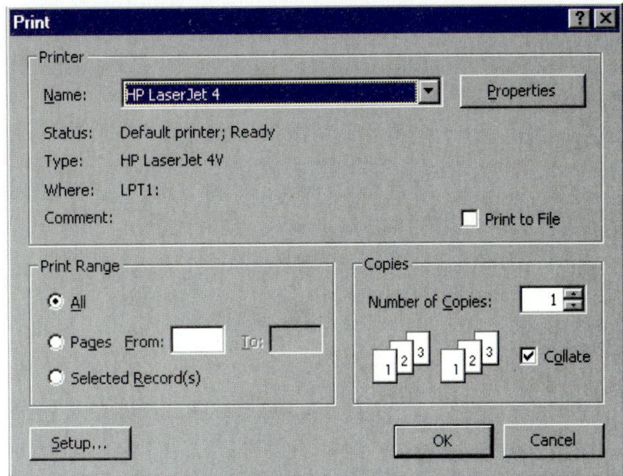

At this point, you can set the dialog box to print the current record or a selection of records (click *Selected Record(s)*), specific pages (of forms), or all records (the default). To print all records in Form view:

9 Click *OK*

10 Close the Form window, and then exit Access

☑ **CHECKPOINT**

Perform these tasks.
1. Describe some techniques to scroll through fields and records in a table and form.
2. Launch Access, open the DCHECK.mdb database file, and then open the Students table.
3. Use the Find command to locate the student "Lee."
4. Use the Replace command to search for all TEST2 grades that equal 88, and change them to 93.
5. Print the Students table, and then exit Access.

SUMMARY

■ A database management system (DBMS) helps you organize data so that they can be easily stored, accessed, modified, and maintained.

■ Data are essentially facts and may include text, numbers, sounds, and objects (graphic images).

■ A database is a collection of related data arranged into fields and records. A field is a single piece of data. A record is a group of related fields. In Access, a database is defined as a collection of one or more related tables and other objects stored in one database file. A table displays data in columnar (column and row) form. Each row represents a single record, and each column, a specific field. The intersection of a column and row is called a cell.

■ The Access window has a title bar, menu bar, toolbar, work area, and status bar. It is the main program window.

■ An Access database file may contain a variety of objects, including tables, queries, forms, reports, pages, macros, and modules. The Database window acts as a menu system for objects stored in a database file. Click the desired *object type* button to display its objects.

■ In creating new tables, a structure is designed that includes a field name, type, and often, size.

■ There are ten field data types. The most commonly used ones are Text, Number, Currency, and Date/Time.

■ A primary key is a field (or set of fields) that uniquely identifies each record in a table. Assigning a primary key will rearrange records in that order. It also prevents you from entering records with duplicate primary key data.

■ The default value option automatically provides a defined field value, which can then be accepted or changed by the user. The validation options enable you to set rules to verify the accuracy of data entered into a field.

■ Objects such as tables or forms may be saved to a database file using the Save or Save As commands. The Save command opens the Save As dialog box for naming and saving a new object or file. Once saved, the Save command resaves the object or file under its original name. The Save As command always opens the Save As dialog box.

■ Data entered into a table are automatically saved when you move from one record to another or when you close the window.

■ The Close command is used to close an object or database window in Access's work area. This frees up system memory.

■ Records can be added in either table or single-record form. A table presents data in rows and columns, whereas a form displays one record on each screen.

■ You can scroll through fields and records by keyboard or mouse. The Find and Replace commands can be used to quickly search for and/or replace field values.

■ Drag and drop techniques can be used to change table column widths or the order of field columns.

■ A table or form can be quickly viewed onscreen using the Print Preview command or printed using the Print command.

KEY TERMS

Shown in parentheses are the page numbers on which key terms are boldfaced.

Close (DB28)	Default value option	Module (DB15)
Data (DB2)	(DB27)	Objects (DB14)
Data Entry (DB36)	Design view (DB30)	Office Assistant (DB17)
Data type (DB23)	Field (DB2)	Primary key (DB24)
Database (DB2)	Field name (DB23)	Print Preview (DB47)
Database management	Field size (DB25)	Properties (DB22)
system (DBMS) (DB2)	Find (DB43)	Query (DB15)
Database window (DB14)	Form (DB15)	Record (DB2)
Datasheet view (DB30)	Macros (DB15)	Replace (DB43)

Report (DB15)

Required (DB25)

Scrolling (DB39)

Shortcut keys (DB6)

Shortcut menus (DB9)

Status bar (DB9)

Table (DB2)

Title bar (DB9)

Toolbar (DB9)

Validation rule (DB27)

Wildcard characters
  (DB45)

UNIT REVIEW

TRUE/FALSE

____ 1. In Access, data are stored in a collection of one or more tables.

____ 2. Table structures are designed in Datasheet view.

____ 3. The Database window is used only to create a new table.

____ 4. Telephone numbers should be stored in a number field.

____ 5. A form presents data in a row and column format.

____ 6. The term data is equivalent to the term field value.

____ 7. A record is a collection of fields.

____ 8. Pressing *Ctrl + Home* will move the selection highlight to the first field in the first record.

____ 9. Pressing *F2* when in a field cell of a table will place the insertion point there for editing.

____ 10. Primary key data does not have to be unique.

MULTIPLE CHOICE

____ 11. Which of the following is not an object in Access?
   a. Form
   b. Table
   c. Report
   d. Data

____ 12. To open a menu by keyboard, you must first press ______ and the underlined letter of the menu bar item.
   a. *Tab*
   b. *Shift*
   c. *Alt*
   d. *Delete*

____ 13. Which of the following field types must include a field size?
   a. Text
   b. Number
   c. Date
   d. Currency

____ 14. All of the following will close a window within Access's work area except
   a. *File, Close*
   b. *File, Exit*
   c. *Ctrl + F4*
   d. Close button of a window

___ 15. To edit the contents of a field by keyboard, you begin by pressing the ________ key.
    a. *Alt*
    b. *F2*
    c. *Edit*
    d. *Insert*

___ 16. What does an ellipsis (...) after a menu command mean?
    a. A dialog box follows.
    b. Another menu follows.
    c. The command will be executed immediately.
    d. An error message will follow.

___ 17. All of the following will move to the next field in a table or form except
    a. *Tab*
    b. Right arrow
    c. *Insert*
    d. *Enter*

___ 18. Which key(s) will quickly move the selection highlight to the first field in the first record?
    a. *Ctrl + 1*
    b. *Alt + Home*
    c. *Ctrl + Home*
    d. *Shift + Home*

___ 19. Characteristics of a field, such as field size or validation rule, are called
    a. Field properties
    b. Field values
    c. Data types
    d. Records

___ 20. Which window can be used to open or create objects in a database?
    a. Table window
    b. Database window
    c. Form window
    d. Help window

MATCHING

Select the term that best matches each feature indicated on the Access screen shown in Figure DB1-A.

___ 21. Access window Close button
___ 22. Click this button to switch to that window
___ 23. Database window
___ 24. Form window
___ 25. Table window
___ 26. Record # indicator
___ 27. Status bar
___ 28. Field
___ 29. Object type buttons
___ 30. Work area

FIGURE DB1-A ■ MATCHING FIGURE

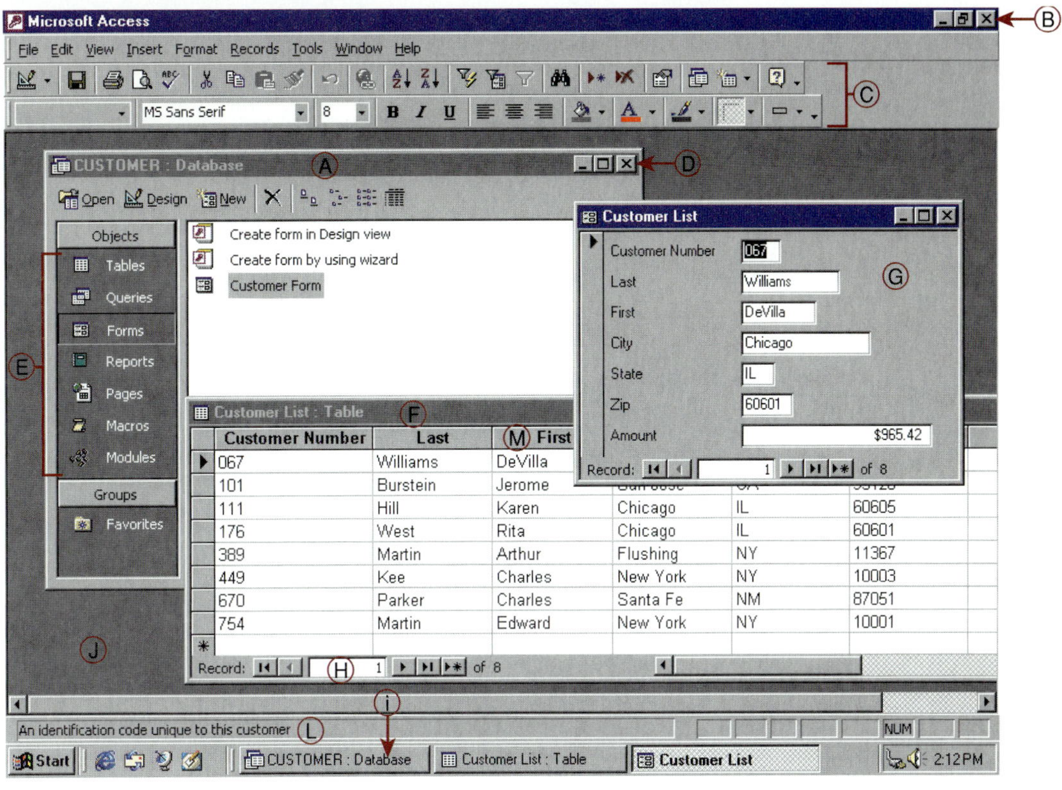

ANSWERS

True/False: 1. T; 2. F; 3. F; 4. F; 5. F; 6. T; 7. T; 8. T; 9. T; 10. F
Multiple Choice: 11. d; 12. c; 13. a; 14. b; 15. b; 16. a; 17. c; 18. c; 19. a; 20. b
Matching: 21. b; 22. i; 23. a; 24. g; 25. f; 26. h; 27. l 28. m; 29. e; 30. j

EXERCISES

I. OPERATIONS

Provide the Access sequence of actions required to do each of the operations shown below. For each operation, assume a system with a hard disk designated as Drive C and a data disk in Drive A.

1. Launch the Access program.

2. Create a new database file named ADDRESS.

3. Create a table structure named ADDRESS LIST with these fields: Last, First, Address, Zip, Phone, and Salary.

4. Add five records to the table.

5. Display all the records in the ADDRESS LIST table; then print them.

6. Create a columnar form named ADDRESS FORM.

7. Add five more records using the ADDRESS FORM.

8. Print Record 8 in the Form format.

9. Move back to the first field in the first record.

10. Save, close all open windows, and exit Access.

II. COMMANDS

Describe what action is initiated or what is accomplished in Access by pressing each series of keystrokes or executing each series of menu commands given below. Assume that each exercise part is independent of any previous parts.

1. Pressing *F1*

2. Clicking the *New* button in the Database window

3. Clicking *File, Exit*

4. Clicking the *Open* button in the Database window

5. Pressing *F2* when in a cell of a table

6. Clicking *View, Datasheet view* when in Design view

7. Clicking the *Find* button

8. Pressing *Ctrl + F4*

9. Pressing *F6* when in the Table Design view

10. Pressing *Alt + F4*

III. APPLICATIONS

Perform the following operations using your computer. You need a hard-disk drive or network with Windows and Access on it. You also need one additional disk on which to store the results of these exercises. In a few words, tell how you accomplished each operation, and describe its result. *Note:* Of the three applications, each relates to school, home, and business, respectively.

APPLICATION 1: DEGREE PLAN

1. Launch Access.

2. Create a database file named DEGREE.

3. Create a table named DEGREE PLAN with the following fields assigning NUMBER as the primary key:

Field Name	Data Type	Field Size
Course	Text	5
Number	Text	5
Grade	Text	1
Completed	Yes/No (Check box)	

4. Enter these five records into the table:

Rec	Course	Number	Grade	Completed
1	CIS	3102	B	Yes
2	CIS	3200	A	Yes
3	ENG	3101	C	Yes
4	MATH	3210		No
5	SPAN	4101	B	Yes

5. Print the table. Close it.

6. Create a columnar form named DEGREE FORM.

7. Enter Records 6 through 10 using the Form window.

Rec	Course	Number	Grade	Completed
6	ACCT	3313		No
7	PE	3304	A	Yes
8	MATH	3213	I	No
9	HIST	3214	C	Yes
10	MUSIC	3333		No

8. Print Record 7 in the Form format.

9. Move back to the first field in the first record.

10. Use the Find command to search for all grades that equal B.

11. Exit Access.

APPLICATION 2: VIDEO COLLECTION

1. Launch Access.

2. Create a database file named VIDEO.

3. Create a table named VIDEO LIST with the following fields assigning VIDEO# as the primary key:

Field Name	Data Type	Field Size
VIDEO #	Number	Long Integer
Volume	Text	3
Start	Text	4
Subject	Text	35
Type	Text	2
Time	Number	Long Integer

4. Enter these eight records into the table and adjust columns as needed:

Rec	VIDEO#	Volume	Start	Subject	Type	Time
1	1000	101	0000	The Rough-Face Girl	C	30
2	1001	101	0650	Will's Mammoth	C	25
3	1002	102	0000	Magic of the 90's	M	120
4	1003	102	1500	Star Trek XXV	SF	128
5	1004	102	3000	Star Warts: Space Frogs	SF	147
6	1005	103	0000	Terminator 15	A	132
7	1006	104	0000	Japanese Ghost Stories	C	45
8	1007	104	4000	Computerized Magician	M	60

5. Create a columnar form named VIDEO INPUT FORM.

6. Enter Records 9 through 12 using the Form window.

Rec	VIDEO#	Volume	Start	Subject	Type	Time
9	1008	105	0000	Using Today's Software	I	125
10	1009	106	0000	Microsoft Made Easy	I	90
11	1010	106	1575	The Magic of Show-Biz	M	120
12	1011	104	1250	Animal Dreaming	C	90

7. Add a record with a video # of 1012, a volume of 108, a start of 0100, your last name as the subject, I for type, and 100 for time.

8. Save and close the Form window.

9. Open the VIDEO LIST table, and then print it.

10. Search and replace all Time fields of 120 with 150.

11. Print the table.

12. Exit Access.

APPLICATION 3: PAYROLL

1. Launch Access.

2. Create a database file named PAYROLL.

3. Create a table named PAYROLL LIST with the following fields assigning SS# as the primary key:

Field Name	Data Type	Field Size
SS#	Text	11
Last	Text	15
First	Text	15
Dept	Text	20
Hours	Number	Long Integer
Rate	Currency	

4. Enter the following four records into the table. (Do not put a hyphen to separate parts of the social security number. This will be added in Unit 2 using Access's Input Mask feature.)

Rec	SS#	Last	First	Dept	Hours	Rate
1	111111111	Brown	Larry	Sales	45	10.25
2	222222222	White	Eileen	Sales	37	9.75
3	333333333	Silver	Steven	Accounting	39	8.75
4	444444444	Gold	Paul	Personnel	35	8.25

5. Save, print, and then close the table.

6. Create a columnar form named EMPLOYEE PAYROLL INFO FORM.

7. Enter Records 5 through 8 using the Form window.

Rec	SS#	Last	First	Dept	Hours	Rate
5	555555555	Brown	Phil	Accounting	35	7.50
6	666666666	Black	Susan	Personnel	42	8.25
7	777777777	Green	Caryn	Accounting	38	6.75
8	888888888	Indigo	Jessica	Personnel	43	5.25

8. Add a record with your name. Assume that you are an employee (SS# 999999999) in Personnel who worked 41 hours at a rate of $9.75.

9. Save and close the Form window.

10. Open the PAYROLL LIST table, and then print it.

11. Search for all Dept fields that display "PERSONNEL" and replace them with "HUMAN RESOURCES"; adjust column widths as needed.

12. Print the table.

13. Exit Access.

DB

MASTERY CASES

The following mastery cases allow you to demonstrate how much you have learned about this software. Each case describes a fictitious problem that can be solved using the skills you have learned in this unit. You are encouraged to design your responses (files, data, lists) in ways that display your personal mastery of the software. Feel free to show off your skills. Use real data from your own experience, or fabricate data if needed.

These mastery cases allow you to display your ability to:

■   Launch the program.
■   Create a database file, table, and form.
■   Enter data.
■   Print records.

CASE 1: TRACKING YOUR DEGREE PROGRAM

You want to keep track of your progress toward graduation. Create a database file and then a table that will store the following data for each course that you must take to complete your degree: department, course number, credits, semester in which course was (or will be) taken, grade, and instructor's name. Include additional fields that you deem important. If you are not enrolled in a degree program, create fictitious data for one of the degree programs offered in your school. Enter data for all courses required for your degree, completing all data as appropriate. Print the table displaying the data for all the courses. Create a form, save, and then print it.

CASE 2: TRACKING YOUR MUSIC COLLECTION

You want to create a catalog to keep track of your music collection. Create a database file and then a table that will include the following data for each music selection in your collection: selection title, artist, album title, type of music (rock, classical, jazz, and so on), and type of media (tape, CD, LP, and so on). Enter data for at least 20 selections representing a mix of different albums, music, and media types. Print the entire list. Create a form. Display your favorite title in the form, and then print it.

CASE 3: TRACKING THE CLIENTELE FOR A BUSINESS

A friend who owns a hair salon asks you to help her keep track of her upscale clientele. Create a database file and then a table that will contain data for each client's name, address, home phone, work phone, date of last visit, service(s) performed, amount charged, name of cosmetologist who performed work, and date of next appointment. Create a form, and then enter data for 15 clients. Print all the records in the Form format.

2

ENHANCING THE DATABASE: MODIFYING STRUCTURE, EDITING DATA, QUERYING, AND REPORTING

<table>
<tr><td colspan="3">OUTLINE</td></tr>
<tr>
<td valign="top">

OVERVIEW

MASTERY SET 2-1: MODIFYING A
   TABLE'S STRUCTURE
Adding Fields
Modifying a Field's Properties
Deleting a Field

MASTERY SET 2-2: LOCATING AND
   EDITING DATA
Editing Data
Sorting Records
Filtering Records

</td>
<td valign="top">

MASTERY SET 2-3: CREATING
   QUERIES
Displaying Selected Fields
Selecting Records
Combining Search Criteria
Creating Summary Statistics

MASTERY SET 2-4: ALTERING
   DATA WITH QUERIES
Modifying Data in All Records
Replacing Data in Selected Records

</td>
<td valign="top">

MASTERY SET 2-5: CREATING
   REPORTS
Creating AutoReports
Duplicating, Renaming, and Deleting
   Reports
Creating a Custom Report

MASTERY SET 2-6: MODIFYING A
   REPORT
Understanding Report Design View
Working with Objects
Adding Calculated Fields and
   Summary Objects

UNIT REVIEW

</td>
</tr>
</table>

OBJECTIVES

After completing the mastery sets in this unit, you will be able to do any or all of the following:

1 Modify a table structure—add and remove fields and change field properties.

2 Locate and edit data and sort, filter, and delete records.

3 Perform simple and custom selections of data (queries).

4 Edit records individually and globally using queries.

5 Create columnar (vertical) and tabular (horizontal) reports.

6 Duplicate, rename, and delete reports.

7 Create custom reports.

8 Modify an existing report.

OVERVIEW

This unit expands on the basic database skills you learned in the previous unit by presenting techniques for modifying table structures, locating and editing data, and creating and using queries and reports. The unit begins with an explanation of table structure modifications—adding, changing, and deleting data fields.

Techniques for editing data and sorting and filtering records follow. This unit then examines methods to create, use, and modify queries and reports.

MASTERY SET 2-1: MODIFYING A TABLE'S STRUCTURE

To prepare for the exercises to follow:

1 Launch Access and, if appropriate, insert your diskette

2 In the Microsoft Access dialog box, click the *Open an existing file* option and then *OK* (or press **Esc** to remove the Access dialog box, and click *File*, *Open*)

3 Click the ▼ button of the *Look in* box, and then the *3 1/2 Floppy (A:)* drive icon (or the folder appropriate for your lab)

Now, open the CUSTOMER file that you saved at the end of the previous unit:

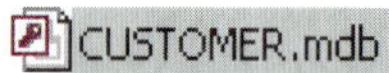

4 Click the *CUSTOMER.mdb* icon in the *Open* list box and then click the *Open* button

5 If needed, click Access's Maximize button

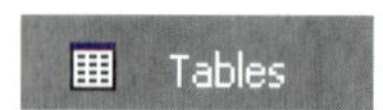

6 If needed, click the *Tables* object type button of the CUSTOMER: Database window

7 Click the *Customer List* icon and then the *Design* button

8 Click the Maximize button of the Customer List: Table window

Your screen should now look like Figure DB2-1a. The Customer List: Table window in Design view enables you to modify its table structure. It looks exactly as it did when you finished designing the Customer List table. You can add fields, change their properties, or delete them using this window.

ADDING FIELDS

You can insert fields either between existing fields or after the last created field. Both techniques are illustrated next.

INSERTING BETWEEN FIELDS. To insert the *Street* field between the *First* and *City* fields:

1 Point to and then click the *City* field row selector (the fourth field) to select it

(*Note:* The row selector is the box on the left of the field name *City*. When you point to it, the mouse pointer changes to a right pointing arrow. Clicking it selects the entire row containing *City*.)

FIGURE DB2-1 ■ MODIFYING A TABLE'S STRUCTURE

(a) The Customer List: Table in Design view allows you to modify a table's structure.
(b) The *Street, Paid,* and *Balance* fields have been added.
(c) The modified table in Datasheet view.

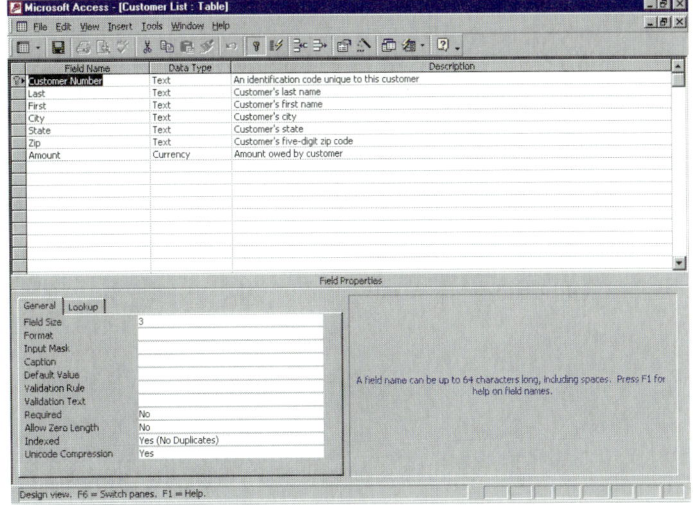

(a)

(b)

Field Name	Data Type	Description
Customer Number	Text	An identification code unique to this customer
Last	Text	Customer's last name
First	Text	Customer's first name
Street	Text	Customer's street
City	Text	Customer's city
State	Text	Customer's state
Zip	Text	Customer's five-digit zip code
Amount	Currency	Amount owed by customer
Paid	Currency	Customer's payment
Balance	Currency	

(c)

Customer Number	Last	First	Street	City	State	Zip	Amount
067	Williams	DeVilla		Chicago	IL	60601	$965
101	Burstein	Jerome		San Jose	CA	95120	$230
111	Hill	Karen		Chicago	IL	60605	$456
176	West	Rita		Chicago	IL	60601	$965
389	Martin	Arthur		Flushing	NY	11367	$65
449	Kee	Charles		New York	NY	10003	$540
670	Parker	Charles		Santa Fe	NM	87051	$450
754	Martin	Edward		New York	NY	10001	$360
							$0

 **2** Press **Insert** or click *Insert, Row*

A new blank row appears. Now, simply complete the field parameters as follows:

3 Click the *Field Name* cell in the new row to place the insertion point there

4 Type **Street** and press ↵

The highlight moves to the *Data Type* column. The default data type is Text. To keep this setting:

5 Press ↵

6 Type **Customer's street**

7 Press **F6** or click the *Field Size* box in the lower pane

8 Delete the default width, type `25`, and press `↵`

The new field is completed.

ADDING AT THE END.   Fields can also be added at the end of the structure. For example, to add two new currency fields named "Paid" and "Balance" at the end of the field structure, as in Figure DB2-1b:

1 Click the blank *Field Name* cell below *Amount* in the upper pane to position the insertion point

2 Type `Paid` and press `↵`

3 Click the `▼` button of the *Data Type* cell, click *Currency*, and press `↵`

4 Type `Customer's payment`

5 Press `↵` to move to the *Field Name* cell of the next row

6 Type `Balance` and press `↵`

7 Click the `▼` button of the *Data Type* cell, click *Currency*, and press `↵`

8 Leave the Description cell blank

Figure DB2-1b shows the modified table. Now, to save your changes and to switch to Datasheet view as in Figure DB2-1c:

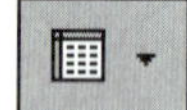

9 Click *View*, *Datasheet View*

A message asks whether you want to save your work.

10 Click *Yes*

The Customer List table should now appear in Datasheet view as in Figure DB2-1c.

11 Use the scroll bar to review your changes

12 If desired, press `Ctrl` + `Home` to move to the first field in the first record

13 Click *File*, *Close*, or click the Customer List: Table window's Close button at the right end of the menu bar   `Ctrl` + `F4`

ADDING FIELDS TO FORMS AND REPORTS.   Although new fields added to a table's structure automatically appear in the related table in Datasheet view, they do not appear in forms or reports you have already created. Because of this, you must either create a new form or report using the revised table, or add the new fields to the existing form or report. Techniques to add fields to a report are discussed later in this unit. You can apply these same techniques to add fields to a form.

MODIFYING A FIELD'S PROPERTIES

You can modify any existing field's properties by using the Table Design window. First you will change the *Zip* field size to 10 and then you will use the Input Mask Wizard to automatically insert a dash between the first five digits and the last four. A **mask** is a pattern that controls the appearance of all data entered into a desired field. Typical standard masks include social security number, date formats, and telephone number.

1 Click the *Tables* object type button of the Database window

2 Click the *Customer List* icon and then the *Design* button

3 If needed, click the Maximize button of the Customer List: Table window

4 Click just before the word "five" in the *Description* cell of the *Zip* field row to position the insertion point

5 Press **Delete** as necessary to delete the "five"

6 Type **nine** and then press **F6** to move to the lower pane

7 For field size, type **10** and press **↵**

8 Click *File, Save* to resave the modified table structure   **Ctrl** + **S**

The field size of 10 allows space for a dash between the first five characters and the last four. The Zip field can now hold a nine-digit zip code. Before you try setting up a mask for the zip code, check with your instructor or lab technician to see if the Input Mask wizard has been installed. If not, skip Steps 9 through 15.

9 Click the *Input Mask* box in the lower pane of the Design Table window to place the insertion point there

Note that an *Input Mask Wizard* icon appears to the right of the Input Mask box. This icon is used to start the Input Mask Wizard.

FIGURE DB2-2 ■ MODIFYING A FIELD'S PROPERTY

The *Zip* field size property has been changed from 5 characters to 10 for a 9-digit zip code with a hyphen.

State	Text	Customer's state
Zip	Text	Customer's nine-digit zip code
Amount	Currency	Amount owed by customer
Paid	Currency	Customer's payment
Balance	Currency	

Field Properties

General | Lookup

Field Size	10
Format	
Input Mask	00000-9999;; _
Caption	

 **10** Click the *Input Mask Wizard* Icon

The wizard's first step offers a variety of preset masks. Its "Try It:" box gives you an opportunity to test the mask before using it. The *Edit List* button can be used to edit a preset mask or to create a customized mask. To select a zip code mask:

11 Click *Zip Code 98052-6399* and then the *Next* button to move to the next step

This step allows you to enter placeholders in the mask. A *placeholder* is a set of characters that is replaced as you enter data into the field. To accept the default setting—no placeholders:

12 Click the *Next* button to move to the next step

Now you can specify whether you want to save the field data with or without symbols in the mask. To save without (the default), and then complete the mask:

13 Click the *Next* button and then the *Finish* button

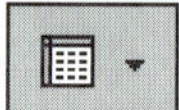 **14** Click *File, Save* to resave the modified table structure   **Ctrl** + **S**

The changes you made should appear as shown in Figure DB2-2. When you enter new zip code data, a dash will automatically appear in the proper position—it need not be typed.

 **15** Click *View, Datasheet View*

Note that a dash appears after the first five digits in the Zip field.

16 Click *File, Close* to close the Customer List: Table window

DELETING A FIELD

Any field and its content can be permanently deleted from a table in either Design view or Datasheet view. Follow these steps to delete the *Balance* field:

 Customer List   **1** Click the *Customer List* icon in the Database window and then the *Design* button

2 If needed, use the vertical scroll bar to display the *Balance* field row

3 Click the *Balance* field row selector to select it

4 Click *Edit, Delete* or *Delete Row*   **Delete**

5 Click *Yes*

6 Click *File, Save*   **Ctrl** + **S**

The *Balance* field (and all associated data) has now been permanently deleted from your table.

7 Click _View_, _Datasheet View_

8 Use the horizontal scroll bar to examine the table, and note that the _Balance_ field column has been deleted

9 Close all windows in Access's work area

10 If you wish to stop for now, exit Access

> **Tip:** To delete a field in Datasheet view, simply click its field label, thus selecting the entire field column, and then click _Edit_, _Delete Column_.

☑ CHECKPOINT

Perform these tasks.

1. If needed, launch Access, and open the DCHECK database created in Unit 1's Checkpoints.
2. Open the Students table in Design view.
3. Add a Social Security field with the appropriate input mask before the _Name_ field. Add the rest of the new fields after the _Test2_ field. Save your modifications:

Field Name	Data Type	Mask
Social Security	Text (11)	Social Security
Test3	Number	
Test4	Number	
Class	Number	

4. Change the _Class_ field's data type to _Text_ and field size to 2, and then save your changes.
5. Delete the _Test4_ field. Save your changes.

DB

MASTERY SET 2-2: LOCATING AND EDITING DATA

To keep a database file current, its data need to be updated, changed, corrected, added to, or deleted. However, before editing data, you must first locate it. This mastery set explores several ways to locate and then edit data. First, you will practice editing data using Form view and then Datasheet view. You then learn how to reorder records for easier access. Next, you will request Access to display only those records you want to see and then edit them.

To prepare for these exercises, you must first delete the old Customer form and then create a new one. This ensures that the new fields you added to the table in the previous mastery set will be available in the new form. (_Note:_ You can also add these new fields to the old form's design; however, this process is more complicated and is discussed later.)

1 If necessary, launch Access, and open the CUSTOMER.mdb database file (saved in the previous unit)

2 If necessary, click the Restore button of the Customer: Database window to reduce it to a smaller window

`Alt` + `-` , `R`

3 Click the *Forms* object type button and then the *Customer Form* icon

4 Press `Delete` , and then click *Yes* to delete the old *Customer Form*

The *Customer Form* icon disappears from the list box. Now, to create a new form:

5 Click the *New* button

6 Click *AutoForm: Columnar*

7 Click the ▾ button for *Choose the table or query where the object's data comes from:*, and then click *Customer List*

8 Click the *OK* button to create the form

The new form should resemble Figure DB2-3. Note that the fields *Street* and *Paid* also appear in the form.

9 Click *File, Save*

`Ctrl` + `S`

10 Type `Customer Form` and then click *OK*

11 Leave the Form view window open for the next exercise

EDITING DATA

In the next exercises, you practice techniques to edit existing data and then add new data.

FIGURE DB2-3 ■ CREATING A REVISED FORM

After a table's structure is modified, any pre-existing form or report must be either recreated or updated to include the changes. Here, the Customer List form has been recreated to include the most recent table structure modifications.

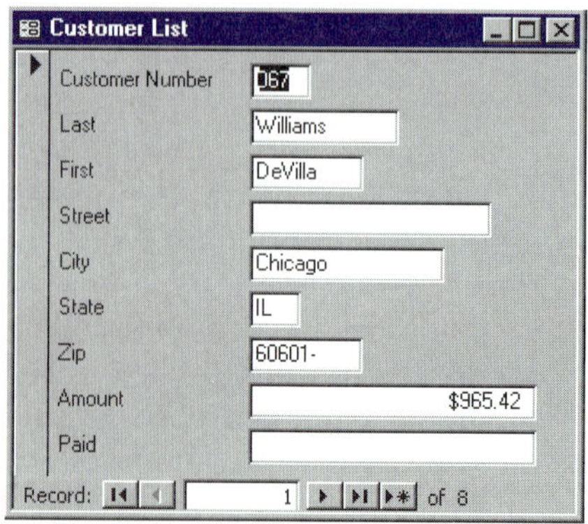

EDITING EXISTING DATA IN FORM VIEW.   To change Record 4's amount of "$965.42" to "$123.45" in Form view, follow these steps:

1 Click the *Next Record* scroll bar button as needed until Record 4 appears (use the window's status bar to help you locate Record 4)   `Pg Dn` as needed

> Tip: You can also click the *Current Record* box in the Form window's status bar, delete its number, type 4, and press *Enter*.

2 Press `Tab` as needed to move to the *Amount* field

Note that the selection highlight is now on *$965.42*. The next character you type will delete the data in the selection highlight. You can also press *Delete* first to remove the highlighted data. For now:

3 Type `123.45` (do not type a dollar sign: Access automatically inserts it because the field's data type is set to *Currency*)

4 Press `↵`

> Tip: Changes to table data are saved when you move the insertion point to another record or close the window. You need invoke the Save command for data changes only if you have changed the table's structure or layout.

FIGURE DB2-4 ■ EDITING EXISTING DATA IN FORM VIEW

(a) Record 6's *Amount* field value has been changed from $945.42 to $123.45.
(b) The Customer List Form window minimized.

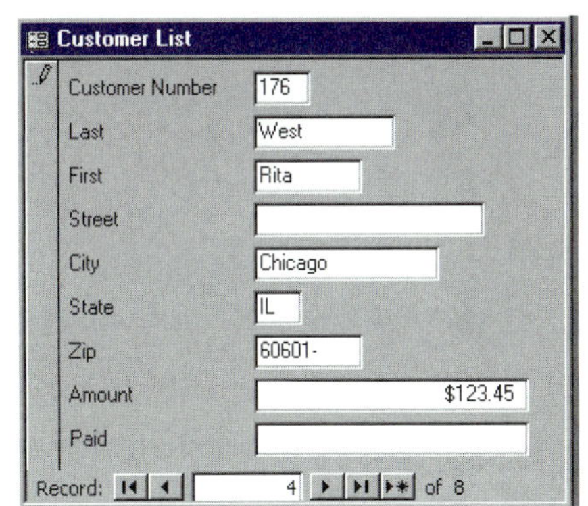

(a)

(b)

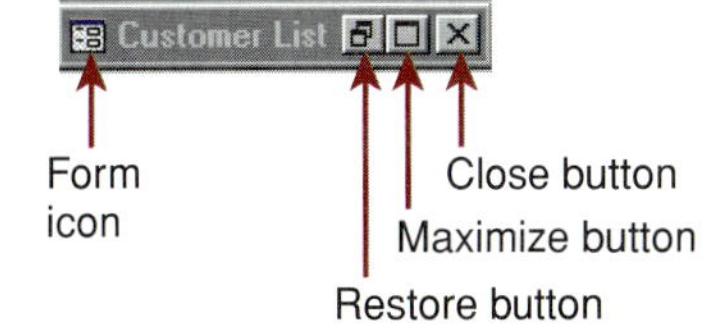

The data in the *Amount* field should now display 123.45 as in Figure DB2-4a. Before practicing editing in Datasheet view, minimize your Form view window. Remember, minimizing reduces a window to an icon and keeps it running at a minimal state. Minimizing also frees up space in a window's workspace and allows you to switch back to an object without reopening it.

5 Click the Minimize button of the Form view window   **Alt** + **-** , **H**

The Form window now shrinks to a small icon in Access's work area as in Figure DB2-4b. This icon resembles a miniature title bar.

FREEZING COLUMNS.   When editing data in Datasheet view, field columns may exceed the current viewing area. The **Freeze Columns** feature freezes columns along the left of a Datasheet view. Once frozen, these cells remain in constant view no matter where you move the insertion point or selection highlight. Although it is not essential for editing, it allows you to see what you are doing more easily. Try this to freeze the *Customer Number* and *Last* field columns:

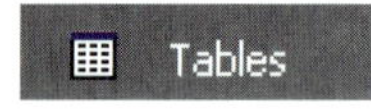

1 Click the *Tables* object type button in the CUSTOMER: Database window

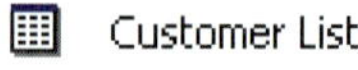

2 Click the *Customer List* icon and then the *Open* button

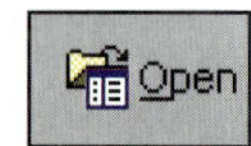

3 Click the Maximize button of the Customer List: Table window   **Alt** + **-** , **X**

4 Click the *Customer Number* column label to select the column

5 **Shift** -click the *Last* column label to select the column

Both the *Customer Number* and *Last* columns are now selected.

6 Click *Format*, *Freeze Columns*

7 Press **Tab** seven times to move to the *Amount* field column

8 Click *File*, *Save*   **Ctrl** + **S**

Your table should appear as in Figure DB2-5a. Note that the *Customer Number* and *Last* columns remain on the screen as you scroll to the *Amount* column. Later, you will turn off the Freeze feature, but for now, leave the feature on.

EDITING EXISTING DATA IN DATASHEET VIEW.   To adjust the "$540.45" in the *Amount* column of Record 6 (Customer Number 449) to "$740.45":

1 Press **↓** as needed to move to *$540.45* in the *Amount* column of Record 6 (Customer Number 449)

The selection highlight is now on *$540.45*. To change the selection highlight to an insertion point:

2 Press **F2**

FIGURE DB2-5 ■ **EDITING EXISTING DATA IN DATASHEET VIEW**

(a) The Freeze columns feature has been turned on to freeze the *Customer Number* and *Last* fields.
(b) Pressing *F2* switches the selection highlight to an insertion point (and vice versa). The insertion point has been positioned between the "5" and "4" to edit "$540.45."
(c) The "$540.45" has been changed to "$740.45."

Freeze Columns feature

Customer Number	Last	Street	City	State	Zip	Amount	Paid
067	Williams		Chicago	IL	60601-	$965.42	
101	Burstein		San Jose	CA	95120-	$230.45	
111	Hill		Chicago	IL	60605-	$456.78	
176	West		Chicago	IL	60601-	$123.45	
389	Martin		Flushing	NY	11367-	$65.30	
449	Kee		New York	NY	10003-	$540.45	
670	Parker		Santa Fe	NM	87051-	$450.75	
754	Martin		New York	NY	10001-	$360.55	
*						$0.00	$0.(

(a)

Amount
$965.42
$230.45
$456.78
$123.45
$65.30
$540.45
$450.75
$360.55
$0.00

(b)

Amount
$965.42
$230.45
$456.78
$123.45
$65.30
$740.45
$450.75
$360.55
$0.00

(c)

Tip: You can switch the selection highlight to an insertion point and back by pressing the *F2* key.

3 Use the arrow keys to move the insertion point between the "5" and "4" in "$540.45" as in Figure DB2-5b

4 Press **Backspace** to delete the "5"

5 Type **7**

6 Press ↵

Your changes should agree with Figure DB2-5c.

Tip: You can also use the Find or Replace commands to help you locate a specific data value and then change it.

ADDING DATA TO RECORDS.   Data can be quickly added to existing records in Form view or Datasheet view. In the next exercise, you use the data in Table DB2-1 to add *Street* and *Paid* data to the CUSTOMER database.

To add the *Street* and *Paid* field values to the first four records using the Customer Datasheet view:

1 Use the arrow keys to move to the *Street* field of Record 1 (Customer Number 067)

2 Type One Dryden Way

Notice that the street text exceeds the current column width. You will adjust this width later.

3 Press Tab as needed to move to the *Paid* field

Note that the Freeze columns feature is still on: The *Customer Number* and *Last* columns remained in view as you moved to the *Paid* column.

4 Type 500 and press ↵

5 Use the same technique to enter the *Street* and *Paid* data for the next three records from Table DB2-1a

Now, to resize the *Street* field column to display its entire contents:

6 Move to the first cell in the *Street* column (any cell in this column will do)

7 Click the *Street* column label to select the entire column

8 Click *Format*, *Column Width* and then the *Best Fit* button

TABLE DB2-1 ■ STREET AND PAID DATA

Record No.	Last Name	Street	Paid
1	Williams	One Dryden Way	500.00
2	Burstein	100 N. 1st Street	100.00
3	Hill	1500 Michigan Avenue	456.78
4	West	75 N. Wacker Drive	0.00

(a)

Record No.	Last Name	Street	Paid
5	Martin	6158 Appleway	10.00
6	Kee	500 Fifth Avenue	0.00
7	Parker	25 Cerillos Road	200.00
8	Martin	50 Carmine Street	130.55

(b)

9 Press any arrow key to remove the selection highlight

The *Street* column has now been resized to display its entire content.

10 Click *File, Save* to save the change in layout   `Ctrl` + `S`

11 Review and, if necessary, edit, your newly entered data

12 Click the Minimize button of the Datasheet window

Now, both the Datasheet and Form windows are minimized at the bottom of your work area. To identify each, examine their icons at the left end of their minimized window icons.

13 Click the Restore button of the Form window's icon (at the bottom left of the work area)

14 Move to Record 5 and then the *Street* field

15 Type 6158 Appleway

16 Move to the *Paid* column of Record 5

17 Type 10 and press ↵

18 Use the same technique to enter the rest of the *Street* and *Paid* data from Table DB2-1b

19 Check that your data for all records matches Table DB2-1b

DELETING RECORDS.   To delete a record in Form or Datasheet view, simply move to any field in the desired record, and then click *Edit, Delete Record*. Try this to delete Record 5 (*Last* = Martin, *First* = Arthur):

1 Move to Record 5

2 Click *Edit, Delete Record, Yes*

Although the record and its record form have been deleted from the Form view, only its data have been deleted from the Datasheet view window. To switch to the Datasheet view window and delete the record row formerly containing Record 5:

3 Click the Minimize button of the Form window

4 Click the Maximize button of the Datasheet window

Note that every field in Record 5 displays *#Deleted*. This message appears *only* because both the table and the form are open at the same time. The record is actually deleted. If you close the table and reopen it, this message and the record that was deleted in the form are gone. If the table is closed when you delete a record using the form, you will not see the *#Deleted* message. Now, to delete the Record 5 row:

5 Click Record 5's row selector to select the entire row

6   Click *Edit, Delete Record* or *Delete, Yes*

Delete , ↵

Only seven records remain.

> **Tip: To delete multiple records in a block (a set of contiguous records), use the Datasheet view, click the row selector of the first desired record, and then *Shift*-click the last desired record in the block; click *Edit, Delete Record* or *Delete, Yes*.**

SORTING RECORDS

Sorting is a process that changes the order of records in a table, form, or other object. To sort the Customer List table by last name in ascending order (lowest to highest), follow these steps:

1   Move to the first cell in the *Last* field column (or any other cell in that column)

 **2**   Click *Records, Sort, Sort Ascending*

Your Customer List table should resemble Figure DB2-6.

At this point, the table can also be reset to its original order, called the **natural order,** by clicking *Records, Remove Filter/Sort.* For now, keep the sort results:

 **3**   Click *File, Save,* to resave the table in this sort order as part of the layout

Try this to place the Customer form in ascending zip code order:

4   Click the Minimize button of the Customer List: Table window

5   Click the Restore button of the Customer Form window icon

Note that the prior sorting operation only affected the table in Datasheet view, not Form view.

6   If needed, move to a *Zip* field (any one will do)

 **7**   Click *Records, Sort, Sort Ascending*

FIGURE DB2-6 ■ **SORTING RECORDS**

The records have been sorted in ascending order by the *Last* field.

Customer Number	Last	Street	City	State	Zip	Amount
101	Burstein	100 N. 1st Street	San Jose	CA	95120-	$230.45
111	Hill	1500 Michigan Avenue	Chicago	IL	60605-	$456.78
449	Kee	500 Fifth Avenue	New York	NY	10003-	$740.45
754	Martin	50 Carmine Street	New York	NY	10001-	$360.55
670	Parker	25 Cerillos Road	Santa Fe	NM	87051-	$450.75
176	West	75 N. Wacker Drive	Chicago	IL	60601-	$123.45
067	Williams	One Dryden Way	Chicago	IL	60601-	$965.42
*						$0.00

8 Scroll through the customer forms and note that the records are in ascending order by zip code

9 Resave the form and then minimize it

FILTERING RECORDS

Access also has the capability of displaying only specific records, hiding all others from view. This feature is called **filtering.** Suppose that you are interested only in customers who live in Illinois. You can instruct Access to display only those records in which the *State* value is "IL" by using Access's filtering feature. The filter feature does not actually remove any records from the database file; it only prevents them from being viewed temporarily.

1 Click the Maximize button of the Customer List: Table window icon

Next, indicate the cell containing the value by which you want to filter:

2 Click (or tab to) the *State* value in Hill's record

3 Click *Records,* then *Filter,* then *Filter by Selection*

Access displays only those records whose *State* value is identical to the value that was selected when you executed the Filter command. You should see a table containing only those three records—Hill, West, and Williams—in which "IL" is the value in the *State* field. Records can be edited, deleted, or printed using the methods you have already learned, but only those records that pass the test imposed by the filter will be displayed on the screen or printer. The filter remains in effect until you cancel it. To cancel this filter:

4 Click *Records,* and then click *Remove Filter/Sort*

All seven records are again displayed. The sort on the last name is also removed. Access remembers the last filter that you used, and it can be applied again at any time. To reimpose the same filter condition as before:

5 Click *Records,* and then *Apply Filter/Sort*

As before, you see the filtered table using the same condition (*State* = IL). Again, to remove the filter:

6 Click *Records, Remove Filter/Sort*

More complicated filters are also possible. Suppose you wanted to view only those records whose zip begins with "1" (like Kee and Martin) or "6" (like Hill, West, and Williams). To accomplish this:

7 Click *Records, Filter,* and then *Filter by Form*

8 If "IL" appears selected in the *State* column, press Delete to remove it ("IL" may appear because you just completed a filter for all records containing that value)

FIGURE DB2-7 ■ FILTERING RECORDS

(a) Searching for zips beginning with the number "1"...
(b) ...or the number "6."

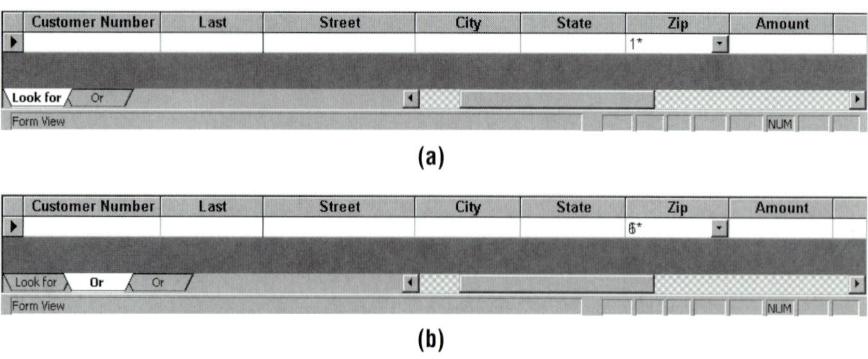

(a)

(b)

A blank, single-row table appears in which you can enter sample values for the records you want to see, edit, or print. Refer to Figure DB2-7a while performing Steps 9 and 10.

9 Place the insertion point anywhere in the *Zip* column by clicking it

10 Type 1*

Recall that the asterisk (*) is a wildcard character. By including it as part of the search, you are asking to see records in which the *Zip* field contains a value beginning with "1" followed by any other characters.

11 Click the *Or* tab at the bottom of the window

You are presented with another blank table in which you can type *the other value* you are looking for. As you see in Figure DB2-7b:

12 Place the text insertion point in the *Zip* column by clicking it

13 Type 6*

Again, by using the wildcard character, you are asking for values that begin with "6" followed by any other characters. To apply the filter:

14 Click *Filter*, Apply *Filter/Sort*

You should see a table containing those records that have zips beginning with "1" or "6." To remove the filter:

15 Click *Records*, *Remove Filter/Sort*

Filters can be designed and applied to screen forms using the same techniques. You can also use words or parts of words in a filter's criteria.

16 Click *Format, Unfreeze All Columns* to turn off the Freeze feature

17 Resort the table by the *Last* field in ascending order (move to the *Last* field column and click *Record, Sort, Ascending*)

18 Resave this change, and then close all windows in Access's work area

19 If you wish to stop, exit Access

☑ CHECKPOINT

Perform these tasks.

1. Launch Access if needed, and open the DCHECK database.
2. Make the following changes in the Students table:

   Note that you do not have to type in the "-" dashes when entering the social security number.

Social Security	Name	Test3	Class
888-88-8888	Smith	85	JR
777-77-7777	Jones	93	JR
666-66-6666	Green	76	SR
555-55-5555	Lee	95	FR
444-44-4444	Kim	82	SO
333-33-3333	Piper	80	SO

3. Sort the records in the Students table by NAME in ascending order, and then re-save it.
4. Filter the table to display only records with TEST2 scores of 93.
5. Remove the filter, and then resave the table.

MASTERY SET 2-3: CREATING QUERIES

A **query** is simply a question that is asked of the table. By using Access's Query feature, you can create a query that restricts the screen display to selected fields and (if you choose) display only those field values that meet search criteria.

Queries provide the true power in a database system. They enable you to view data from different perspectives, ask questions about data values, and manipulate field values into patterns that help you gain insight about your data. Queries can also be used to perform the following functions:

- Insert new values.
- Modify field values.
- Perform calculations on field values.

Because of their importance, queries are presented in some depth in the following exercises. At first, you will use the Query feature simply to restrict fields in a display; then you will extend your selection capabilities. To prepare for this section:

> **1** If necessary, launch Access, and then open the CUSTOMER database file

> **2** Click the *Queries* object type button

DISPLAYING SELECTED FIELDS

A quick way to display only selected fields is to use Access's Simple Query Wizard. Try this to display only the *First* and *Last* field columns:

> **1** Double-click the *Create query by using wizard* icon

The Simple Query Wizard appears. At this point, you select any fields for display in any order.

> **2** If needed, click the ▾ button of the *Tables/Queries* drop-down box and then *Table: Customer List* to set the query's source

> **3** Click *First* in the *Available Fields* list box, and then click the > button

> **4** Click *Last* in the *Available Fields* list box, and then click the > button

> **Tip:** You can also double-click a field in the *Available Fields* list box to select it. Clicking the >> button will select all fields, the < button deselects a single field, and the << button deselects all fields.

Your selections in the Wizard should agree with those shown in Figure DB2-8a. Also review this figure to understand the functions of the Wizard components.

> **5** Click the *Next >* button to move to the Wizard screen

This dialog box lets you name your query and specify whether you would like to view the query's information (default) or modify its design. Normally, you assign a query name that indicates what the query displays. However, for now, to accept the default query name and to view its information:

> **6** Click the *Finish* button

The results of your query should agree with those shown in Figure DB2-8b. The result of a query is called a **dynaset,** which looks and acts like a table but is really a selection of the data in an underlying table. Changes made to the dynaset are passed on to the table, so you can edit the records that your queries find.

The query procedure can also search for selected field values and perform mathematical calculations on number fields, as you will see in the next portion of this exercise. To remove the dynaset from the screen:

>  **7** Click *File, Close* or click the Query window's Close button   

Note that a query icon named *Customer List Query* appears in the list box of the CUSTOMER: Database window.

FIGURE DB2-8 ■ **CREATING A SIMPLE QUERY**

(a) This dialog box is used to select fields to be displayed in a query.
(b) The result of the query.

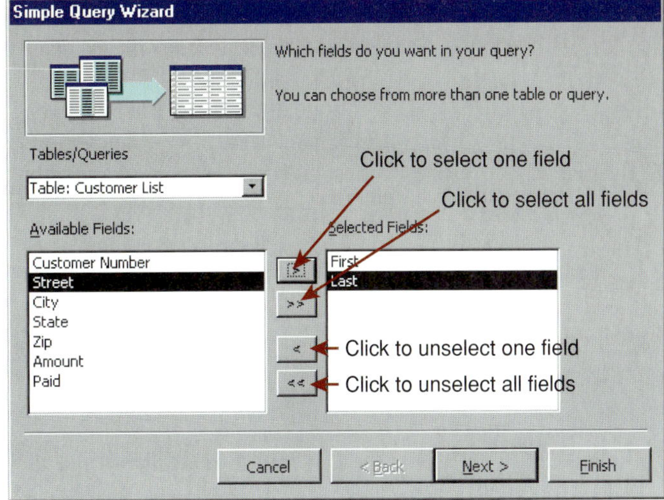

(a)

First	Last
DeVilla	Williams
Jerome	Burstein
Karen	Hill
Rita	West
Charles	Kee
Charles	Parker
Edward	Martin

(b)

SELECTING RECORDS

A simple query restricts the fields displayed in the dynaset but still includes all records from the Customer table. By adding a conditional expression to the query, however, you can instruct Access to select only those records that meet the stated condition (**criterion**), as you did in the filtering operation earlier. Although criteria can be used to display particular field values, they can also modify the effects of many other Access commands, such as reporting, deleting, updating, replacing, and copying (as you will see).

Conditional selections fall into a number of categories. You can select records that match criteria exactly, fall within an acceptable range of values, fit a pattern, come close to selection values, or are unlike the selection criteria entirely. You can also combine criteria, depending on your needs. The following exercises examine some of these techniques.

SELECTING RECORDS USING AN EXACT MATCH.   To select records with field values that match a particular value, you simply place the fields you want displayed in the dynaset using a drag-and-drop method and then type the desired value in the criteria row of the appropriate field column. Any record that matches the query (or search) criteria will be selected. For example, suppose you wanted to display the name and street information about those customers whose state is "New York":

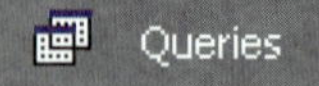

1 If needed, click the *Queries* object type button

2 Double-click the *Create query by Design view* button

The Show Table dialog box appears. This dialog box has three tabs: *Tables, Queries,* and *Both.* These tabs are for selecting tables, queries, or both tables and queries for use in a query. Once selected, the fields from the selected tables/queries will be used in the query. For now, select only the Customer List table:

3 Click *Customer List* in the *Tables* tab and then the *Add* button

> **Tip:** You can select several tables and queries for a query operation. Simply click the first item and either *Ctrl*-click each additional item or *Shift*-click the desired last item to select a block (contiguous group).

4 Click the *Close* button in the Show Table dialog box

Your Query window should resemble Figure DB2-9a. To select the field *Last:*

5 Click the *Last* field in the *Customer List* box in the upper pane of the Query window

6 Drag and drop the *Last* field into the *Field* row of the first column of the lower pane (grid)

The first column in the lower pane should now resemble Figure DB2-9b. To select the *First, City,* and *State* fields as in Figure DB2-9c:

7 Click the *First* field in the *Customer List* box in the upper pane of the Query window

8 Drag and drop the *First* field into the *Field* row of the second column of the lower pane

9 Use the Customer List box's scroll bar to display both *City* and *State* fields

Now, try this to move a block of fields at one time:

10 Click the *City* field, and then **Shift** -click the *State* field to select them both

11 Drag and drop the selection to the *Field* row of the third column of the lower pane

> **Tip:** You can also double-click a field to insert it into the query window's lower pane.

Your Query window should look like the one shown in Figure DB2-9c.

So far, you've simply identified the field columns that will appear in the answer (query result). Now, you can restrict the records that will appear by specifying the search criteria as follows:

12 In the *State* column, click the *Criteria* cell, and then type **NY** as in Figure DB2-10a

13 Press ↵ or **Tab** and note that Access automatically inserts quotes around text criteria

(a) The Query window in Design view lets you define a query's criteria.
(b) To place a field in the lower pane, simply drag and drop it from the *Customer List* box.
(c) The *Last, First, City,* and *State* fields have been selected for the query.

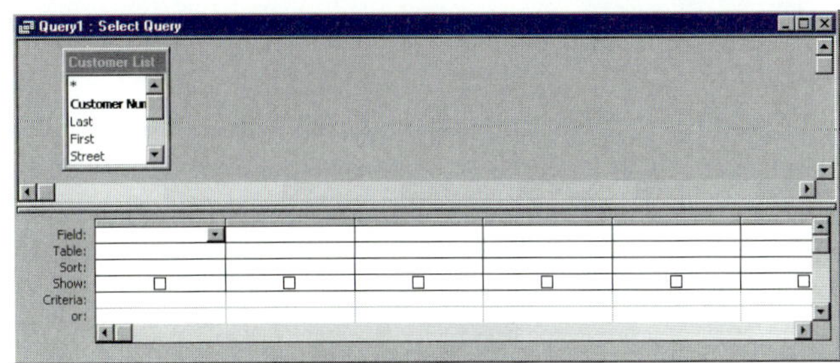

(a)

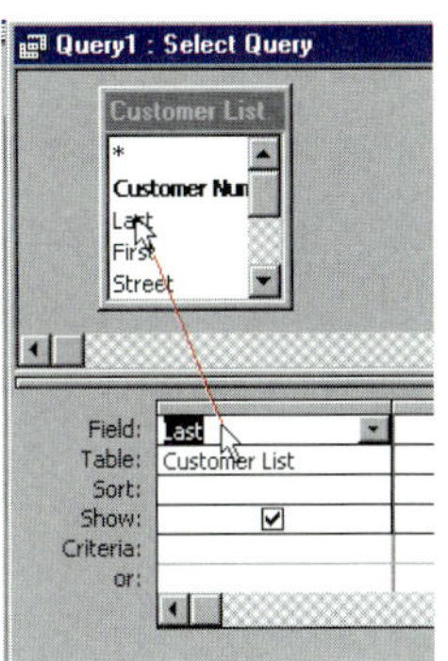

(b)

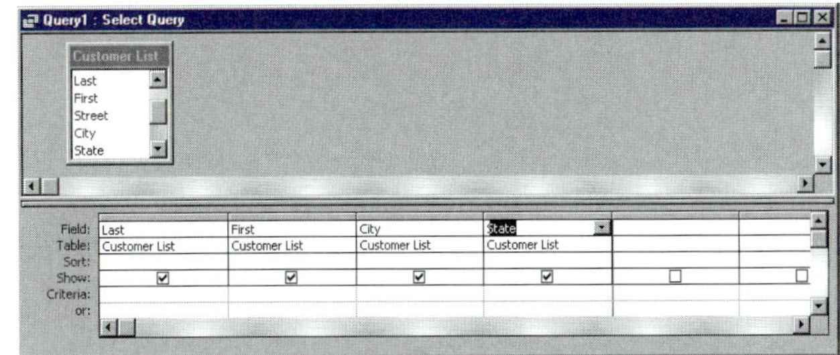

(c)

14   Click *Query, Run*

The answer to this query appears on your screen, as shown in Figure DB2-10b. Note that only those records whose field value for *State* exactly matches the "NY" search criterion are listed. Note, too, that only the *Last, First, City,* and *State* fields are shown.

15   Close (but do not save) the query

Tip: Although many of the query exercises are run without saving, you can also save queries so that you can rerun them at a later date to display updated data. In general, one-time queries need not be saved. Those that you expect to use regularly should be saved.

It is easy to add additional criteria. Suppose you wanted to find a resident of New York state whose last name is "Martin." To ask Access to find any matching records for you:

16　Double-click the *Create query in Design view* button

17　Click *Customer List* in the *Tables* tab and then the *Add* button

18　Click the *Close* button in the Show Table dialog box

You again see the Select Query design window.

19　Repeat Steps 5 through 12 to select the *Last, First, City,* and *State* fields and to set the criteria for *State* as "NY"

Your window should again appear as in Figure DB2-10a.

20　Click the *Criteria* cell of the *Last* field column, and then type　Martin

Note: "Martin" and "NY" must be in the same criteria row.

21　Click *Query, Run*

Now, only those records that match both criteria (*Last* = "Martin" and *State* = "NY") are displayed.

22　Close the Query window without saving

SELECTING RECORDS WITHIN AN ACCEPTABLE RANGE.　At times you will want to select records that fall within a range of values, not just one particular value. You can accomplish this by using a relational operator as part of the search criteria. A relational operator lets you specify a range of criteria to be used in the search. Table DB2-2 lists the relational operators used in queries.

FIGURE DB2-10　■　SETTING CRITERIA

(a) The query criteria "NY" is entered in the *Criteria* cell of the *State* column.
(b) The results of the query display only those fields identified in the query design whose records' *State* field = NY.

Field:	Last	First	City	State	
Table:	Customer List	Customer List	Customer List	Customer List	
Sort:					
Show:	☑	☑	☑	☑	☐
Criteria:				NY	
or:					

(a)

Query1 : Select Query

Last	First	City	State
Kee	Charles	New York	NY
Martin	Edward	New York	NY

(b)

TABLE DB2-2 ■ RELATIONAL OPERATORS USED IN ACCESS QUERIES

Operator	Example	Explanation
<	<500	Less than
>	>500	Greater than
=	=500	Equal to
<=	<=500	Less than or equal to
>=	>=500	Greater than or equal to
AND	>5 AND <10	Logical "AND" connector; both conditions must be true
OR	>100 OR <10	Logical "OR" connector; either condition must be true
NOT	NOT 500	Logical "NOT" expression; all values except 500

To specify a range of values in a query, you simply enter an initial relational operator in the *Field* column, followed by the value to be searched. For example, to select records whose *Amount* field value is "$300" or more, do this:

1 If needed, click the *Queries* object type button

2 Double-click the *Create query in Design view* button

3 Click *Customer List* in the *Tables* tab and then the *Add* button

4 Click the *Close* button in the Show Table dialog box

You again see the Select Query design screen.

5 Use the drag-and-drop techniques learned in the previous exercise to add the *Customer Number*, *Last*, *Amount*, and *State* fields to the *Fields* row of the lower pane

6 Click the *Criteria* row of the *Amount* column and type >=300

This last entry asks for only those records whose *Amount* value is greater than or equal to $300. Note that you do not enter the currency symbol, nor would you enter commas to set off thousands in large amounts.

An additional feature the Select Query screen offers is sorting. It would be reasonable to want the resulting dynaset to be sorted by customer number. To accomplish this, follow these steps:

7 Click the *Sort* cell of the *Customer Number* column

8 Click the ▼ button of the *Sort* cell, and then *Ascending*

FIGURE DB2-11 ■ **SELECTING RECORDS WITH AN ACCEPTABLE RANGE**

(a) The query has been set to display only the *Customer Number, Last, Amount,* and *State* fields whose *Amount* is greater than or equal to 200 in ascending order by *Customer Number.*

(b) The result of the query.

(a)

Field:	Customer Number	Last	Amount	State
Table:	Customer List	Customer List	Customer List	Customer List
Sort:	Ascending			
Show:	✓	✓	✓	✓
Criteria:			>=300	
or:				

(b)

Query1 : Select Query

Customer Number	Last	Amount	State
670	Parker	$450.75	NM
449	Kee	$740.45	NY
754	Martin	$360.55	NY
067	Williams	$965.42	IL
111	Hill	$456.78	IL
		$0.00	

Compare your screen with Figure DB2-11a; then:

9 Click *Query, Run*

As shown in Figure DB2-11b, only those records whose field values for *Amount* are 300 or more are listed. Note, too, that only the *Customer Number, Last, Amount,* and *State* fields are shown and that the dynaset is sorted by customer number.

10 Close the Query window without saving

PATTERN SEARCH.   You can also search for patterns or a series of characters. Access provides the same wildcard characters for queries that are used in the Find procedure discussed earlier. Assume, for example, that you want to see records whose *City* field value starts with an "S." Try this query:

1 Double-click the *Create query in Design view* button

2 Click *Customer List* in the *Tables* tab and then the *Add* button

3 Click the *Close* button in the Show Table dialog box

You again see the Select Query design screen.

4 Click the *Last* field and then Ctrl -click the *City* field in the *Customer List* box

This selects the two fields as a group.

5 Drag and drop the selected fields to the *Field* row of the lower pane

6 In the *Criteria* cell of the *City* column, type S* and press Tab

FIGURE DB2-12 ■ PATTERN SEARCHES

(a) The query has been set to search for all records whose *City* begins with "S."
(b) The result of the query.
(c) The query has been set to search for all records whose *City* begins with "S" but also includes "t."
(d) The result of the query.

(a)

(b)

(c)

(d)

When the active area is moved, Access automatically changes the display to read *Like "S*"*. The "*" in "S*" is a wildcard character that represents one or more characters. Compare your screen with Figure DB2-12a; then:

7 Click *Query*, *Run*

Those cities that begin with an "S" (Santa Fe and San Jose) are shown as in Figure DB2-12b. Add this change to search for records whose *City* field value starts with an "S" but also includes a "t":

8 Click *View*, *Design View*

9 Delete the content in the *Criteria* cell of the *City* column

10 In the *Criteria* cell of the *City* column, type S*t* and press Tab

Compare your settings with Figure DB2-12c; then:

11 Click *Query*, *Run*

As in Figure DB2-12d, only one city (Santa Fe) matches the modified criteria. Pattern searches are useful when you are looking for particular telephone area codes (as in 718*), or dates in a certain year (as in ??/??/94) or month (as in 11/??/??). The "?" is the wildcard character that represents only one character. You can devise many other possibilities once you know how to use patterns to search records.

12 Close the Query window without saving

COMBINING SEARCH CRITERIA

What if you want to include records whose amount meets or exceeds $200 but only if the value in the *State* field is "IL"? For such needs, conditions can be combined with AND or OR connectors. Note that the **AND connector** finds records that meet both conditions, while the **OR connector** finds records that meet either condition.

USING THE "AND" CONNECTOR.   The first query uses an AND connector to find those records whose *State* equals "IL" and *Amount* equals or exceeds "200." To create this query:

1 Double-click the *Create query in Design view* button

2 Click *Customer List* in the *Tables* tab and then the *Add* button

3 Click the *Close* button in the Show Table dialog box

4 Drag and drop the *Last, First, Amount,* and *State* fields from the *Customer List* box to the *Field* rows of the first four columns

5 Click the *Show* check boxes on the *Amount* column and then the *State* column to remove the check marks (this instructs Access to not display these columns in the dynaset)

6 In the *Criteria* cell of the *Amount* column, type `>=200`

7 In the *Criteria* cell of the *State* column, type `IL` (this must be in the same row as you used in Step 6)

8 Set the *Sort* cells of both the *Last* and *First* columns to *Ascending*

Compare your screen with Figure DB2-13a. Then:

9 Click *Query, Run*

Only those records that match both criteria are displayed, as shown in Figure DB2-13b. Note, too, that fields used in criteria searches need not appear in the dynaset.

10 Close the Query window without saving

> **Tip:** When performing complicated queries, it may be helpful to first leave the *Show* boxes checked, run the query to verify the results, and then remove the checks in the desired *Show* boxes and rerun the query.

Now, using *Customer Number* and *Amount* as displayed fields, create queries to match the rest of the examples given. The first of these queries uses an AND connector in the same field. It finds records whose amount equals or exceeds "200" AND is less than "800."

11 Double-click the *Create query in Design view* button

12 Click *Customer List* in the *Tables* tab and then the *Add* button

FIGURE DB2-13 ■ USING THE *AND* CONNECTOR

(a) The query's criteria has been set to search for all records whose *Amount* is greater than or equal to 200 AND whose *State* is IL.
(b) The result of the query.
(c) The query's criteria has been set to search for all records whose *Amount* is greater than 200 and is less than 800.
(d) The result of the query.

(a)

Field:	Last	First	Amount	State
Table:	Customer List	Customer List	Customer List	Customer List
Sort:	Ascending	Ascending		
Show:	☑	☑	☐	☐
Criteria:			>=200	"IL"
or:				

(b)

Query1 : Select Query

Last	First
Williams	DeVilla
Hill	Karen

(c)

Field:	Customer Number	Amount
Table:	Customer List	Customer List
Sort:		
Show:	☑	☑
Criteria:		>200 AND <800
or:		

(d)

Query1 : Select Query

Customer Number	Amount
670	$450.75
101	$230.45
449	$740.45
754	$360.55
111	$456.78
	$0.00

13 Click the *Close* button in the Show Table dialog box

14 Drag and drop the *Customer Number* and *Amount* fields from the *Customer List* box to the *Field* row in the lower pane

15 In the *Criteria* cell of the *Amount* column, type **>200 AND <800**

The lower pane of your Select Query window should look like the one in Figure DB2-13c.

16 Click *Query, Run*

Check to be sure each record in the dynaset conforms to the criteria as in Figure DB2-13d.

17 Close the window without saving

USING THE "OR" CONNECTOR.   The next query uses an OR connector with two fields. In this example, you will find records whose state is "IL" OR whose amount equals or exceeds "200."

1 Perform Steps 1 through 3 of the previous exercise to display the Design Query window

2 Drag and drop the *Customer Number, State,* and *Amount* fields from the *Customer List* box to the *Field* row of the lower pane

3 Click the *Show* check box of the *State* column to remove its check

The *State* field used to express criteria will not be displayed.

4 Click the *Criteria* cell of the *State* column and type IL

5 Click the *or* cell of the *Amount* column and type >=200

Compare your lower pane with Figure DB2-14a, and be sure they match. Note that you should type the criteria for the *Amount* column on a different row from the criteria for the *State* column. This is the way the OR connector is expressed between values found in different fields.

6 Click *Query, Run*

USING THE *OR* CONNECTOR

FIGURE DB2-14 ■ USING THE *OR* CONNECTOR

(a) The criteria is set to search for records whose *State* equals IL OR whose *Amount* is greater than or equal to 200.
(b) The result of the query.
(c) The criteria is set to search for records whose *State* equals IL or NM.
(d) The result of the query.

(a)

Field:	Customer Number	State	Amount
Table:	Customer List	Customer List	Customer List
Sort:			
Show:	☑	☐	☑
Criteria:		"IL"	
or:			>=200

(b)

Query1 : Select Query

Customer Number	Amount
370	$450.75
101	$230.45
449	$740.45
754	$360.55
176	$123.45
067	$965.42
111	$456.78
*	$0.00

(c)

Field:	Last	First	State
Table:	Customer List	Customer List	Customer List
Sort:			
Show:	☑	☑	☑
Criteria:			"IL"
or:			"NM"

(d)

Query1 : Select Query

Last	First	City	State
Parker	Charles	Santa Fe	NM
West	Rita	Chicago	IL
Williams	DeVilla	Chicago	IL
Hill	Karen	Chicago	IL
*			

Your query should resemble Figure DB2-14b.

7 Close the Query window without saving

The last query uses an OR connector within one field to list records whose value in the *State* field is either "IL" or "NM":

1 Create a query with *Last, First, City,* and *State* fields and *State* Criteria of IL Or NM, as in Figure DB2-14c

2 Run the query, and compare your results with Figure DB2-14d

3 Close the Query window without saving

As you have seen in these four queries, AND connects two criteria in the same field column, as does OR. When combining criteria in different fields, those on the same row indicate an AND connector, whereas those on separate rows indicate an OR connector.

CREATING SUMMARY STATISTICS

You can also use queries to generate **summary statistics** for an entire file (or selected records) using the Sum, Average, and Count commands. The following exercise demonstrates this application.

THE SUM COMMAND. The **Sum command** totals selected numeric fields in the table. As with most other commands, the Sum command can be used with conditions to limit its scope. The following exercise presents three examples of the Sum command. Use Figure DB2-15a as a guide.

1 Double-click the *Create query in Design view* button

2 Click *Customer List* in the *Tables* tab and then the <u>A</u>dd button

3 Click the *Close* button in the Show Table dialog box

4 Click the *Totals* toolbar button (this adds another row named "Total" to the lower pane)

5 Drag and drop the *Amount* and *Paid* fields from the *Customer List* box to the *Field* row of the first two columns of the lower pane

6 Click the *Total* cell of the *Amount* column; click the ▾ button and then *Sum*

7 Click the *Total* cell of the *Paid* column; click the ▾ button and then *Sum*

8 Click <u>Q</u>uery, <u>R</u>un

Access displays the sums of the two fields as in Figure DB2-15b. To return to the Query Design screen:

9 Click <u>V</u>iew, <u>D</u>esign View

FIGURE DB2-15 ■ **CREATING SUMMARY STATISTICS**

(a) The query has been set to sum the *Amount* and *Paid* columns.
(b) The result of the query.
(c) The query has been set to sum the *Amounts* for records whose *Paid* field value equals 0.
(d) The result of the query.

(a)

(c)

(c)

(d)

Now, using Figure DB2-15b as a guide, add a feature that will total only those records with a zero in the *Paid* field:

10 Type **0** in the *Criteria* cell of the *Paid* column

11 Move to the *Total* cell of the *Paid* column, click its ▼ button, and then click *Where* (use the scroll bar to locate the *Where* option if needed)

The English translation of this query is, "Sum the Amount fields *where* Paid is zero." Your selections should agree with those in Figure DB2-15c.

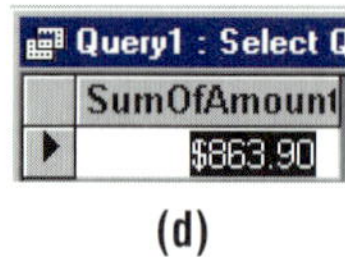

12 Click *Query, Run*

As in Figure DB2-15d, a total is shown in the *Amount* field, but only for those records whose *Paid* fields were equal to 0. Perform one more query using Sum:

13 Click *View, Design View*

14 Move to the *Field* cell in the *Paid* column and delete "Paid"

15 Type **City**

16 Move to the *Total* cell in the *City* column, click the ▼ button of the *Total* cell, and then click *Group By* (use the scroll bar if needed)

17 Click the *Show* check box in the *City* column to place a check there

18 In the *Criteria* cell, delete the "0," type **New York**, and press **Tab**

19 Click *Query*, *Run*

This query displays a sum amount of $1,101.00 for those records whose *City* field value is "New York."

20 Close all windows in the Access work area without saving

21 If you wish to stop, exit Access

THE AVERAGE COMMAND.   The **Average command** computes the arithmetic mean (average) of all numeric fields or expressions. It is invoked in a fashion similar to that of the Sum command but replaces Sum with Avg. Refer to your online help to use this command.

THE COUNT COMMAND.   The **Count command** tabulates the number of records that meet a stated condition. Like the Sum and Average commands, it can be used in the query form to tabulate any desired condition. For example, if you were to select *Count* in the *State* field, Access would count the number of records with entries (nonblank values) in the *State* field in the table. (All seven records have entries, so the resulting count would be 7 in this case. However, if one customer's state had not been recorded, the count would be 6.)

☑ CHECKPOINT

Perform these tasks and answer these questions.
1. Open the DCHECK database file, and create a simple query displaying only the *Name* and *Test2* fields and save it as Test2 Query.
2. Create a query that displays only those students whose Test2 grades are greater than or equal to 90. Save the query as Test2>=90.
3. What are summary statistics?
4. Create a query that displays all students whose Test1 AND Test2 scores are greater than 90. Save the query as Test1 AND Test2>90.
5. Average those records whose Test1 grades are less than 80. Save the query as AVG Test1<80. (*Hint:* The *Test1* field will need to be placed in the Query design lower pane twice: once with *Average* and once with *Where.*)

MASTERY SET 2-4: ALTERING DATA WITH QUERIES

Editing is fine for individual record changes, but it can be tedious when performing the same update on many records. For example, perhaps you want to change all zip codes that start with 100 to 113 or add $20 to all *Amount* fields. You can use the Update Query feature to alter data in specified fields of the table.

> **Warning: Altering data in a group of records is a potentially hazardous technique, for one mistake can inadvertently change thousands of records. It is advisable to create a backup (copy) of your table for safekeeping before attempting update queries.**

To prepare for the exercises in this mastery set:

1   If necessary, launch Access, and open the CUSTOMER.mdb database file

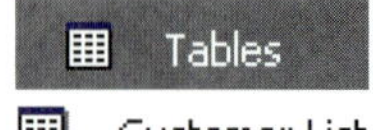

2   If necessary, click the *Tables* object type button and the *Customer List* icon

3   Click *Edit, Copy*   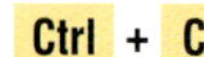 **Ctrl + C**

4   Click *Edit, Paste*   **Ctrl + V**

When asked to name the new table:

5   Type Customer List Backup , and then click the *Structure and Data* option and *OK*

Access has made a copy of Customer List so that if an error is made in the next procedure, you could copy from Customer List Backup to Customer List.

> **Tip: No two objects may be assigned the same name.**

MODIFYING DATA IN ALL RECORDS

This first exercise appends (adds) the characters "0000" to the end of each current zip code. Because you already changed the size of the *Zip* field in Mastery Set 2-1, it can hold the additional characters.

1   Click the *Queries* object type button, and double-click the *Create query In Design view*

2   Click the *Tables* tab, *Customer List,* the *Add* button, and then the *Close* button in the Show Table dialog box

3   Click *Query, Update Query*

The Update Query Design screen appears. An update query is used to change field values.

4   Locate the *Zip* field in the *Customer List* box by using its vertical scroll bar

5   Drag and drop the *Zip* field from the *Customer List* box to the *Field* cell in the first column of the lower pane

6   Click the *Update To* cell of the *Zip* column to place the insertion point there

7   Type [Zip]+"0000" and press ↵ (*note:* If you did not use the Mask feature, you will need to type [Zip]+"-0000" instead)

As shown in Figure DB2-16a, the field name must be in square brackets. The literal string "0000" contains the four characters (zeros, not the letter "O") that will be added to each zip code value. A **literal string** is a series of characters that always print or display without variation.

FIGURE DB2-16 ■ MODIFYING DATA IN ALL RECORDS

(a) The Update Query window is used to define the criteria to update the *Zip* field values with "-0000."
(b) The results of the update.

(a)

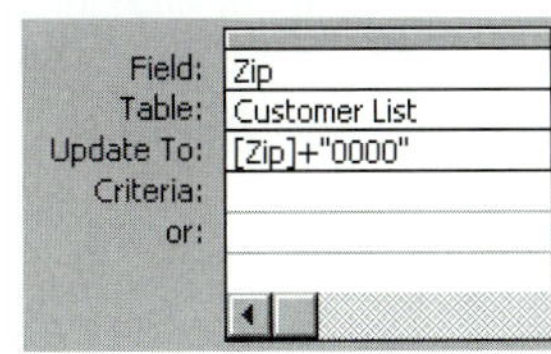

(b)

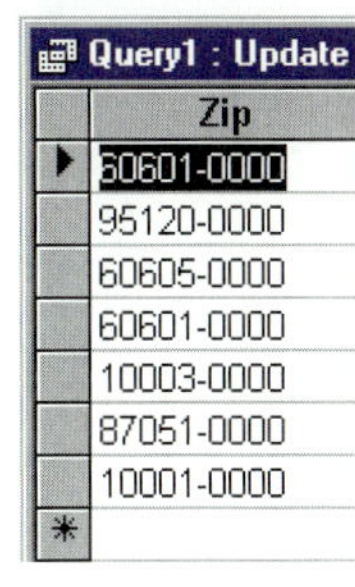

8 Click *Query, Run*

Access displays a box informing you that seven records are about to be updated. This gives you a chance to cancel the procedure in case you made a mistake.

9 Click *Yes*

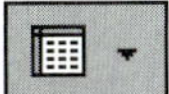

10 Click *View, Datasheet View*

As in Figure DB2-16b, each zip code should have been changed so that the last five characters are "-0000."

> **Tip: If you open the Customer List table, it should also reflect the change. (The backup table, however, does not reflect the change.)**

When you finish viewing:

11 Close the query window without saving

REPLACING DATA IN SELECTED RECORDS

You can use the Update Query feature to replace the contents of fields that meet set criteria. The criteria can be set in the same search field or in a different search field. A *search field* is a field in which you instruct Access to look. The update query changes the data in a table when it is run.

REPLACING DATA WITHIN THE SAME FIELD.   This exercise changes the data in *City* fields that read "New York" to "New York City." It does not change all records, but only those that meet the stated condition.

1 Repeat Steps 1 through 3 in the previous exercise

2 Locate the *City* field in the *Customer List* box by using its vertical scroll bar

3 Drag and drop the *City* field from the *Customer List* box to the *Field* cell of the first column of the query

4 Click the *Update To* cell of the *City* column, and type `New York City`

5 Click the *Criteria* cell of the *City* column, type `New York` , and press ↵

Compare your settings with those in Figure DB2-17a. This condition translates as, "Change the City field for each record whose city is New York to New York City."

> **Tip: To change all records, simply omit the search criteria.**

6 Click *Query, Run*

The screen displays a message that two records will be changed. Note that the Datasheet view will also display the two records that will be updated.

7 Click *Yes*

8 Close the query window without saving

9 Click the *Tables* object type button, the *Customer List* icon, and then the *Open* button

10 Maximize the Customer List: Table

Your window's *City* column should agree to Figure DB2-17b.

FIGURE DB2-17 ■ REPLACING DATA WITHIN THE SAME FIELD

(a) The *Update To* and search *Criteria* have been set in the same field.
(b) The results of the update.

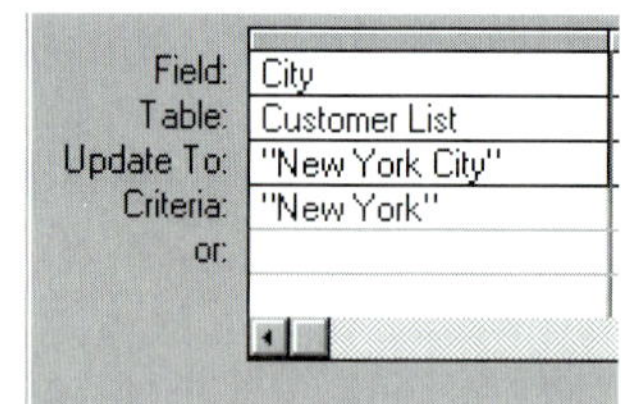

(a)

	Customer Number	Last	First	Street	City	State	Zip	
▶	101	Burstein	Jerome	100 N. 1st Street	San Jose	CA	95120-0000	
	111	Hill	Karen	1500 Michigan Avenue	Chicago	IL	60605-0000	
	449	Kee	Charles	500 Fifth Avenue	New York City	NY	10003-0000	
	754	Martin	Edward	50 Carmine Street	New York City	NY	10001-0000	
	670	Parker	Charles	25 Cerillos Road	Santa Fe	NM	87051-0000	
	176	West	Rita	75 N. Wacker Drive	Chicago	IL	60601-0000	
	067	Williams	DeVilla	One Dryden Way	Chicago	IL	60601-0000	
*								

(b)

11 Close the Customer List: Table window

USING A DIFFERENT SEARCH FIELD.   Using a separate search field can also achieve a desired result. For example, assume that you want to add $15 to the *Amount* field of anyone who has not yet paid:

1 Open an update query window with Customer List as the table

2 Drag and drop *Amount* from the *Customer List* box to the *Field* cell in the first column of the lower pane (if needed, use the scroll bar of the *Customer List* box)

3 Move to the *Update To* cell of the *Amount* column, and type [Amount]+15

As written, this change will affect all records in the table. Because you do not want that to occur, you must add a search condition as follows:

4 Drag *Paid* to the *Field* cell in the second column of the query

5 Move to the *Criteria* cell of the *Paid* column, and type 0 (zero)

The selections in your Update Query window should match those in Figure DB2-18a. The query will now find all records whose *Paid* field is 0, and for those records only, add $15 to the *Amount* field.

6 Click *Query, Run*

The screen displays a message that two records will be changed because two customers have *Paid* amounts of zero: Kee and West.

7 Click *Yes*

8 Close the Update Query window without saving

9 Click the *Tables* object type button, the *Customer List* icon, and then the *Open* button

---

FIGURE DB2-18 ■ REPLACING DATA IN A FIELD DIFFERENT FROM THE SEARCH FIELD

(a) The *Update To* criteria is specified in the Amount column *Field,* and the search *Criteria* is defined in the *Paid* column.
(b) The result of the update.

(a)

Field:	Amount	Paid
Table:	Customer List	Customer List
Update To:	[Amount]+15	
Criteria:		0
or:		

Amount	Paid
$230.45	$100.00
$456.78	$456.78
$755.45	$0.00
$360.55	$130.55
$450.75	$200.00
$138.45	$0.00
$965.42	$500.00
$0.00	$0.00

(b)

10 If necessary, use the horizontal scroll bar to display the *Amount* and *Paid* columns

Your *Amount* and *Paid* columns of the Customer List: Table window should resemble Figure DB2-18b. Note that 15 has been added to the *Amount* fields of Kee, $755.45, and West, $138.45 (formerly $740.45 and $123.45). These two records' *Paid* field value equals 0.

11 Close the Customer List: Table window

12 If you wish to stop for now, exit Access

There are thousands of ways to use update queries to modify current entries or change them entirely.

CHECKPOINT

Perform these tasks.
1. If needed, launch Access, and open the DCHECK database.
2. Use an update query to change the name "Smith" to "Frank" in the Students table. Do not save the query.
3. Use an update query to add three points to Test2 and two points to Test3. (*Hint:* Because Test scores are numeric fields, do not use quotes in the criteria.) Do not save the query.
4. Use an update query to add five points to any score in Test1 that falls below 50. Do not save the query.
5. Review your changes in Datasheet view. Close all windows in the Access work area.

MASTERY SET 2-5: CREATING REPORTS

A **report** is a view that presents data from records in a manner the user specifies and organizes. Although its results can appear on the screen, it is generally used to produce a printed output. You can create a report from a table or a query. The process is the same. In the next exercises, Access's AutoReport Wizard is used to help you quickly create a new report. To prepare for the exercises in this mastery set:

1 Launch Access if needed, and open the CUSTOMER.mdb database file

2 Open the Customer List table and check that it is sorted by the *Last* field in ascending order (if necessary, click the *Last* column field label to select the column, and then click *Records*, *Sort*, *Sort Ascending*), and then close the table

3 Click the *Reports* object type button of the CUSTOMER: Database window

CREATING AUTOREPORTS

Access offers two AutoReport formats: **Columnar Report** (list fields vertically) or **Tabular Report** (list fields horizontally). Once you create an AutoReport, you can edit it.

CREATING A COLUMNAR REPORT.   To create an AutoReport: Columnar format:

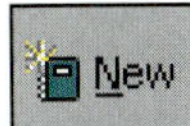

1 Click the *New* button

2 Click *AutoReport: Columnar*

3 Click the [▼] button of *Choose the table or query where the object's data comes from:*, click *Customer List,* and then click *OK*

> **Tip:** You can also select a query in Step 3 instead of a table.

4 Click the Maximize button of the Report window

5 Use the window's scroll bars to reposition the report's view as in Figure DB2-19a

Note that the report is displayed as a Print Preview. This lets you see the report as it would appear on paper. As you move the mouse pointer in the work area of the screen, its shape resembles a magnifying glass. When a minus sign appears in it, clicking an

---

FIGURE DB2-19 ■ CREATING AUTOREPORTS

(a) An AutoReport: columnar format.

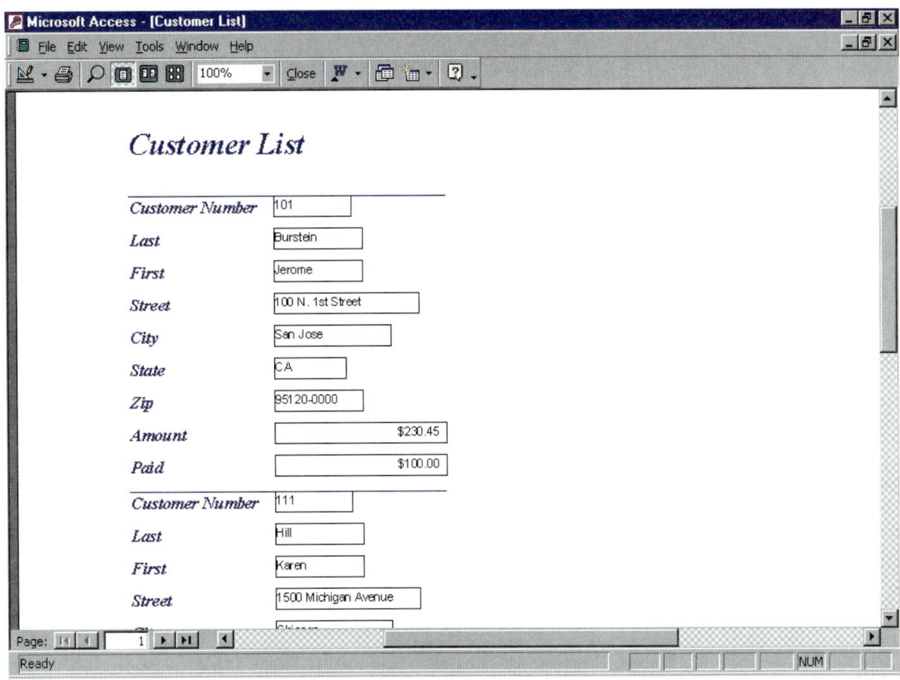

(a)

(continued)

FIGURE DB2-19 ■ CREATING AUTOREPORTS CONTINUED

(b) An AutoReport: tabular format.

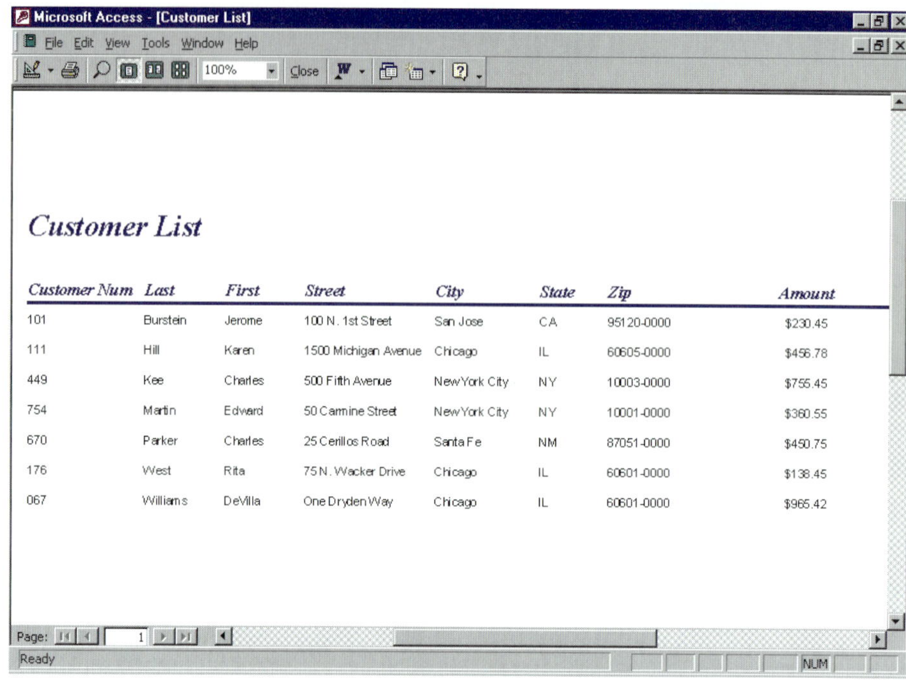

(b)

area of the report will shrink its view. Similarly, when a plus sign appears in the pointer, clicking the report will enlarge its view. Try this:

6 Click the report title—*Customer List*

7 Click it again to return it to its original size

Note that the title "Customer List" appears at the top of the first page only. The current date and page number will appear at the bottom of every page.

8 Use the scroll bars to move through the report and examine its content (you can also use the arrow keys and **Pg Up** or **Pg Dn** keys to scroll through the report)

9 Reposition the report's view to match the one in Figure DB2-19a

10 Click the *Close* toolbar button to switch to the Report Design view window

You'll use this window later to modify a report.

11 Click *File*, *Save*   **Ctrl** + **S**

12 Type **Customer Columnar Report**, and click *OK*

 **13** Click *File, Close*, or click the *Close* button at the right end of the menu bar to close the window

> Tip: A reopened, saved report will display updated database data.

CREATING A TABULAR REPORT. To create an AutoReport: Tabular format, follow these steps:

1 Click the *New* button

2 Click *AutoReport: Tabular*

3 Click the ▼ button of *Choose the table or query where the object's data comes from:*, click *Customer List*, and then click *OK*

4 Use the scroll bars to move through the report and examine its content (you can also use the arrow keys and `Pg Up` and `Pg Dn` keys to scroll through the report)

5 Reposition the report's view to match that in Figure DB2-19b

6 Click the *Close* toolbar button to switch to the Report Design view window

 **7** Click *File, Save*   `Ctrl` + `S`

8 Type `Customer Tabular Report` and click *OK*

 **9** Click *File, Close*, or click the *Close* button at the right end of the menu bar to close the window

DUPLICATING, RENAMING, AND DELETING REPORTS

As with any object in Access, reports can be duplicated, renamed, and deleted. The operations discussed in this section can be applied to any object created in the Database window.

DUPLICATING A REPORT. Earlier you duplicated a table using the Copy and Paste commands. These commands can also copy any object in the Access window. For example, to duplicate the Customer Tabular Report:

Customer Tabular Report   **1** Click the *Customer Tabular Report* icon in the Database window's List box tab

 **2** Click *Edit, Copy*   `Ctrl` + `C`

 **3** Click *Edit, Paste*   `Ctrl` + `V`

4 Type `Customer List Report` in the Paste As dialog box, and then click *OK*

A copy of the Customer Tabular Report has now been created with a different name.

RENAMING A REPORT. A report or any other object can be renamed. To rename the Customer List Report as "Customer Report," do this:

1 If needed, click the *Customer List Report* icon to select it

2 Click *Edit, Rename*

3 Move the insertion point after the "t" in "List"

(Remember, pressing an arrow key when data is selected removes the selection highlight.)

4 Press **Backspace** five times to remove "List," and the space before it

5 Press ↵ to accept the revised name

> **Tip:** After selecting the *Customer List Report* icon (Step 1), you can simply click the *Customer List Report* icon title to place it in edit mode for renaming or press *F2*.

DELETING A REPORT.   The Delete command as used earlier to remove a form can also be applied to a report or other object. To delete the Customer Report:

1 Click the *Customer Report* icon

2 Click *Edit, Delete*   **Delete**

3 Click Y*es*

The report disappears from the window's list box.

CREATING A CUSTOM REPORT

Suppose you want to create a report with all fields from the Customer List table except *Customer Number.* You would also like the report to be grouped by city, sorted by last name, and have summary statistics for the *Amount* and *Paid* columns. Access's Report Wizard is the answer to this complicated task.

1 If needed, click the *Reports* object type button

2 Double-click the *Create report by using wizard* icon

The Report Wizard's first dialog box is used to select the Tables/Queries and then the fields that you want to include in the report. Although you can choose fields from more than one table/query, only the Customer List table will be used in the next exercise.

3 If needed, click the ▼ button of the *Tables/Queries* drop-down box, *Table: Customer List*

4 Click the *Last* field in the *Available Fields* box and then the > button

5 Click the *First* field in the *Available Fields* box and then the > button

6 Repeat Step 3 to select the *Street, City, State, Zip, Amount,* and *Paid* fields

> **Tip:** Instead of performing Step 3, you can also double-click each desired field in the *Available Fields* box to select them.

As with other wizards, clicking the >> button selects all fields. Clicking the < button deselects a single field, and clicking the << button deselects all fields.

Your selections should resemble Figure DB2-20a.

7 Click the *Next* > button

The selections in this dialog box are optional and can be used to rearrange data in the report by one or more fields so that records containing the same data (in that field) can be displayed as a **group.** These groups, if desired, can then be subtotaled separately.

> **Tip:** To skip an optional dialog box, click the *Next* > or *Finish* button. *Next* > will take you to the next dialog box, and *Finish* will create the report using the current selections.

For this report, group all customers by the *City* field:

8 Click *City* in the *Do you want to add grouping levels?* list box, and then click the > button

Your dialog box should now match the one in Figure DB2-20b.

9 Click the *Next* > button

This dialog box is for setting sorting order and placing summary statistics in your report. These tasks are optional; however, to see their effect, make the following selections:

10 Click the ▼ button of the *number 1* drop-down box, and then click *Last* to sort by this field

Your dialog box should resemble Figure DB2-20c. Note that you can sort in up to four levels. Each level can also be sorted in ascending (default) or descending order. Use the *Sort* button to the right of the sort level box to define the sort order. Now, to add summary statistics to the *Amount* and *Paid* columns:

11 Click the *Summary Options* button to display its dialog box

12 Click the *Sum* check box for the *Amount* field

13 Click the *Sum* check box for the *Paid* field

Your selections should match those in Figure DB2-20d. This dialog box also lets you set the report to show "Detail and Summary" (default) or "Summary Only" in the report and a percentage of the total for sums.

14 Click *OK* to return to the previous dialog box, and then click the *Next* > button

This dialog box lets you set the layout of your report. Currently, the dialog box is set to create a report in **portrait** orientation (8 1/2" by 11"). To change the orientation to **landscape** (11" by 8 1/2") as in Figure DB2-20e:

DB

15 Click the *Landscape* option

16 Click the *Next* > button for the Style selection dialog box

---

FIGURE DB2-20 ■ **CREATING A CUSTOM REPORT WITH THE REPORT WIZARD**

(a) This dialog box is used to select fields to be displayed on a report.
(b) This dialog box is used to define field groupings.
(c) Up to four levels of sorting can be defined in this dialog box. Clicking *Summary Options* will open its dialog box.

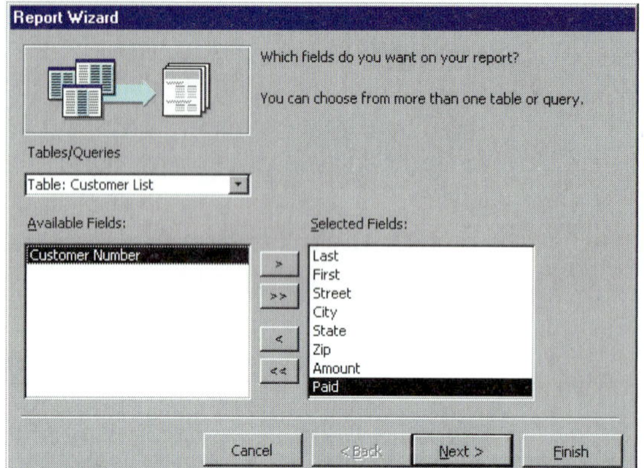

(a)

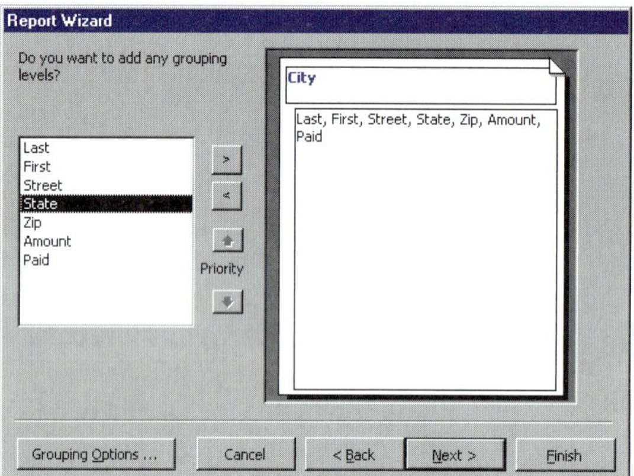

(b)

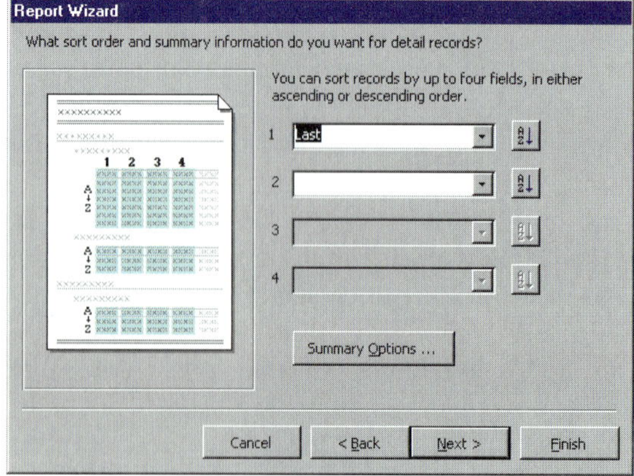

(c)

(continued)

FIGURE DB2-20 ■ CREATING A CUSTOM REPORT WITH THE REPORT WIZARD CONTINUED

(d) Summary options selected here will appear in the report footer.
(e) Layout and orientation settings are defined here.
(f) Report style options can be selected here.

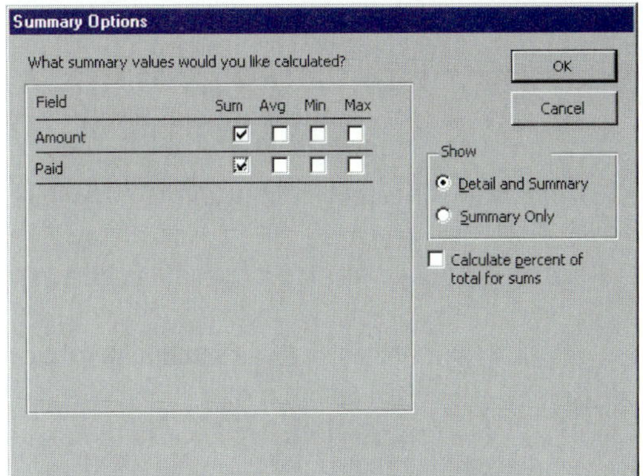

(d)

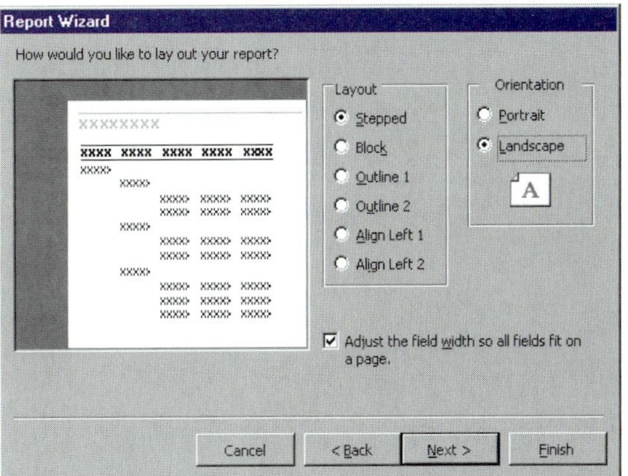

(e)

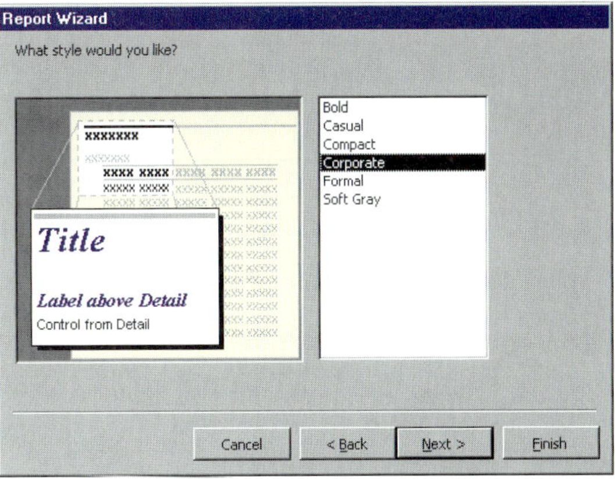

(f)

Currently, this dialog box is set to Corporate style (the default). A sample of its look appears in the left side of the dialog box, as in Figure DB2-20f. At this point, you can select another style by clicking it or keep the default style. To keep the Corporate style:

17 **If needed, click *Corporate***

18 Click the _Next >_ button

19 Type **Customer By City Report** in the _"What title do you want for your report?"_ box

This is the last dialog box of the Wizard. It is used to name the report. You can also specify the way you will first see the report (Print Preview or Design view). To create the report and display it in Print Preview:

20 Click the _Finish_ button

21 Click the Maximize button of the Print Preview window   **Alt** + **-** , **X**

22 Use the window's scroll bars to view its content

The top left portion of your report should resemble Figure DB2-21. As you scroll to the _Paid_ and _Grand Total_ fields, note that they maybe only partially displayed. If so, you'll correct this in the next mastery set.

23 Turn on your printer

24 Click _File, Print, OK_ to print the report   **Ctrl** + **P** , ↵

25 Click _File, Close_ or the _Close_ button of the Print Preview window   **Ctrl** + **F4**

26 Close all windows in Access's work area

FIGURE DB2-21 ■ THE COMPLETED CUSTOM REPORT

Customer By City Report

City	Last	First	Street	State	Zip	Amount	Pa
Chicago							
	Hill	Karen	1500 Michigan Avenue	IL	60605-0000	$456.78	$456.7
	West	Rita	75 N. Wacker Drive	IL	60601-0000	$138.45	$0.0
	Williams	DeVilla	One Dryden Way	IL	60601-0000	$965.42	$500.0
Summary for 'City' = Chicago (3 detail records)							
Sum						$1,560.65	$956.7
New York City							
	Kee	Charles	500 Fifth Avenue	NY	10003-0000	$755.45	$0.0
	Martin	Edward	50 Carmine Street	NY	10001-0000	$360.55	$130.5
Summary for 'City' = New York City (2 detail records)							
Sum						$1,116.00	$130.5
San Jose							
	Burstein	Jerome	100 N. 1st Street	CA	95120-0000	$230.45	$100.0
Summary for 'City' = San Jose (1 detail record)							
Sum						$230.45	$100.0
Santa Fe							

☑ CHECKPOINT

Perform these tasks and answer these questions.

1. Open the DCHECK database. Create columnar and tabular AutoReports using the Students table. Name them "Student Columnar Report" and "Students Tabular Report."
2. Duplicate the Students Tabular Report and call it "Copy of Students Tabular Report."
3. Use the Report Wizard to create a custom report from the Students table. Use all fields grouped by Class and sorted by name.
4. Include average summary statistics for the test grades, and name the report "Detail Students Report."
5. Print the Detail Students Report, and then close the database.

MASTERY SET 2-6: MODIFYING A REPORT

All items that make up a report or form are also considered to be objects. You can rename, rearrange, insert, delete, or copy them. Their properties, such as font (typeface), format (numbers), alignment, and size can also be adjusted. You will now use a copy of the Customer By City Report to learn how to make these modifications. To prepare for this mastery set:

1 **Open the CUSTOMER.mdb database and if needed, click the *Reports* object type button**

2 **Click the *Customer By City Report* icon**

 **3** **Click *Edit, Copy***   `Ctrl + C`

 **4** **Click *Edit, Paste***   `Ctrl + V`

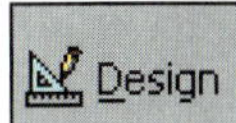 **5** **Type** Customer Report - By City **in the Paste As dialog box, and then click *OK***

6 **Display the Customer Report - By City in Design view and, if needed, maximize its window**

7 **Drag and drop the toolbox title bar until the box is positioned as in Figure DB2-22**

Your window should resemble Figure DB2-22. For a description of each toolbox's button, see the appendix.

> **Tip: To display the toolbox if it is not on the screen, click *View, Toolbox*.**

UNDERSTANDING REPORT DESIGN VIEW

As shown in Figure DB2-22, a report's structure is divided into bands: *Report Header, Page Header, City Header* (optional group header), *Detail, City Footer* (optional group footer), *Page Footer,* and *Report Footer.* A **band** is a separate section of a report. The bar at the top of each band identifies and separates the band and is called the band's *title*

FIGURE DB2-22 ■ **WORKING IN REPORT DESIGN VIEW**

(a) The Report Design View window.
(b) Toolbox buttons.

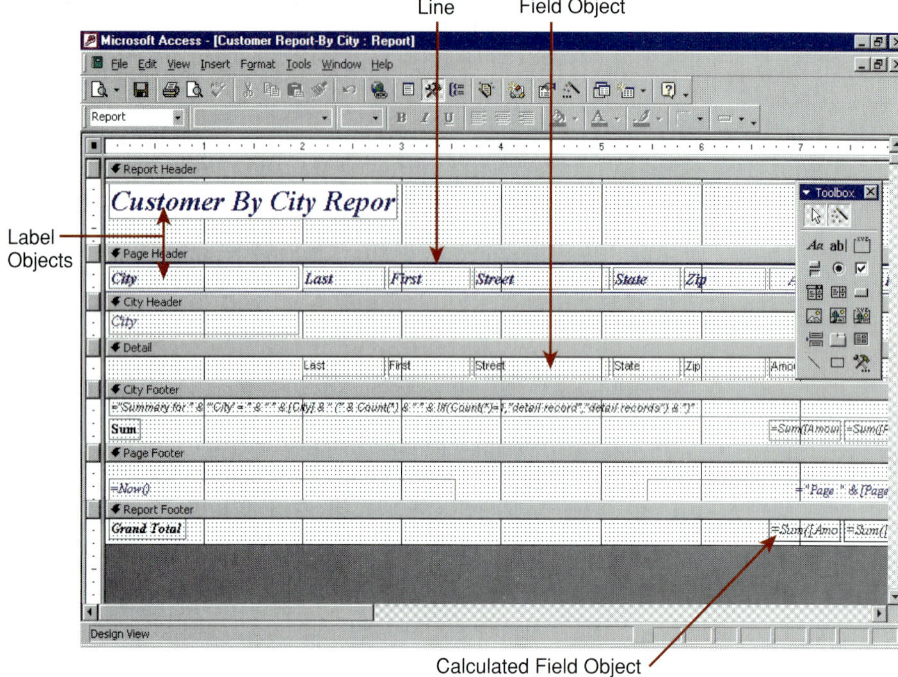

line. See Table DB2-3 for a description of each band's function. To select (highlight) a band, click its title line. The selected band is the one in which you are currently working. You can use keyboard commands to edit the objects in this band.

All graphical objects within a band are called controls. A **control** includes text boxes, list boxes, check boxes, option buttons, command buttons, lines, and rectangles. A **label control** is used for descriptive titles. A **text box** displays field data (**field object**) or the result of a mathematical equation (calculated control). Controls are grouped into three categories: *bound, unbound,* and *calculated.* A **bound control** is one that displays field data from an underlying table or query such as a field object. An **unbound control** is a descriptive or decorative control, such as a label object, line, or rectangle. A **calculated control** displays the result of a mathematical equation, for example, a summary statistic. Figure DB2-22 identifies some of these objects.

WORKING WITH OBJECTS

In these next exercises, you learn how to resize, add, and rearrange objects in your report. These techniques can be equally applied to a form.

RESIZING OBJECTS.   To resize label, field, and calculated field objects, you first select them and then drag one of their **selection handles** (small square boxes) located along each object's border. Try this to resize the *City* objects in the Page Header and City Header bands:

TABLE DB2-3 ■ REPORT BANDS

Band	Description
Report Header band and Report Footer band	Form the top and bottom base layers of the report. Items in these bands print only once in the entire report. Items placed in the report header appear at the start of the report; items placed in the report footer appear at the end of the report.
Page Header band and Page Footer band	Print once on each page. Items placed in the page header appear at the top of each page; items placed in the page footer appear at the bottom of each page.
Detail band	Forms the body of the report. When a report is created, this band is filled with data from the table associated with the report.
Group band	An optional band created when records are grouped within the report. Group identification is typically placed at the top of the band; summary statistics are placed at the bottom.

1 Click the *City* label object in the Page Header band to select it

2 **Shift** -click the *City* field object in the City Header band to select it

Both objects should now be selected. Note that selection handles appear on their borders.

3 Slowly point to the center selection handle on the right border of the *City* label object until the pointer appears as a resizing pointer (double-arrow) as in Figure DB2-23a

4 Using the ruler bar as a guide, drag the selection handle to the left to the 1 1/4-inch horizontal mark as in Figure DB2-23b (note that the ruler bar becomes highlighted as you drag)

5 Click outside the selection to deselect

 **6** Click *File, Save* to resave the report   **Ctrl** + **S**

Objects can also be sized to fit their data, to a grid, and to the tallest, shortest, widest, and narrowest data. The Size submenu of the Format menu offers these options, which you will use later.

ADDING A FIELD.   Add fields to a report's design by using the Field List dialog box. Try this to add the *Customer Number* field:

 **1** Click *View, Field List*

The *Field List* box displays fields from the underlying table.

FIGURE DB2-23 ■ RESIZING OBJECTS

(a) Click the first object, and then *Shift*-click each additional object to create a multiple selection.
(b) The *City* objects have been resized.

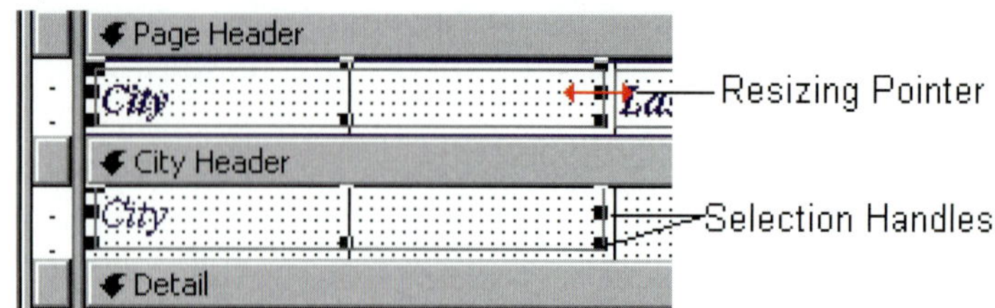

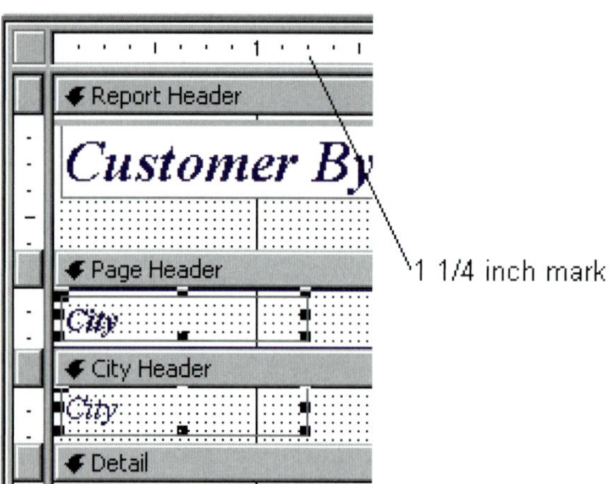

2 Click *Customer Number* in the *Field List* box to select it

> **Tip:** You can select additional fields to be placed at the same time by *Ctrl*-clicking each additional field in the *Field List* box. You can also select fields in a block (contiguous group) by clicking the first field and then *Shift*-clicking the last field of the block.

3 Drag and drop the *Customer Number* field in the Detail band at about the 1-inch horizontal mark as in Figure DB2-24a

4 Click outside the selection to deselect it

Note that in Step 3, Access inserted the field object and its associated label. Because you do not need this label here:

5 Click only the *Customer Number* label object (left object) to select it, and then press **Delete**

You will add a different label for the customer number shortly.

FIGURE DB2-24 ■ **ADDING A NEW FIELD**

(a) Dragging and dropping a field or group of fields from the *First* list box will place its label and field objects in the report.
(b) Dragging a selection handle will resize an object.

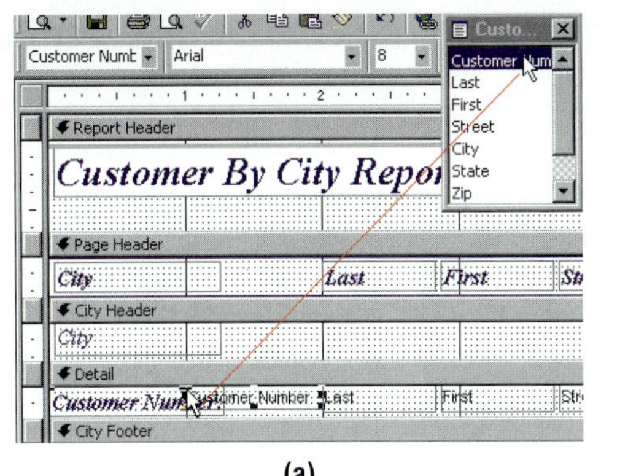

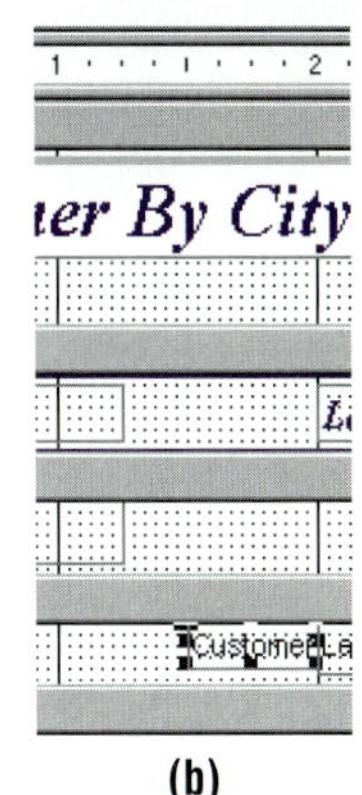

(a)   (b)

Tip: If you place the field object in the wrong band, simply select it and press *Delete.* Then repeat Steps 1 through 4.

6 Click the *Close* button of the *Field List* box

7 Click the *Customer Number* field object to select it, and then drag the center selection handle of the left border to the 1 1/2-inch mark as in Figure DB2-24b (the actual position of your *Customer Number* field object may differ slightly)

8 Click outside the object to deselect it

9 Resave the report

SIZING, SPACING, AND ALIGNING AN OBJECT WITH OTHERS.   When you first place a new object in a report, it may not be the same size as other objects, or it might not be spaced properly or aligned with other objects. To resize, space, and align the *Customer Number* field object as in Figure DB2-25:

1 Click the *Customer Number* field object, and then **Shift** -click the *Last* field object

FIGURE DB2-25 ■ **SIZING, SPACING, AND ALIGNING**

The *Customer Number* field has been resized, spaced, and aligned. Note that only the "Customer" of the "Customer Number" field name appears in the box after it is resized.

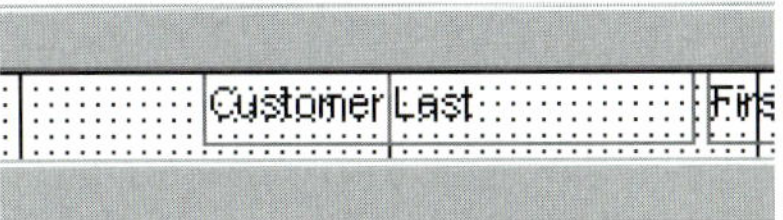

2 Click *Format,* (if needed, ), *Size, To Tallest*

If the objects are not spaced properly, try the following:

3 Click outside the selected objects to deselect them

4 Click the *Customer Number* field object to select it

5 Point anywhere within the object until the pointer appears as a small hand

6 Drag and drop the object as needed so that space occurs between it and the *Last* field object similar to other spaces in the band

> **Tip:** The Horizontal Spacing and Vertical Spacing submenus of the Format menu also offer a variety of spacing options that you can apply to a selection of objects.

7 Deselect the object

Now, to better align the objects:

8 Select both the *Customer Number* and *Last* objects

9 Click *Format, Align, Top*

Your *Customer Number* field object should now be sized, spaced, and aligned as in Figure DB2-25.

10 Deselect the objects and resave the report

ADDING A LABEL.   To add a the label object "ID#" to the Page Header band as in Figure DB2-26a:

1 Click the *Label* button in the toolbox

2 Position the +A portion of your pointer at about the 1 1/2-inch horizontal mark, near the Page Header title line

3 Drag diagonally to create a rectangular label box similar to the one in Figure DB2-26a

> **Tip:** Instead of performing Steps 2 and 3, you can simply click the 1 1/2-inch horizontal mark and start typing.

4 Type **ID#** and press 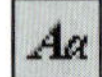

5 If needed, use the techniques in the previous exercise to resize, space, or align the label object

6 Resave the report

7 Click *View, Print Preview* to view your changes

FIGURE DB2-26 ■ ADDING A LABEL OBJECT

(a) The *ID#* field object has been inserted into the report windows.
(b) The *ID#* column as it appears with the new field.

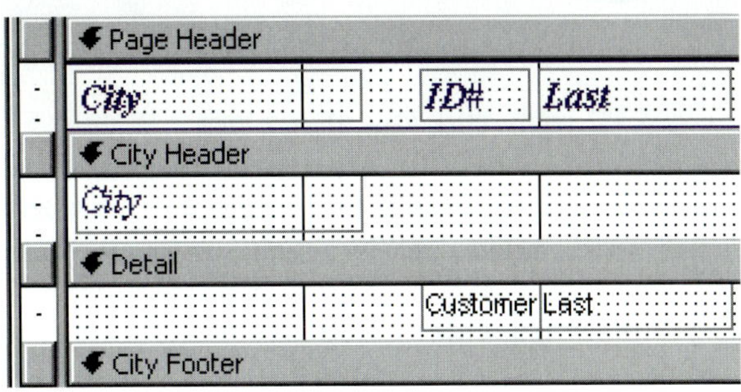

(a)

(b) Sum

The first grouping of the *ID#* column should resemble Figure DB2-26b.

RENAMING A LABEL.   The contents of any existing label object can be changed. For example, to change the report's title to "Customer Report - By City":

1 Click *View, Design*

2 Click the report title label object (which currently displays "Customer By City Report") to select it

3 Click just after the word "Customer" to place the insertion point there

4 Press **Delete** as needed to remove "By City" and any extra space between "Customer" and "Report"

5 Move the insertion point to the end of "Report"

6 Press **Spacebar** and then type **- By City**

7 Click outside the title label object to deselect it

8   **Resave the report**

9   Click *View, Print Preview* to view your change

Your new report title should read "Customer Report - By City" as in Figure DB2-27.

10   Click *View, Design View*

DELETING OBJECTS AND UNDOING AN ACTION.   You can delete any selected object by simply pressing the Delete key or clicking *Edit, Delete*. Try this:

1   **Click the report title label object to select it**

2   **Click *Edit, Delete***   `Delete`

Although the report title label object disappears, it is not yet permanently gone.
Access's **Undo** command can reverse your last action. Try this:

3   **Click *Edit, Undo Delete***   `Ctrl` + `Z`

The report title label object reappears.

4   **Close the Report window without saving**

ADDING CALCULATED FIELDS AND SUMMARY OBJECTS

Columns in a report can contain expressions that perform calculations on numeric
fields. For example, the following exercise shows you how to make Access calculate
the difference between the *Amount* and *Paid* fields and place the result in the last column with a heading of "Due." You will also add a summary field object (calculated
control) in the City Footer and Report Footer bands to sum the *Due* column.

ADDING A CALCULATED CONTROL.   First, insert an object in the Detail band
that describes the calculation you want Access to make each time the report is printed
(Amount – Paid).

The report title has been
changed.

Customer Report – By City

City		ID#	Last	First
Chicago				

FIGURE DB2-28 ■ POSITIONING YOUR SCREEN FOR NEW OBJECTS

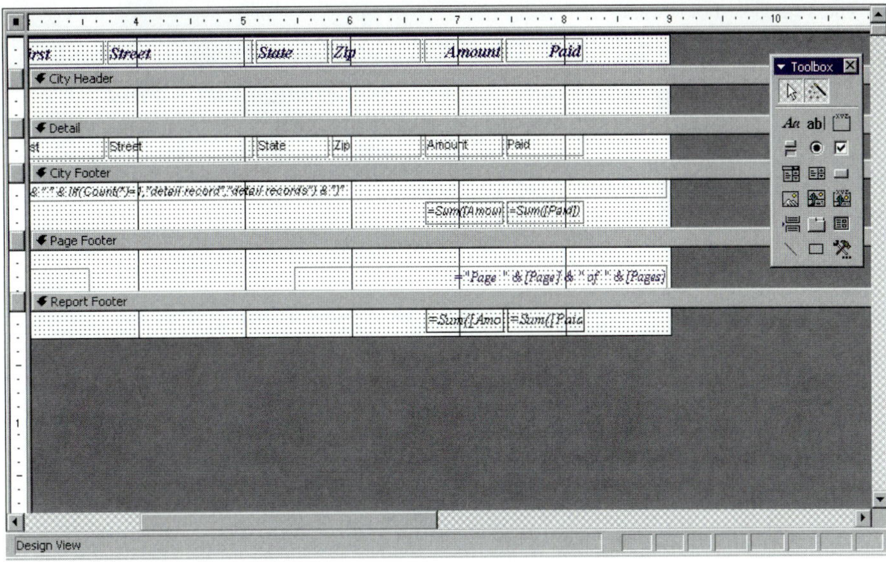

1   If needed, launch Access, open the CUSTOMER.mdb database, click the *Reports* object type button, and then open the Customer Report - By City report in Design view

2   Use the scroll bars to reposition the display, and drag and drop the toolbox as in Figure DB2-28 (the position of some objects may differ in your report)

Use the following steps to add the summary statistic objects and adjust your objects' positions as needed.

3   Click the *Text Box* button on the toolbox (your pointer changes to a "+abl")

4   Using Figure DB2-29a as a guide, position the "+" portion in the Detail band where the top left corner of the field object should appear (at the 8 1/4-inch horizontal mark), and then click

As in Figure DB2-29a, two objects should now appear: a label object (left) displaying "Text#" and an object displaying "Unbound" (right). "Unbound" simply indicates that the object is currently not associated with (bound to) any field in the table. You will change this shortly by adjusting this new object's *properties*. An object's properties are its characteristics or behavior. Before binding a field to this object, do the following to remove the "Text#" label object:

5   Click outside the selected objects to deselect them

6   Click only the *Text#* label object, and press **Delete**

7   Click the *Unbound* field object to select it

FIGURE DB2-29 ■ **ADDING CALCULATING FIELDS**

(a) The Text Box tool is used to create these objects.
(b) The Properties dialog box.
(c) The result of adding the *Due* objects.

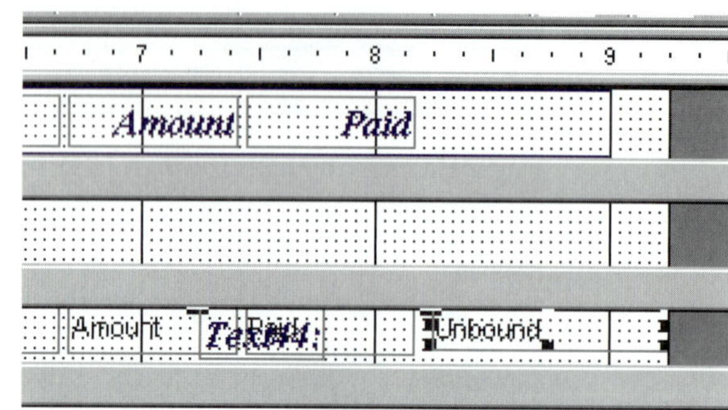

(a)

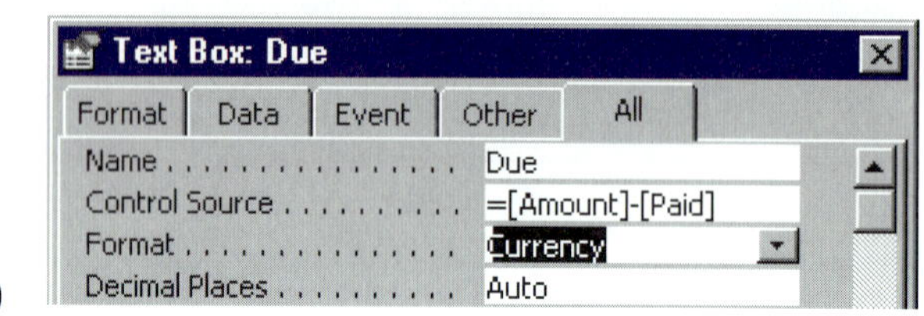

(b)

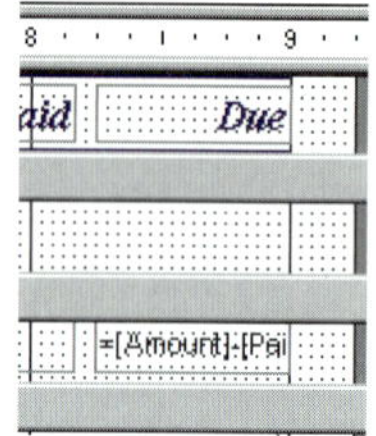

(c)

8 Drag the center selection handle of the right border to the left until it aligns with the 9-inch mark

9 Click *View*, *Properties* to display its dialog box

> Tip: Instead of performing Steps 7 through 9, you can double-click the *Unbound* field object to open its Properties dialog box.

10 Click the *All* tab

Note that an object's Properties dialog box contains several tabs. Each tab's function is described in Table DB2-4.

Now, make the following changes to the properties of the new unbound object:

11 Click the *Name* box to place the insertion point there and then delete its content

12 Type **Due** and press ↵

13 Type **=[Amount]-[Paid]** in the *Control Source* row and press ↵

The *Control Source* property specifies which data should appear in a control. Access field names are enclosed in brackets in expressions. Next, indicate to Access that this value is to be displayed as currency:

14 Click the  button of the *Format* box, use the scroll bar to locate *Currency*, and then click it

TABLE DB2-4 ■ TEXT BOX PROPERTIES DIALOG BOX TABS

Tab	Description
Format	This group of properties controls the way the object appears on the screen or page, determining font name, font size, format, number of decimals, and so forth.
Data	This group of properties controls the data that the object displays, where the data comes from or how it is calculated, its input mask, and so forth.
Event	These properties are used by advanced users to develop more sophisticated applications that will not be covered in this manual.
Other	The most important of these properties is *Name,* which allows an object to be named so that it can be referred to in subsequent calculations or procedures
All	Displays all properties in order of importance so that the user can scroll up and down the list adjusting any of the properties.

Your dialog box entries should match those in Figure DB2-29b.

 **15** Click the *Close* button of the Properties dialog box

16 If needed, resize, space, or align the object

Next, place a label object with the caption "Due" in the Page Header band, as in Figure DB2-29c:

 **17** Click the *Label* button on the toolbox

18 Point to the top left corner of where the label should appear in the Page Header band (starting at the 8 1/4-inch mark), and then drag to create a rectangular box between the 8 1/4-inch and 9-inch marks, type Due , and then press ↵

 **19** Click the *Align Right* toolbar button

20 Click outside the label object to deselect it

21 If needed, move and resize the label object to match Figure DB2-29c

 **22** Click *File, Save*   Ctrl + S

Now, look at the results of your modifications:

 **23** Click *View, Print Preview*

If your display is in Portrait orientation (8 1/2" wide × 11" high), it will not display all of the reports columns on the same page. As such, to switch to Landscape (11" × 8 1/2") orientation,

24 If necessary, to switch to landscape orientation, click *File*, *Page Setup*, *Page* tab, the *Landscape* option and then *OK*

ADDING SUMMARY STATISTICS.   Summary statistics are created by placing calculated controls in Footer bands. In the following exercise, you place calculated controls in the City Footer and Report Footer bands that will sum the *Due* column.

 **1** Click *View*, *Design View*

2 Use the scroll bars to reposition the report's display so that the *Amount*, *Paid*, and *Due* columns are visible, similar to Figure DB2-28

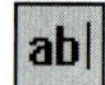 **3** Use the *Text Box* button on the toolbox to place an object in the City Footer band beneath the appropriate column starting at the 8 1/4-inch mark, as in Figure DB2-30a

4 Delete the label object (*Text#*) to the left of the *Unbound* field object

5 Click the *Unbound* control object to select it, resize its width to be between the 8 1/4-inch and 9-inch marks, resize its height and alignment to agree to the *Paid* object on its left

 **6** Click *View*, *Properties*

7 Click the *All* tab, and press `Ctrl` + `Home` to move to the *Name* box

8 Type `Sum of Due By City` and press `↵`

9 Type `=Sum([Amount])-Sum([Paid])` and press `↵`

10 Click the `▼` button of the *Format* box, and then click *Currency*

11 Move (scroll) down to the *Font Italic* box, click the `▼` button, and then click *Yes*

12 Keep the Properties dialog box open, and move it as needed by dragging its title bar as you perform the next steps

13 Repeat Steps 3 through 5 to place an *Unbound* control object in the Report Footer band

Note that the Properties dialog box was open but changed focus to the new unbound control.

14 Click the title bar of the Properties dialog box

15 Move to the *Name* box, type `Sum of Due`, and press `↵`

16 Repeat Steps 9 and 10

17 Move (scroll) down to the *Border Style* box, click the `▼` button, and then click *Solid* to place a solid-line border around the object

FIGURE DB2-30 ■ **ADDING SUMMARY STATISTICS**

(a) An unbound object is placed in the City Footer band for a summary statistics formula.

(b) Summary statistic formulas have been placed in the City Footer and Report Footer bands.

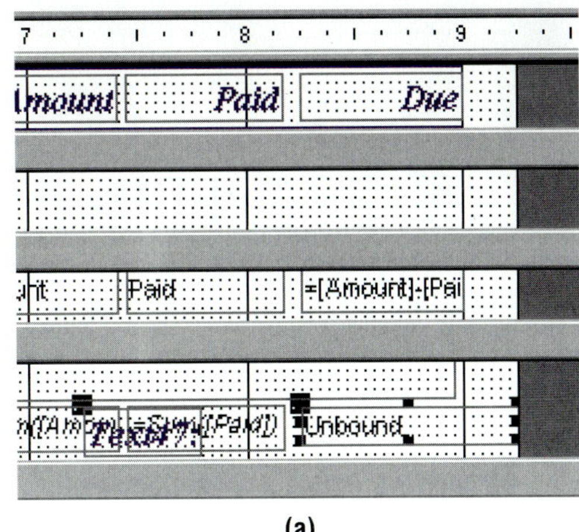

(a)

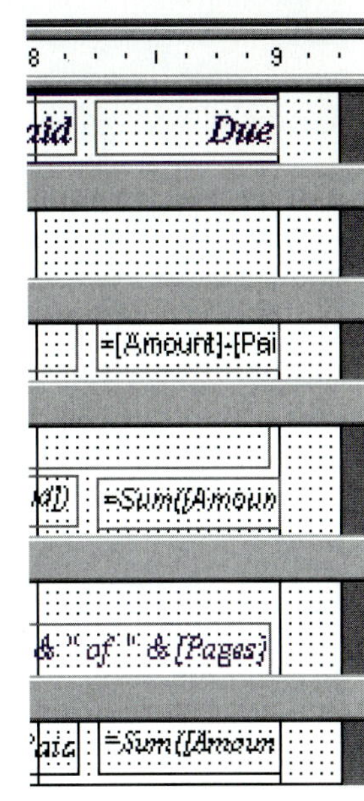

(b)

18 Move (scroll) down to the *Font Name* box, click the [▼] button, use the scroll bar to locate *Times New Roman,* and then click it

19 Move to the *Font Size* box, click the [▼] button, and then click *10*

20 Move to the *Font Italic* box, click the [▼] button, and then click *Yes*

21 Click the *Close* button of the Properties dialog box

22 Click outside the selected object to deselect it

23 Resave the report

The two new summary statistic objects that you added to the City Footer and Report Footer bands should now appear, similar to those shown in Figure DB2-30b.

 **24** Click *View, Print Preview*

25 If needed, to switch to Landscape orientation, click *File, Page Setup, Page* tab, the *Landscape* option and then *OK*

Your complete modified Report should resemble Figure DB2-31.

26 Click any desired portion of the report to resize its view

FIGURE DB2-31 ■ THE MODIFIED REPORT

Customer Report - By City

City	ID#	Last	First	Street	State	Zip	Amount	Paid	Due
Chicago									
	111	Hill	Karen	1500 Michigan Avenue	IL	60605-0000	$458.73	$458.73	$0.00
	178	West	Rita	75 N. Wacker Drive	IL	60601-0000	$193.45	$0.00	$193.45
	087	Williams	DeVito	One Dryden Way	IL	60601-0000	$285.42	$50.00	$485.42
Summary for City = Chicago (3 detail records)									
Sum							$1,530.45	$253.73	$60.33?
New York City									
	449	Kee	Charles	500 Fifth Avenue	NY	10009-0000	$155.45	$0.00	$155.45
	754	Martin	Edward	50 Commerce Street	NY	10001-0000	$285.55	$19.55	$250.00
Summary for City = New York City (2 detail records)									
Sum							$1,748.00	$1,30.55	$253.45
San José									
	101	Burston	Jerome	100 N. 1st Street	CA	95120-0000	$250.45	$100.00	$150.45
Summary for City = San Jose (1 detail record)									
Sum							$250.45	$100.00	$150.45
Santa Fe									
	870	Parke	Charles	25 Cerrillos Road	NM	37051-0000	$450.75	$200.00	$250.75
Summary for City = Santa Fe (1 detail record)									
Sum							$450.75	$200.00	$250.75
Grand Total							$3,357.85	$1,387.33	$1,970.52

Thursday, January 07, 1999   Page 1 of 1

27 Turn on your printer, click *File*, *Print*, *OK*   `Ctrl` + `P`

28 Examine the printed report and if needed, switch back to Design view and use the techniques discussed earlier to resize, move, or align the objects, and then resave the report

29 Close all windows in Access's work area

30 If you wish to stop, exit Access

☑ CHECKPOINT

Answer these questions and perform these tasks.

1. What are bands and controls?
2. Define the terms *label object* and *field object*. How do you create a calculated control?
3. Open the DCHECK database file, and then open the Detail Students Report.
4. Modify the Detail Students Report by changing the properties of Test3's label in the Page Header band to Average and its field objects, the properties of the Test 3 field object to: Name-Average, and Control Source—enter the formula =([Test1]+ [Test2])/2, and then delete the =Avg([Test3]) in the Class Footer band. (*Hint:* You must delete the object with the average of Test3 in the footer band before you

change the name of the detail object from Test3 to Average. If you don't, you will get an error message when you preview the results before deleting the object from the footer.) Right-align the results.

5. Resave and print the report.

SUMMARY

- Modifying a table's structure involves working in the Table Design view to alter or delete existing fields or add new fields.
- A table's data can be edited (changed, deleted, or added to) in Form view or Datasheet view. Pressing the *F2* key switches the selection highlight to/from an insertion point.
- When editing in Datasheet view, you can freeze specific columns on the left so that they remain constant no matter where the insertion point or selection highlight is positioned.
- Records can be deleted from a table in Database or Form view by first selecting the record and then clicking *Edit, Delete Record.*
- Records can be sorted in ascending or descending order. These sort commands can be applied to a Datasheet, Form, Query, and Report view.
- Filtering is a process of hiding the display of all records except those that meet specified criteria.
- A query is a question asked of a database. You can create queries to display selected fields and records that match criteria you specify.
- In a query, the AND connector searches for records that meet two or more conditions, whereas the OR connector locates records that meet either condition.
- Summary statistics are commands that provide sum, average, count, and other summary calculations on a query or report.
- The Update Query feature can be used to modify data in all records and replace data in selected records.
- The AutoReports feature can quickly create a Columnar or Tabular Report from a table or query.
- A report's structure is divided into bands (sections). Each band may contain controls (graphical objects) that can be edited. A label control is used for descriptive titles. A text box can contain a label (title) object or a field (data) object.
- Controls are grouped into three categories: bound (displays field data), unbound (displays a label, line, or rectangle), or calculated (displays the result of a mathematical operation).
- Controls may be resized, moved, renamed, or deleted. Most changes are made through a control's Properties dialog box.
- The Undo command can be used to reverse your last action.

KEY TERMS

Shown in parentheses are the page numbers on which key terms are boldfaced.

AND connector (DB84)	Control (DB104)	Freeze Columns (DB68)
Average command (DB89)	Count command (DB89)	Group (DB99)
Band (DB103)	Criterion (DB77)	Label control (DB104)
Bound control (DB104)	Dynaset (DB76)	Landscape (DB99)
Calculated control (DB104)	Field object (DB104)	Literal string (DB90)
Columnar Report (DB94)	Filtering (DB73)	Mask (DB63)

Natural order (DB72)	Selection handles (DB104)	Text box (DB104)
OR connector (DB84)	Sorting (DB72)	Unbound control (DB104)
Portrait (DB99)	Sum command (DB87)	Undo (DB110)
Query (DB75)	Summary statistics (DB87)	
Report (DB94)	Tabular Report (DB94)	

UNIT REVIEW

TRUE/FALSE

____ 1. Table structures are designed and modified using the same view.

____ 2. A mask is a pattern that you can set for all data entered into a desired field

____ 3. The *Sort Ascending* button places text fields in alphabetical order.

____ 4. Queries can be used only to display selected fields.

____ 5. A report's data source can be a table or query.

____ 6. Filtering sorts records in ascending or descending order.

____ 7. The Detail band forms the body of the report.

____ 8. Grouped reports show only totals—no detail.

____ 9. The Report Wizard can be used to create only simple reports.

___ 10. Objects in a report or form are called controls.

MULTIPLE CHOICE

___ 11. Which feature would you use to create a pattern for entering social security numbers (000-00-0000)?
   a. Insert Mask Wizard
   b. Insert Social Security format
   c. Format Wizard
   d. Field Control

___ 12. Which command allows records in a table to be shown in another sequence?
   a. Locate
   b. Place field
   c. Arrange
   d. Sort

___ 13. In which band of a report's Design view can you set titles that will appear on each page?
   a. Page header
   b. Report header
   c. Table band
   d. Group band

___ 14. How can the width of a control in a report be changed?
   a. Select the *Width* button
   b. Select *Width* on the Edit menu
   c. Drag and drop a selection handle on the object's border
   d. Delete and reinsert the object at the new width

___ 15. A query feature that can be used to modify existing records is
   a. Simple query
   b. Search

c. Update
d. Summary statistics

___ 16. Which connector finds records that meet either of two conditions?
a. OR
b. AND
c. EITHER
d. NOR

___ 17. Sections of a report are called
a. Controls
b. Field lines
c. Field objects
d. Bands

___ 18. To resize a selected object in Report Design view,
a. Click *Edit, Resize*
b. Double-click it
c. Click *Tools, Resize*
d. Drag and drop one of its selection handles

___ 19. The contents of many records can be changed at one time using which of the following?
a. Report
b. Query
c. Form
d. Properties

___ 20. When referred to in reports, field names are placed in which of the following?
a. {Braces}
b. (Parentheses)
c. [Brackets]
d. "Quotation marks"

MATCHING

Select the term that best matches each feature indicated on the Access screen shown in Figure DB2-A.

___ 21. Created by the grouping feature.
___ 22. Area to specify a condition of a selection.
___ 23. Objects created in this band appear only at the end of a report.
___ 24. Data source of a query.
___ 25. A label control.
___ 26. Enter by dragging and dropping the field from a table list box.
___ 27. A calculated object that currently displays a summary formula.
___ 28. The selected object.
___ 29. Objects contained in this band are the main content of a report.
___ 30. Use to place a text box in a report.

ANSWERS

True/False: 1. T; 2. T; 3. T; 4. F; 5. T; 6. F; 7. T; 8. F; 9. F; 10. T
Multiple Choice: 11. a; 12. d; 13. a; 14. c; 15. c; 16. a; 17. d; 18. d; 19. b; 20. c
Matching: 21. e; 22. c; 23. j; 24. a; 25. d; 26. b; 27. g and k; 28. h; 29. f; 30. m

FIGURE DB2-A ■ **MATCHING FIGURE**

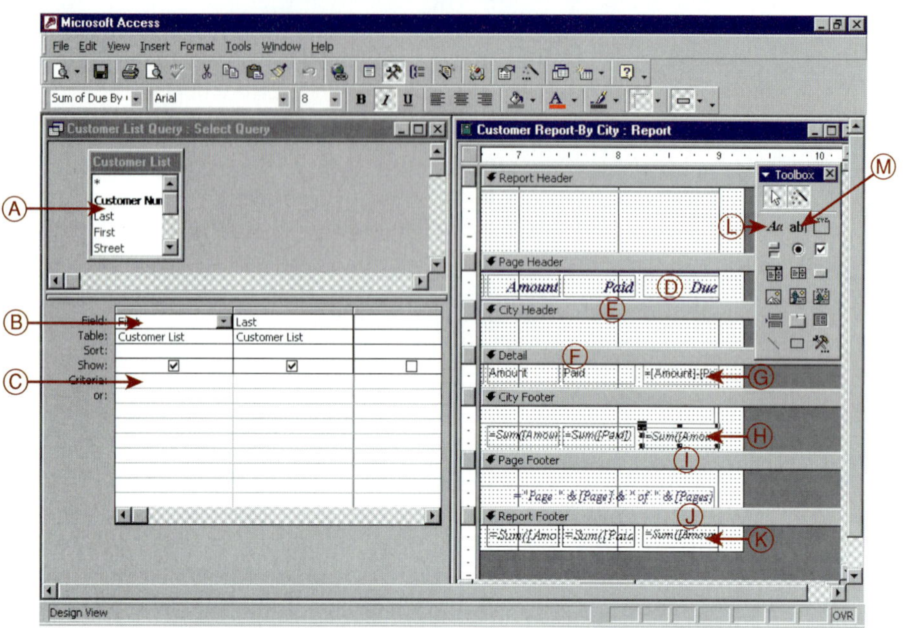

EXERCISES

I. OPERATIONS

On a separate piece of paper, provide the Access actions required to perform each of the following operations. Assume that your data will be stored in the root directory of Drive A. Further assume that your data disk contains a table named ADDRESS, which has the following structure:

Field	Name	Data Type	Field Size
1	Last	Text	15
2	First	Text	12
3	Phone	Text	12
4	Street	Text	25
5	City	Text	20
6	State	Text	2
7	Zip	Text	5
8	Size	Number	

1. Display the ADDRESS table in Datasheet view.

2. Modify the table structure in ADDRESS to include a text field named "Title," four characters in width, in Field 3 of the structure. Place the Title field between the *First* and *Phone* fields.

3. Change the *City* field to hold a maximum of 25 characters.

4. Copy the ADDRESS table and name it ADDRESS2. Next, sort and then resave the table in city order.

5. Create a query that displays only the *Last, First,* and *Phone* fields from the AD-DRESS2 table.

6. Use the query feature to change all *City* fields with "New York" to "Manhattan" in the ADDRESS2 table.

7. Create a report named "Phone List 1." Have the report display the *Last, First,* and *Phone* fields.

8. Modify the report to add a column (between the *First* and *Phone* fields) to show the Size field *without totals.*

9. Print preview the report.

10. Create and print a report using the same layout for those records whose phone number begins with a 718 area code. (*Hint:* First create a query and then use it to create the report.)

11. Copy the report to "Phone List 2." Add a column for "State" at the right side. Print the report.

12. In Datasheet view, locate the record whose last name is Smith and then change the first name to Mary.

13. Add 10 to all values in the *Size* field.

14. Change the *Size* data values that are less than 500 to a new value of 0.

15. Place an asterisk after the *City* field values for those people whose state is New York.

16. Calculate the sum and average of the *Size* field for the entire database file and then count the number of records whose size equals 0.

II. COMMANDS

Describe what is accomplished in Access by the actions described below. Assume that each exercise part is independent of any previous parts.

1. Clicking the *Design View* button

2. In the Table Design view, when a row is selected (highlighted), pressing *Insert*

3. Clicking an object

4. Clicking *Query, Run*

5. Dragging and dropping a field from the upper to the lower pane of a Query Design window

6. Clicking the *Sort Ascending* button

7. Dragging a selection handle

8. Dragging an object in Report Design view

9. Clicking the *Print Preview* button on the Report Design view window

10. Using an AND connector in a query

11. In a Query Design view, typing **Sum** in the *Total* row of the *Pay* column and **Santa Fe** in the *Criteria* row of the *City* column

12. Typing **New York** in the *Criteria* row and in the *State* column of a Query screen

13. Typing **[Pay]*1.05** in the *Update* column of a Query screen

14. Placing a formula in the Control Source box of an object's Properties box

15. Using the Copy and Paste commands on an object in the *Reports* tab of the Database window

III. APPLICATIONS

Perform the following operations using your computer. You need a hard-disk drive or network with Windows and Access on it. You also need your data disk for retrieval and for storing the results of these exercises. Save the database file after completing any design changes. *Note:* Of the three applications, each one relates to school, home, and business, respectively.

APPLICATION 1: CREATING A DEGREE PROGRESS REPORT

1. Launch Access, and open the DEGREE database you created for Unit 1.

2. Create a query that lists the Course, Number, and Grade fields for only CIS courses. Save the Query as CIS COURSES.

3. Create a query to limit the searches to courses with an "I" grade. Use the query to list these courses, showing all fields. Save the query as COURSES WITH "I" GRADE.

4. Back up the degree plan table by copying it as Degree Plan Copy before performing the following delete query. Open the COURSES WITH "I" GRADE query and then delete them. Print the DEGREE PLAN table. (*Hint:* After running the query, select all records in the query, and then click *Edit, Delete Record.*)

5. Create a report named PROGRESS from the DEGREE PLAN table. Include all four fields as columns sorted by course order. Be sure the report has two title lines and that your name is included on the second line.

6. Save and print the report.

7. Create another report named PROGRESS2 with all four fields as columns sorted by grade order. Save and print the report.

8. Using Table Design view, modify the structure of the DEGREE PLAN table so that a new fifth field is added: Name = Points, Data Type = Number. This field will hold the grade points that you are given for each grade.

9. Using Datasheet view, enter the following data for the Points column: 4 for each A Grade, 3 for each B Grade, 2 for each C Grade, 1 for each D Grade, and 0 for each F Grade.

10. Modify the PROGRESS2 report to include the Points field and reorder the columns as follows: *Grade, Points, Course, Number.* Delete the *Completed* column from the report.

11. Save and then print PROGRESS2.

12. Sort the DEGREE PLAN table into descending points order. Resave the table and print it.

13. Exit Access.

APPLICATION 2: UPDATING THE VIDEO LIST TABLE

1. Launch Access, and open the VIDEO database file.

2. Add these four records to the VIDEO LIST table:

VIDEO#	Volume	Start	Subject	Type	Time
1013	107	0000	Word	I	75
1014	107	3000	The Marx Brothers	O	125
1015	101	1125	The Boys and the Seals	C	45
1016	101	2050	Dear as Salt	C	50

3. Using Table Design view, modify the table structure to add a field named Rating directly after the Subject field. Data Type = Text, and Field Size = 4.

Use the VIDEO LIST table as the source table for Steps 4 through 16.

4. Create a report named VIDEO TYPE REPORT from the VIDEO LIST table displaying all fields sorted in ascending order by type and subject. Print the report.

5. Use a query to display the *Volume, Start,* and *Subject* fields for those tapes whose type is C. Save the query as TYPE C QUERY, and then print it.

6. Create a query for tapes whose time exceeds 60 minutes. List only the *Volume, Subject,* and *Time* fields. Save the query as SUBJECTS EXCEEDING 60 MINUTES, and then print it.

7. Using the query feature, search for records whose subject is "Microsoft Made Easy," and then delete them. Do not save the query. (*Hint:* After running the query, select all records in the query, and then click *Edit, Delete Record.*)

8. Using the query feature, search for records whose time is 132 minutes, and then delete them. Do not save the query.

9. Create a Tabular report in landscape orientation called VIDEO REPORT 1. Include your name on the second line of the title that appears at the top of each page. (*Hint:* To increase the width of a band, drag the lower band's title row as needed. Also, for this exercise, use two Label controls, one for each title.) Create columns that display all the fields in the structure but no totals. Print the report in volume and start (counter) order.

10. Create a report named TYPE C REPORT to include only those records whose type is C, and then print it. Create a second report named TIME > 60 REPORT for records whose time exceeds 60. Save and print it. (*Hint:* Use the queries created in Steps 5 and 6 as the source for these reports.)

11. Use the query feature to replace all Rating data with "****" in the VIDEO LIST table. Then replace the Rating data field with "**" only for those records with a volume of 106. Do not save the queries. Print the updated VIDEO LIST table.

12. Modify VIDEO REPORT 1 to remove the Rating column and include another column with a heading of "Hours" that displays the result of dividing the *Time* field by 60. Format this as fixed with two decimals. Print the report.

13. Add summary statistics to VIDEO REPORT 1 for the *Time* and *Hours* columns to show totals in the Report Footer. Format numbers as Fixed with 2 decimals. Resave and then print the report. (*Hint:* To get the total for hours you must enter **=SUM([TIME])/60.**)

14. Create a report in landscape orientation called VIDEO REPORT 2 with data grouped in the *Volume* field (create a group header and footer) and sorted by *Subject*. Add a summary statistic for *Time*. Print the results.

15. Locate each of the following records and make the indicated edit to its data:

For: VOLUME	Change: START
101 (0650)	Start to 0750
104 (0000)	Time to 65
107 (3000)	Subject to Word and Time to 85

Sort the table in *Subject* order, and then print and save it.

16. Use an update query to update the VIDEO LIST table by reducing the *Time* field by 5; then use another update query to set all *Rating* fields to a blank (" "). (*Note:* This procedure can also be done in the same query.) Print the updated VIDEO LIST table.

17. Exit Access.

APPLICATION 3: ADJUSTED PAYROLL

1. Launch Access, and open the PAYROLL database file.

2. Using the Table Design view, modify the PAYROLL LIST table structure by first adding a field named BONUS directly after the *DEPT* field. Data Type = CURRENCY. Next, increase the *SS#* Field Size to 11 and then create a social security mask (000-00-000).

3. Copy the structure and data of the PAYROLL LIST table to a new table called PAY RATE, and sort the new table by rate in ascending order. Resave and then print the contents of the table.

4. Using the PAYROLL LIST table, create a query named HUMAN RESOURCES > 40 with the names and rates of employees whose department is Human Resources and who worked more than 40 hours. Save and print the query.

5. Create a query named NON-SALES EMPLOYEES that will display all records except those in Sales. List employees' names and departments using this query. Save and print the query.

6. Create a query named ACCOUNTING-RATE >= 7.50 to limit searches to employees in Accounting whose rate is $7.50 or more. Use the query to list those employees, showing all fields. Save and print the query.

7. Find and delete Caryn Green's record.

8. Use the Update Query feature to update the database by reducing the *HOURS* field by 5, and then use another update query to set all BONUS fields to 0. Do not save the query.

9. Use the filter feature to display only records for the Sales department. Select the records displayed and then delete them.

10. Using the PAYROLL LIST table, create a tabular report in landscape orientation named PAY REPORT. Include your name on the second line of the title that appears at the top of each page. Create columns that display each of the seven fields in the structure. Group data in the *DEPT* field, and sort in alphabetical order by last and then first name. Add summary statistics for the *Bonus, Hours,* and *Rate.* Print the report.

11. Use the PAYRATE table to create a query named SALES DEPT to include all fields for only those employees in the Sales department. Use this query to create an Autoreport called PAY REPORT-SALES DEPT. Create another query named SALES DEPT >40 HOURS to include those employees whose hours exceed 40 and then an Autoreport from this query named PAY REPORT-SALES DEPT >40 HOURS. Print each report.

12. Using the PAYROLL LIST, replace all BONUS data with $20. Then replace the BONUS data with $40 only for those employees in ACCOUNTING. Do not save the query. (*Hint:* Use the Update Query feature.)

13. Modify the PAY REPORT report to include an eighth column with a heading of "Gross" that displays the result of multiplying the *HOURS* field by the *RATE* field. Format as *Currency.* Resave and then print the report.

14. Locate each of the following records in the PAYROLL LIST table and make the indicated edit to its data. List the table in alphabetical order by the *LAST* field, resave and then print it.

For:	Change:
Black	DEPT to ACCOUNTING
Brown	HOURS to 41

15. Exit Access.

MASTERY CASES

The following mastery cases allow you to demonstrate how much you have learned about this software. Each case further extends a problem from Unit 1 and can be solved using the skills you have learned in this unit. If you do not have the table referred to in a case, create it by following the instructions in Unit 1. Although minimum acceptable outcomes are specified, you are encouraged to design your response (files, data, lists) in ways that display your personal mastery of the software. You may have to restructure your table (add or adjust fields) to adequately respond to a case.

These mastery cases allow you to display your ability to:

- Modify a table's structure.
- Locate and edit data, and rearrange and filter records.
- Create queries.
- Use queries to update records.
- Create reports.
- Modify reports.

CASE 1: UPDATING YOUR DEGREE PROGRAM TABLE

You want to amend the table structure and data you created in the graduation progress database file in Unit 1. First, add additional fields and data (such as quality points earned) that will let you calculate your grade point average using the accepted procedure of your school. Enter appropriate data for all courses. Next, use the query feature to list courses with your highest grade. Create a report that lists all courses in the order in which they were taken, grouped by semester, with semester and cumulative grade point average calculations.

CASE 2: UPDATING YOUR MUSIC COLLECTION TABLE

You have received an offer to program music shows for a local disc jockey and need to amend the database file you created for the music catalog in Unit 1. Modify the table's structure to contain a field for the play length (to the nearest minute) of each selection. After updating each record to reflect the new data, create and print a separate query for each type that lists all fields for each type of media. Create a report from the table, grouped by type of music, sorted by album title, both by group and in total. Place your letterhead in the top of the report, save it, and print it.

CASE 3: UPDATING THE CLIENTELE TABLE

Your cosmetologist would like to be able to offer her clients a free manicure on their birthdays. Amend the database file's table structure you created for her in Unit 1 to accomplish this goal. After you update the records, create and print a query that displays each client's name and birthday in ascending order by birthday. Next, create and print a report grouped by service, listing clients alphabetically by last name, with their home phone numbers and birthdays.

DATABASE MANAGEMENT, LABELS, RELATIONAL DATABASES, CHARTS, AND SHARING DATA

OUTLINE

OBJECTIVES

After completing the mastery sets in this unit, you will be able to do any or all of the following (based on your selection of mastery sets):

1. Duplicate, rename, delete, and create a reference to a database file.
2. Create a reference to an object with a database file.
3. Copy and append records.
4. Explain the techniques for creating, modifying, and printing labels.
5. Describe the procedures for creating, modifying, and using customized forms.
6. Explain the steps necessary to use multiple tables in a relational database—creating main and subforms by using one-to-many and many-to-one relationships.
7. Prepare line, bar, and pie charts from table records.
8. Link data from other applications.
9. Prepare Access files for and download files from the World Wide Web.
10. Export files to and import files from other applications.

OVERVIEW

This unit presents additional topics of interest to the Access user. Each topic is presented as a separate mastery set that can be studied independently of the others. Study the mastery sets that are most useful to you. Mastery Set 3-1 presents database management techniques—various methods to duplicate, rename, delete, and refer to files and objects, and copy and add records. Mastery Set 3-2 explains the creation and use of printed labels—a procedure much like those for reports and forms. Techniques for customizing data entry forms are presented in Mastery Set 3-3. Mastery Set 3-4 looks at true relational database techniques, where separate tables are linked together on the same Form to act as one large database. Mastery Set 3-5 introduces charts in Access. Mastery Set 3-6 shows how to prepare data to be transferred between Access and other programs.

A file named MAGICAL is required for use with some of the mastery sets in this unit. This file reduces the amount of basic keystroking you must do. If desired, data are supplied as needed so that you can create it yourself.

The MAGICAL file may be found in the Access subdirectory on Harcourt Brace's Web site, on a separate disk, or on your LAN (check with your instructor). The MAGICAL file is identified at the beginning of each exercise that requires it.

MASTERY SET 3-1: DATABASE MANAGEMENT

Database management is an important aspect of controlling data. As seen earlier, an Access database file may contain a variety of objects, including tables, queries, forms, reports, pages, macros, and modules. Both database files and the objects within them can be duplicated, renamed, deleted, or referenced. *Duplicating* a file or object is the process of making a copy. *Renaming* involves changing a file or object's name. *Deleting* removes the file from a disk or the object from a file. *Referencing* involves creating a **shortcut icon** to access the file or object from a different location. Techniques to accomplish these tasks are discussed first, followed by a look at copying and appending data to records.

MANAGING FILES

You can open, copy, move, delete, rename, or reference Access database files by using the Open or Export dialog box, My Computer, or Windows Explorer. Only the Access Open or Export dialog box technique is discussed here. Refer to your Windows online help to use the other two methods.

To prepare for this section:

1 **Start Windows, and launch Access**

2 **Click the *Cancel* button of the Microsoft Access dialog box** **Esc**

DUPLICATING FILES. Most duplicating in Windows requires that you first select the desired item(s) to be copied, then invoke the Copy command, move to the desired destination, and then invoke the Paste command. When you use the Copy command, the selection is copied to the Windows Clipboard, a temporary holding area for the selection until it is pasted. The Paste command copies the selection from the Clipboard to a desired destination.

Try this to duplicate the CUSTOMER.mdb database file on the same diskette (or folder):

1 Click *File, Open* for its dialog box   **Ctrl** + **O**

2 If necessary, insert your diskette

3 Use the *Look in* drop-down box to switch to your 3 1/2-inch floppy drive (or the drive or folder appropriate for your system)

4 Click the *CUSTOMER.mdb* database file icon (not the icon's title)

> Note: If you accidentally click the file icon's title instead of its icon, the "CUSTOMER.mbd" will appear highlighted (selected) in a black rectangular border. This allows you to edit the title. To select the file icon instead, press ↵ and then click the file icon to the left of the title.

(a) Right-clicking a file icon in the Open dialog box opens this shortcut menu.
(b) Right-clicking an object icon in the Export window opens this shortcut menu.

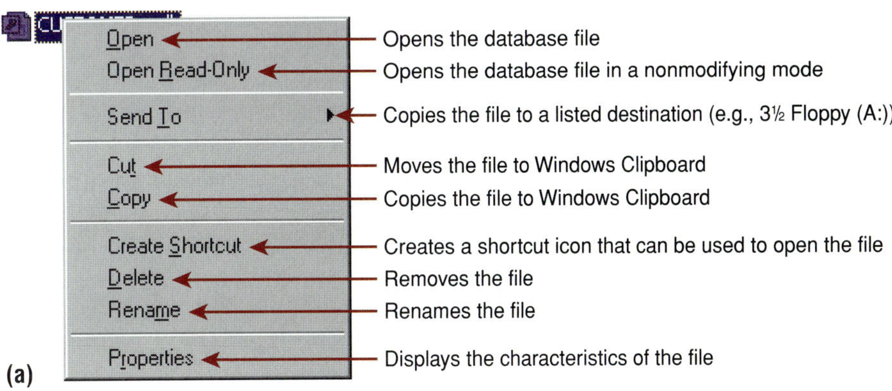

(a)

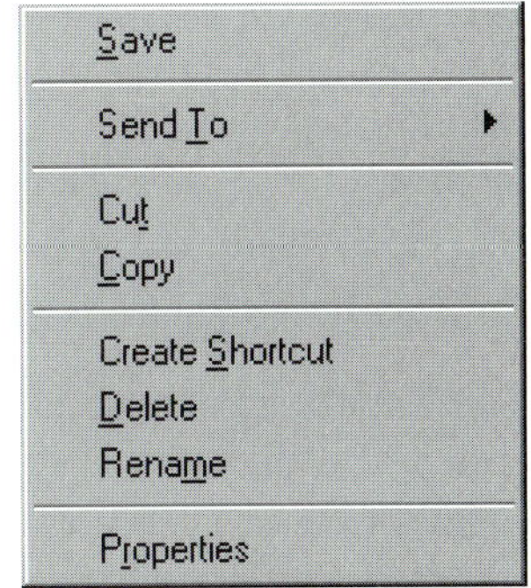

(b)

5 Right-click the *CUSTOMER.mdb* database file icon to display its shortcut menu, as in Figure DB3-1

This shortcut menu contains a variety of commands, as described in Figure DB3-1.

6 Click *Copy* to copy the file to the Windows Clipboard

> **Tip:** To move the file, click *Cut* instead of *Copy* in Step 6.

7 Right-click the blank (white) area of the Files list box, and click *Paste*

> **Tip:** Instead of Step 7, you can also click the blank (white) area of the Files list box, and then press *Ctrl + V* to paste the file into the same folder.

A new file icon, automatically named *Copy of CUSTOMER,* now appears in the dialog box. (When you copy a file to the same folder, it cannot have the same filename.) So that you do not have unnecessary files occupying space on your disk, do the next step to delete the Copy of CUSTOMER.mdb file before proceeding to the next copy exercise.

8 Click the *Copy of CUSTOMER.mdb* file icon (not the icon's title), press **Delete** , and then click *Yes*

> **Tip:** You can also right-click the file icon and then click *Delete* to remove it.

The same technique works for copying a file to a *different* folder (which also may be in a different drive). First, you will use the Open dialog box to create a new folder named "Backup." This and the Export dialog box have a toolbar button for creating a *New Folder* in the current folder. After that, you will move the CUSTOMER.mdb database file there.

 **9** Click the *New Folder* toolbar button in the dialog box

You can use the *New Folder* toolbar button any time to create a new folder, not only for a copy-and-paste operation.

10 Type **Backup** and press ↵

A new folder named "Backup" appears in the Look in box of the dialog box. Now, to go back to the previous folder:

 **11** Click the *Up One Level* toolbar button

Now, try this exercise to copy the CUSTOMER.mdb file from the root (or "main") folder of your diskette or folder to the Backup folder:

 **12** Right-click the *CUSTOMER.mdb* icon to display its shortcut menu

This shortcut menu, as shown in Figure DB3-1, appears again.

13 Click *Copy* to copy the file to the Clipboard

14 Double-click the *Backup* folder icon to open it

> **Tip:** You can also use the *Save in* or *Look in* drop-down box to switch a desired destination folder.

15 Right-click an empty area of the list box and then click *Paste*   `Ctrl + V`
to paste the Customer file in the Backup folder

Note that this time, the file copies with the name *CUSTOMER.mdb,* not *Copy of CUSTOMER.* This is because you copied the file to a different folder, thus the same name can be used.

16 Click the *Cancel* button to exit the dialog box

RENAMING A FILE.   The process of renaming a file is similar to renaming any icon in Windows. You use its shortcut menu or click it. Try this to rename the *Copy of CUSTOMER* file to *CUSTOMER - Copy 1:*

 **1** Click *File, Open*   `Ctrl + O`

 **2** Examine the Look in box to see if it is displaying the *Backup* folder; if not, change it to your *3 1/2-inch floppy drive* (or the drive or folder appropriate for your system) and then double-click the *Backup* folder

3 Click the *CUSTOMER.mdb* file icon

4 Right-click the *CUSTOMER.mdb* icon, and then click *Rename*   `F2`

> **Tip:** Instead of Step 4, you can click the text *CUSTOMER.mdb* to the right of its icon.

5 Type `CUSTOMER - COPY.mdb` and press ↵

Your file has now been renamed. Leave the dialog box open for the next exercise.

CREATING A SHORTCUT.   *Shortcut icons* enable you to open a file or program from a different location. Shortcut icons are not the file or programs themselves, but rather a reference that can be used to open the file or program to which they refer. The Create Shortcut command first creates a shortcut icon in the same folder, and you then use the Cut and Paste commands to move the icon to a different location. Try this to create a shortcut icon for the CUSTOMER file and move it to the Backup folder:

 **1** Click the *Up One Level* toolbar button to move back one folder

2 Right-click the *CUSTOMER.mdb* icon, and then click *Create Shortcut*

An icon named *Shortcut to CUSTOMER.mdb* appears. Now, move it to the *Backup* folder:

3 Right-click the *Shortcut to CUSTOMER.mdb* icon, and then click *Cut*   `Ctrl + X`

4 Double-click the *Backup* folder icon to switch to it

5 Right-click an empty area of the list box and then
click *Paste* to paste the shortcut there   **Ctrl** + **V**

You can now use this shortcut icon to open the CUSTOMER file in the root folder of
your disk from the *Backup* folder.

6 Click the *Shortcut to CUSTOMER.mdb* icon, and then click the *Open* button

The CUSTOMER database window reappears in Access's work area. Now, to delete
the *Backup* folder (and its contents) before proceeding to the next mastery set:

7 Close the CUSTOMER database window

8 Click *File, Open*   **Ctrl** + **O**

9 Click the *Up One Level* icon to move back to the root folder

10 Right-click the *Backup* folder icon, and then click *Delete*   **Delete**

11 Click *Yes*

The *Backup* folder and its contents have now been removed.

12 Click the dialog box's *Cancel* button   **Esc**

13 If you desire, exit Access

MANAGING OBJECTS

The techniques you practiced in the "Duplicating, Renaming, and Deleting Reports"
section of Mastery Set 2-5 also apply to any object in the Database window. Table
DB3-1 reviews these and other related commands.

COPYING A TABLE.   Unlike copying other objects in the Database window, Access offers three options for copying a table: *Structure Only, Structure and Data,* and
Append Data to Existing Table. Earlier, you used the *Structure and Data* option, which
copied the entire table and its contents. The *Structure Only* option copies only the field
structure of a desired table to a new table. The *Append Data to Existing Table* option
copies only a table's data to another table. The following exercise copies only the structure of the *Customer List* table to a new table called *Names.*

1 Launch Access

2 Open the CUSTOMER.mdb database file

3 Click the *Tables* object type button and then the *Customer List* icon

TABLE DB3-1 ■ WORKING WITH OBJECTS WITHIN THE DATABASE WINDOW

Task	Actions
Select an Object	Click the object
Select Additional Objects	*Ctrl*-click each additional object
Select a Block (contiguous group)	Click the first object and then *Shift*-click the last object
Copy a Selection	Click *Edit, Copy,* move to destination, click *Edit, Paste,* type new object name if pasting within the same tab, click *OK*
Move a Selection	Click *Edit, Cut,* move to destination, click *Edit, Paste*
Rename an Object	Right-click the object, click *Rename*
Delete a Selection	Press *Delete* or click *Edit, Delete*

4 Click *Edit, Copy*   `Ctrl` + `C`

5 Click *Edit, Paste*   `Ctrl` + `V`

6 Type **Names** in the *Table Name* box

7 Click the *Structure Only* option

The Paste Table As dialog box should resemble Figure DB3-2. This indicates to Access that you want to copy the original table's structure but not its data (records).

8 Click *OK*

FIGURE DB3-2 ■ COPYING A TABLE

The Paste Table As dialog box appears when you invoke the Copy and Paste commands on a table.

DB

To verify that the copy was properly made:

9 Click the *Names* icon and then the *Design* button

You should see the same list of field names, types, and properties that you typed into Customer List. Now, switch to Datasheet view to see that there are no records in this table:

10 Click *View, Datasheet*

To close the table:

11 Click the Names table's *Close* button

Because Access does not allow you to copy or append records to a table that contains records with the same primary key (customer number in this table), you need to turn off this feature for the rest of the exercises in this section. Note that in normal practice, records with different data would be copied or appended to a table. For the following demonstrations, however, you use only the Customer List and Customer Backup tables, which include the same records.

To turn off the primary key feature:

12 Click the *Customer List* icon and then the *Design* button

13 Click the *Primary Key* toolbar icon to turn off the feature (the *Primary Key* icon should disappear to the right of the *Customer Number* field name)

14 Click the *Close* button of the Customer List table and then *Yes*

15 Repeat Steps 12 through 15 for the Customer List Backup table

To append data to an existing table, the receiving table must have the same field structure. Try this to append the records from the Customer List (source) table to the Customer Backup (destination) table:

16 Click the *Customer List* icon

17 Click *Edit, Copy*   `Ctrl` + `C`

18 Click *Edit, Paste*   `Ctrl` + `V`

19 Type Customer List Backup in the *Table Name* box

20 Click the *Append Data to Existing Table* option and then *OK*

21 Open the Customer List Backup table in Datasheet view

22 If the Clipboard window appears, click its *Close* button

Note that as in Figure DB3-3, there are duplicates of each record. This is because the data in the Customer List and Customer List Backup tables are the same.

FIGURE DB3-3 ■ **THE APPENDED CUSTOMER LIST BACKUP TABLE**

Customer Number	Last	First	Street	City	State	Zip
449	Kee	Charles	500 Fifth Avenue	New York	NY	10003-
176	West	Rita	75 N. Wacker Drive	Chicago	IL	60601-
449	Kee	Charles	500 Fifth Avenue	New York City	NY	10003-00
176	West	Rita	75 N. Wacker Drive	Chicago	IL	60601-00
101	Burstein	Jerome	100 N. 1st Street	San Jose	CA	95120-
101	Burstein	Jerome	100 N. 1st Street	San Jose	CA	95120-00
754	Martin	Edward	50 Carmine Street	New York	NY	10001-
754	Martin	Edward	50 Carmine Street	New York City	NY	10001-00
670	Parker	Charles	25 Cerillos Road	Santa Fe	NM	87051-
670	Parker	Charles	25 Cerillos Road	Santa Fe	NM	87051-00
111	Hill	Karen	1500 Michigan Avenue	Chicago	IL	60605-
111	Hill	Karen	1500 Michigan Avenue	Chicago	IL	60605-00
067	Williams	DeVilla	One Dryden Way	Chicago	IL	60601-
067	Williams	DeVilla	One Dryden Way	Chicago	IL	60601-00

Record: 1 of 14

23 Close the Customer List Backup window

Tip: Use the Find Duplicates Query Wizard to locate duplicate records. At that point, if desired, you can delete them.

CREATING A SHORTCUT TO AN OBJECT.   To create a shortcut to an object on the desktop (default) or in a desired folder, simply right-click the object, and then click *Create Shortcut.* Try this to create a shortcut for the Customer List table:

1 If needed, open the CUSTOMER.mdb database file

2 Click the *Tables* object type button

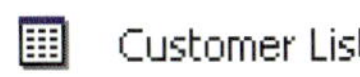

3 Click the *Customer List* table icon

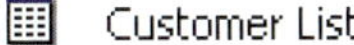

4 Right-click the *Customer List* table icon for its shortcut menu

Note that the options available here are similar to those in the Open dialog box's shortcut menu (in Figure DB3-1a).

5 Click *Create Shortcut*

The Create Shortcut dialog box appears, as in Figure DB3-4. This dialog box lets you specify the desired location of the shortcut. If you like, you can use the *Browse* button to change the location of the shortcut. For now, though, accept the default—the desktop:

This dialog box is used to set the location of a database window's shortcut icon.

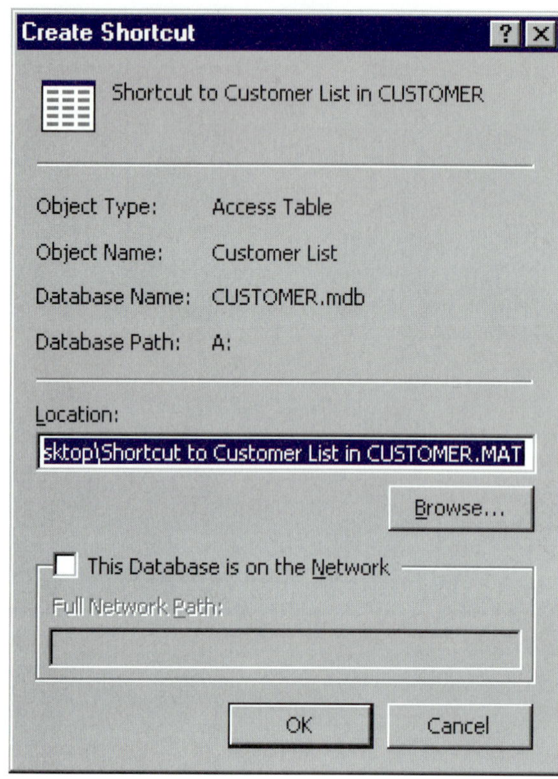

6 Click *OK*

7 Exit Access

8 Exit or minimize any other open program so that your desktop is visible

A *Shortcut to Customer List in CUSTOMER* icon should now appear on your desktop. Now, to use the shortcut icon to open the Customer List table.

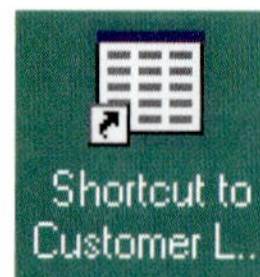

9 Double-click the *Shortcut to Customer List in CUSTOMER* icon

The Customer List table opens with Access.

10 Close the Customer List: Table window

Once a shortcut icon has been made, you can copy or move it using the Copy or Cut and Paste commands. This will enable you to open a desired table and Access from any desired folder.

COPYING AND APPENDING RECORDS

The *Append Data to Existing Table* option of the Paste Table As dialog box is perfect for copying all records from one table to another. However, you may at times want to copy only certain records, either into a new table or into another existing table. The next exercises explore techniques to accomplish this. Remember, in normal practice, records with different data would be copied or appended to a table. For this demonstration, however, you will use only the Customer List table.

COPYING SELECTED RECORDS TO A NEW TABLE.   If you want to create a separate table of customers in New York City (or another city) who have not yet paid in full, use the Make Table Query command. For example, to create a new table called Past Due - New York City that contains only customers in New York City:

1   If needed, open the CUSTOMER: Database window

2   Click the *Queries* object type button

3   Double-click the *Create query In Design View* icon

4   Click *Customer List,* the *Add* button, and then the *Close* button

5   Click (on the menu bar) *Query,* (if needed, the *More* button), *Make-Table Query* for its dialog box

6   Type   `Past Due - New York City`   in the Table Name dialog box

Your dialog box should resemble Figure DB3-5a. The Make-Table Query creates a new table within the same database file (default) or in another database file. For now, place the table in the current database (default) as follows:

7   Click *OK*

8   Click the Maximize button of the Query window

9   Click *Customer Number* in the *Customer List* box (upper pane), and press   `Shift` + `End`   to select all fields

10   Drag and drop the selection to the *Field* row in the lower pane

11   Click the *Criteria* cell of the *City* column

12   Type   `New York City`   and press   `↵`

Your Query window should resemble Figure DB3-5b. Note that Access automatically places quotation marks around "New York City."

Tip: Any condition or combination of conditions can be used in the Query screen to limit the records that will be copied to the new table. In addition, you can also restrict the fields that will be displayed. To do so, click the *Show* check box of the field you do not want to show to remove its check.

FIGURE DB3-5 ■ COPYING SELECTED RECORDS TO A NEW TABLE

(a) The Make Table-Queries dialog box can be used to create a new table for selected records.
(b) Setting the criteria for the new table-query.
(c) The new table with only the records whose *City* equals "New York City."

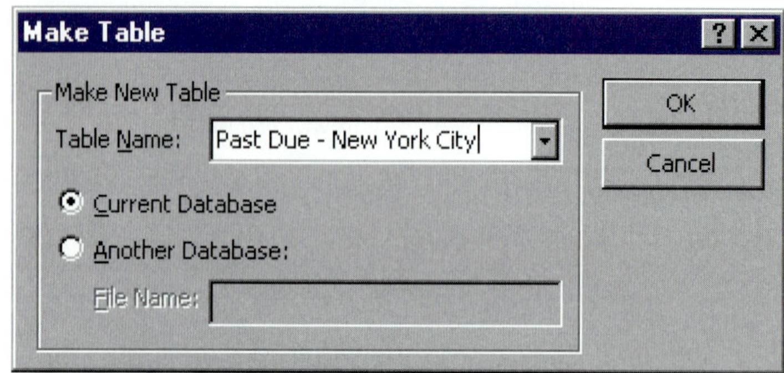

(a)

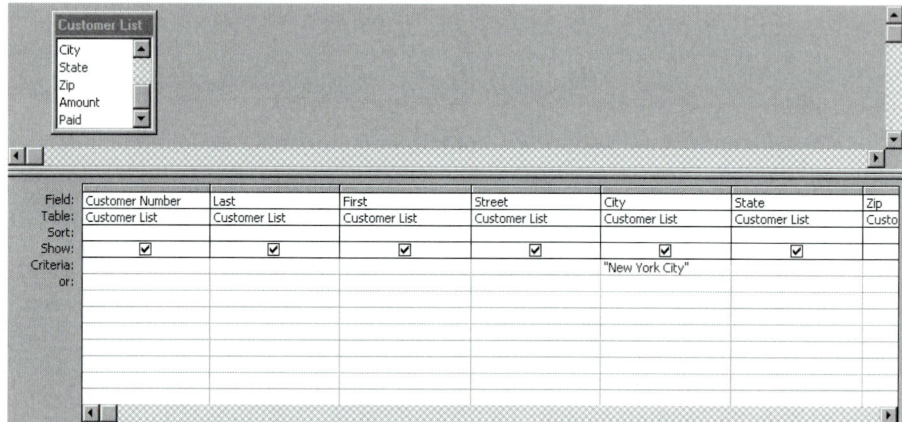

(b)

Customer Num	Last	First	Street	City	State	Zip	Amount
449	Kee	Charles	500 Fifth Avenue	New York City	NY	100030000	$755.45
754	Martin	Edward	50 Carmine Stre	New York City	NY	100010000	$360.55

(c)

13 Click *Query, Run*

In this example, only two records meet the stated condition. When Access asks you to confirm the addition of these two records to the table:

14 Click *Yes*

15 Close the Query window without saving the query

Next, verify that Access performed the query according to your expectations:

16 Click the *Tables* object type button

17 Click the *Past Due - New York City* icon and then the *Open* button

Your Past Due - New York City table should resemble Figure DB3-5c. It should contain only the Kee and Martin records (the only two New York City customers). Note that some Table properties such as the zip code mask or the Customer Number column width did not transfer. At this point, if desired, you can go into Design view to add the mask. When you are finished:

18 **Close the Past Due - New York City: Table window**

ADDING RECORDS.   You can also copy records from one table to another using the Copy and Paste commands. The only restriction is that the fields in both the source table and the destination table must be of the same type and in the same order. The Paste procedure will place data from the first column of the source in the first column of the target, and so on. This next exercise demonstrates how to append records of Illinois residents from the Customer List table to the Copy of Customer List table.

1 **Copy the structure and data of the *Customer List* table to a table named Copy of Customer List**

2 **Open the Customer List table**

3 **Move to the *State* column (any cell will do)**

4 **Click *Records*, *Sort*, and then *Sort Ascending***

Now the records are grouped by state.

5 **Click the row selector of the first record whose state = "IL" (111, Hill)**

6 **Shift -click the row selector of the last record whose state = "IL" (176, West)**

Your selection should match the one in Figure DB3-6a.

7 **Click *Edit*, *Copy***   Ctrl + C

The records have been copied to the Clipboard. Next, display the destination table:

8 **Click *Window*, *1 CUSTOMER: Database* to switch to the database window**   Ctrl + F6

9 **Open the Copy Of Customer List table**

10 **Click *Edit* (if necessary, click the *More* button first), and then *Paste Append***

Access asks you to confirm the insertion of three records.

11 **Click *Yes***

Your modified Copy of Customer List table now contains ten records, as shown in Figure DB3-6b.

12 **Press any arrow key to deselect**

FIGURE DB3-6 ■ ADDING RECORDS

(a) Clicking Hill's row indicator and then *Shift*-clicking West's row indicator selects the records as a block.

(b) The selected records have been added to the Copy of Customer List table.

Customer Number	Last	First	Street	City	State	Zip	
101	Burstein	Jerome	100 N. 1st Street	San Jose	CA	95120-0000	
111	Hill	Karen	1500 Michigan Avenue	Chicago	IL	60605-0000	
067	Williams	DeVilla	One Dryden Way	Chicago	IL	60601-0000	
176	West	Rita	75 N. Wacker Drive	Chicago	IL	60601-0000	
670	Parker	Charles	25 Cerillos Road	Santa Fe	NM	87051-0000	
754	Martin	Edward	50 Carmine Street	New York City	NY	10001-0000	
449	Kee	Charles	500 Fifth Avenue	New York City	NY	10003-0000	

(a)

Customer Number	Last	First	Street	City	State	Zip	
449	Kee	Charles	500 Fifth Avenue	New York City	NY	10003-0000	
176	West	Rita	75 N. Wacker Drive	Chicago	IL	60601-0000	
101	Burstein	Jerome	100 N. 1st Street	San Jose	CA	95120-0000	
754	Martin	Edward	50 Carmine Street	New York City	NY	10001-0000	
670	Parker	Charles	25 Cerillos Road	Santa Fe	NM	87051-0000	
111	Hill	Karen	1500 Michigan Avenue	Chicago	IL	60605-0000	
067	Williams	DeVilla	One Dryden Way	Chicago	IL	60601-0000	
111	Hill	Karen	1500 Michigan Avenue	Chicago	IL	60605-0000	
067	Williams	DeVilla	One Dryden Way	Chicago	IL	60601-0000	
176	West	Rita	75 N. Wacker Drive	Chicago	IL	60601-0000	

(b)

13 Close all windows in Access's work area

14 Exit Access

☑ CHECKPOINT

Perform these tasks.

1. Create a copy of the DCHECK file.
2. Rename the copy DCHECK UNIT3.
3. Open the DCHECK UNIT3 database file and copy only the table structure of the Students table to a table named TEST1.
4. Copy only the social security, names, and TEST1 scores from the Student table to the TEST1 table. (*Hint:* Select the appropriate columns by clicking the first column indicator and then *Shift*-clicking the last desired column indicator.)
5. Create a shortcut to access the TEST1 table from your desktop.

MASTERY SET 3-2: CREATING LABELS

Printing labels is an important activity for organizations that do a lot of mailing or shipping, and many Access users maintain mailing lists of employees, customers, subscribers, and so on. Labels are also useful for inventory items in a warehouse or for file folders in a records department. To make the process of printing labels easier, Access includes a Label Wizard feature that walks you through the process of designing (in effect) a report that prints data on adhesive-backed, precut labels (of course, you would need to load your printer with the appropriate label sheets). Once printed in the appropriate positions, labels can then be affixed to letters, packages, or files as needed.

USING THE LABEL WIZARD

The following exercise demonstrates how to create and print data from the Customer List table on mailing labels. You need not have labels to perform this exercise—you can print the data on regular paper as well.

1 **Launch Access**

2 **Open the CUSTOMER.mdb database file**

3 **Click the *Reports* object type button and then the *New* button**

4 **Click *Label Wizard* and then the ▼ button of the *Choose the table or query where the object's data comes from:* drop-down list; click *Customer List* and then *OK***

> **Tip: You can use a query instead of a table in Step 4.**

You should now see the first in a series of Label Wizard dialog boxes that will walk you through the process of designing labels. For this exercise, you will use the label size *Avery number 5096,* as in Figure DB3-7a:

5 **Click the *Filter by manufacturer:* ▼ button and then click *Avery***

6 **If needed, click the *English Unit of Measure* option**

7 **If needed, use the vertical scroll bar of the *What label size would you like?* box to locate the label type 5096**

8 **Click *5096* to select it, as in Figure DB3-7a**

9 **Click the *Next >* button**

This dialog box (as shown in Figure DB3-7b) lets you set the font and color of the text that will appear on the label. To accept the default:

10 **Click the *Next >* button**

This dialog box is where you select the fields that will appear on the label. To make the selections as in Figure DB3-7c:

11 **If needed, click the *Prototype Label* box to place the insertion point there**

12 **Type ID# and press Spacebar**

> **Note: To insert fields into the Prototype label, you can either click the desired field in the *Available Fields* list box and then click the > button or just double-click the desired field.**

FIGURE DB3-7 ■ **CREATING LABELS**

(a) This dialog box is used to select the type of label size.
(b) This dialog box is used to set the font and text color.
(c) This dialog box is used to set a prototype label.

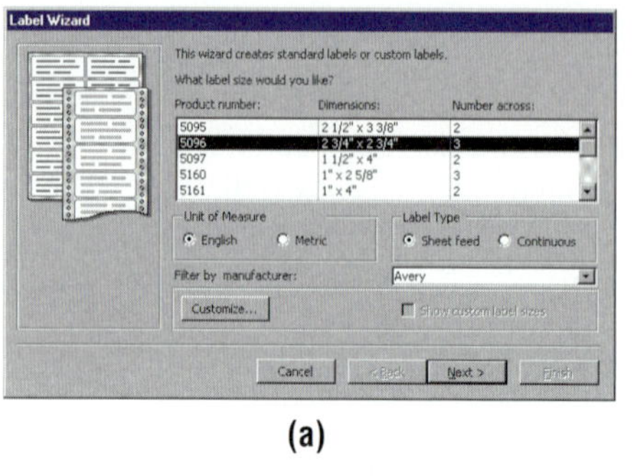

(a)

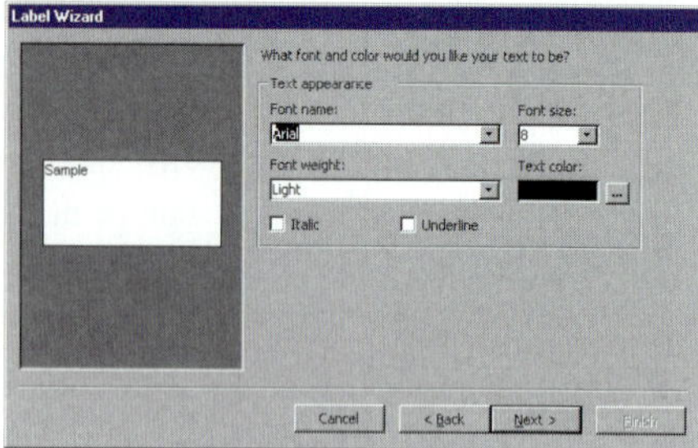

(b)

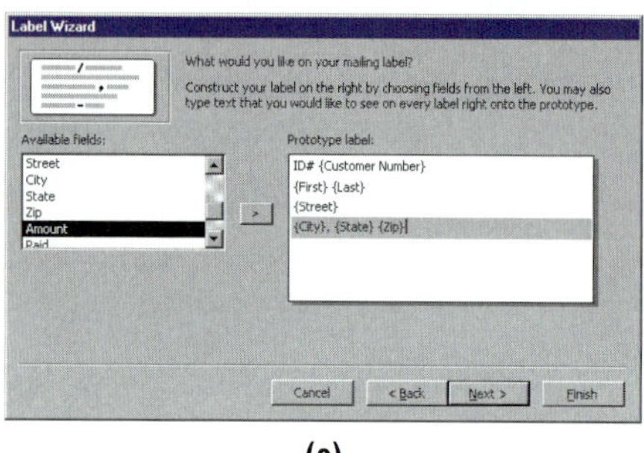

(c)

13 Click *Customer Number* in the *Available Fields* list box and then the > button

14 Press ↵ to move to the next line

15 Double-click *First* in the *Available Fields* list box

16 Press **Spacebar** to place a space between the first and last names

17 Double-click *Last* in the *Available Fields* list box

18 Press ↵ to move to the next line

19 Double-click *Street* and then press ↵

20 Double-click *City*, type **,** (comma), and press **Spacebar**

21 Double-click *State* and press **Spacebar**

22 Double-click *Zip*

The selections and entries that you just made should match those in Figure DB3-7c.

23 Click the *Next* > button

This dialog box is for defining sorting order. To sort the labels by Zip:

24 Click *Zip* and then the > button

25 Click the *Next* > button

26 Type Customer Labels by Zip Code in the *What name would you like for your report?* box

At this point, you can either request to see the labels as they would appear printed (default) or look at them in Design view. To print preview them:

27 Click the *Finish* button

Your screen should resemble Figure DB3-8.

28 Use the scroll bars to view other parts of the screen

29 Turn on your printer, and then if desired, insert Avery 5096 label paper (regular paper will do fine for this exercise)

 **30** Click *File*, *Print*, OK   **Ctrl** + **P** , **↵**

 **31** Click *File*, *Close*, or click the Close ("X") button of the Print Preview window   **Ctrl** + **F4**

MODIFYING LABELS

Labels are like any other report. They can be copied and modified for other uses.

1 Click the *Customer Labels By Zip Code* icon and then the *Design* button

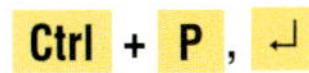

FIGURE DB3-8 ■ **THE COMPLETED LABELS**

The completed labels in Report view.

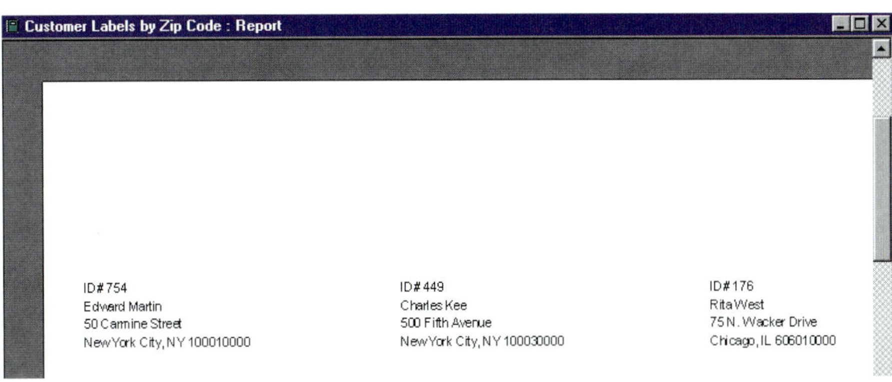

2 If necessary, click the Maximize button and drag and drop the Toolbox and Report properties windows as needed

Access displays the label report in Design view. As you can see, it consists of a variety of objects that you could delete, edit, or move. The objects all have properties that can be altered. Of course, whether the Customer Labels report prints names in one, two, three, or more columns depends on the label product that you told Access you intended to use. Access stores the measurements of the most popular labels and uses them to design a report that will print properly on the label product you designate. If you purchase labels that are not on the list that comes with Access, you can enter the measurements of the new product.

3 Close the Design View window

4 Exit Access

☑ CHECKPOINT

Perform these tasks.
1. Using Design View, change the field name "Name" in the Students table of the DCHECK UNIT 3 database file, to "Student Name."
2. Using the Students table of the DCHECK UNIT 3 database file, create a two-line label report named "Student Test1 Labels" that will print the name on line 1 and the words "Test 1:" on line 2 followed by the Test1 grade. Select a label product that prints one label across. Sort the Labels by Student Name. Print Student Test1 labels.
3. Create a query for those students whose Test1 grade exceeded 80.
4. Create labels for the Student Name and Test1 grade from the query.
5. Using the Label Wizard, create another label report with all the fields. Name the report Student Labels, and use a label product that prints three labels across. Instruct Access to sort the labels by Test2 score. Print all labels.

MASTERY SET 3-3: CREATING CUSTOMIZED FORMS

Using the *AutoForm* feature, Access can quickly create a form for any table or query. As you have seen, a form presents a single record at a time. Although the AutoForms feature may be sufficient for most uses, you may want to design a screen that better suits your needs (or the needs of other users). You might want to rearrange the order of fields for easier input or use prompts that more clearly describe the data to be entered rather than the actual field names themselves. You may also want to title the form or add or remove fields.

USING THE FORM WIZARD

The Form Wizard is a great tool to help you begin creating a customized form. It guides you through selecting fields, layout, and style for your form. To create the form in Figure DB3-9 using the Form Wizard:

1 Launch Access, and open the CUSTOMER.mdb database file

Forms

2 Click the *Forms* object type button

3 Double-click the *Create form by wizard* icon

4 In the Form Wizard, click the ▼ button of the *Tables/Queries* drop-down box, and then *Table: Customer List*

This dialog box is used to select the fields that you want to include in your form. You'll select all fields except the *Customer Number* field to place on the form.

5 Click *Last* in the *Available Fields* list box, and then click the > button

6 Repeat Step 5 to select the *First, Street, City, State, Zip, Amount,* and *Paid* fields

> **Tip:** Remember, you can also double-click the desired fields in the *Available Fields* list box instead of clicking them and then clicking the > button.

7 Click the *Next* > button

This dialog box lets you select the layout of your form. Layout options include *Columnar* (default), *Tabular, Datasheet,* and *Justified.* Clicking an option displays a sample of its layout on the left side of the dialog box. Create a justified form by following these steps:

8 Click the *Justified* option and then the *Next* > button

In this dialog box, you define the Form's style. To view a sample of each form style, simply click the desired style. For this exercise, choose the following:

9 Click *Standard* for style and then the *Next* > button

10 Type `Customer Data Form` in the *What title do you want for your form?* box

At this point, you can elect to view the form for data entry (Form view) or in Design view for editing. To display in Form view (the default):

11 Click the *Finish* button

FIGURE DB3-9 ■ CREATING A FORM WITH THE FORM WIZARD

This form was created from the Customer List table using the Form Wizard.

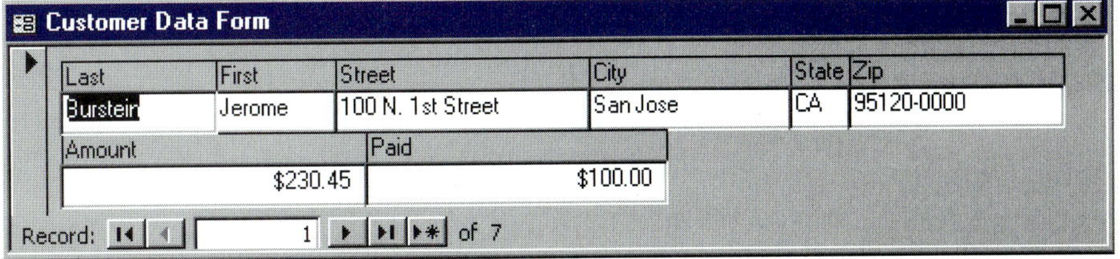

12 **If needed, switch to Form view**

Your Customer Data Form should resemble Figure DB3-9. Now you are ready to make some modifications.

13 **Close the Form window**

14 **Copy the form by clicking the *Customer Data Form* icon, *Edit*, *Copy*, *Edit*, and *Paste*, typing** Copy of Customer Data Form **, and then clicking *OK***

UNDERSTANDING FORM DESIGN VIEW

Working in Form Design View is similar to Report Design View. As you will soon see, all the same tools are available to edit your form.

1 **If needed, click the *Forms* object type button**

2 **Click the *Customer Data Form* icon**

3 **Click the *Design* button**

4 **Click the Maximize button of the Form Design window**

5 **If needed, click *View, Toolbox* to display its toolbar**

6 **Move the toolbar to the same position, as in Figure DB3-10**

As in Figure DB3-10, a form's structure is divided into bands: *Form Header, Page Header* (optional), *Detail, Page Footer* (optional), and *Form Footer.* As in a report, a band is a separate section of a form. The line at the top of each band identifies and separates the band and is referred to here as the *band's title line.* See Table DB3-2 for a description of each band's function. To select a band, click its title line to highlight it. The selected band is the one in which you are currently working. You can use keyboard commands to edit the objects in this band.

As you work in Form Design view, remember that all objects within a band are called *controls.* Controls may include labels, text boxes, list boxes, check boxes, option

FIGURE DB3-10 ■ THE FORM DESIGN VIEW WINDOW

The Customer Data form in Form Design view is ready to be modified.

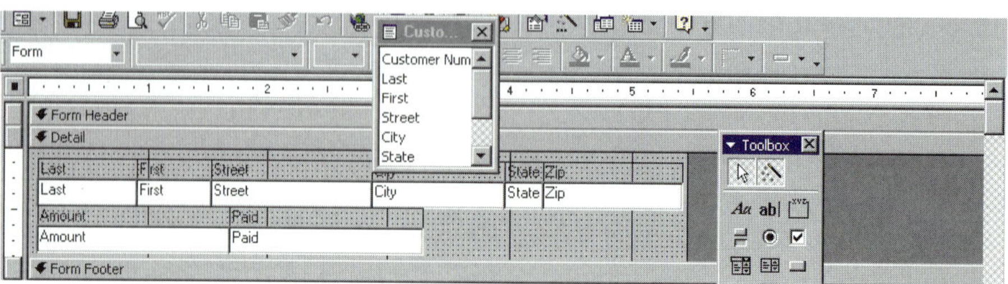

TABLE DB3-2 ■ FORM BANDS

Band Description

Form Header band and Form Footer band — The top and bottom base layers of a form. Items in these bands print only once in the entire form. However, they appear on the top or bottom of every form in Form View on the screen. Items placed in the form header appear at the start of the form; items placed in the form footer appear at the end of the form.

Page Header band and Page Footer band — Print once on each page. Items placed in the page header appear at the top of each page; items placed in the page footer appear at the bottom of each page.

Detail band — Forms the body of the form. When a form is created, this band is filled with data from the table associated with the form.

buttons, command buttons, lines, and rectangles. A *bound control* displays field data such as a *field object*. An *unbound control* displays a title or a graphic and includes a label object, line, or rectangle. A *calculated control* displays the result of a mathematical equation, such as a *calculated field object*.

FIGURE DB3-11 ■ THE COMPLETED CUSTOMER FORM

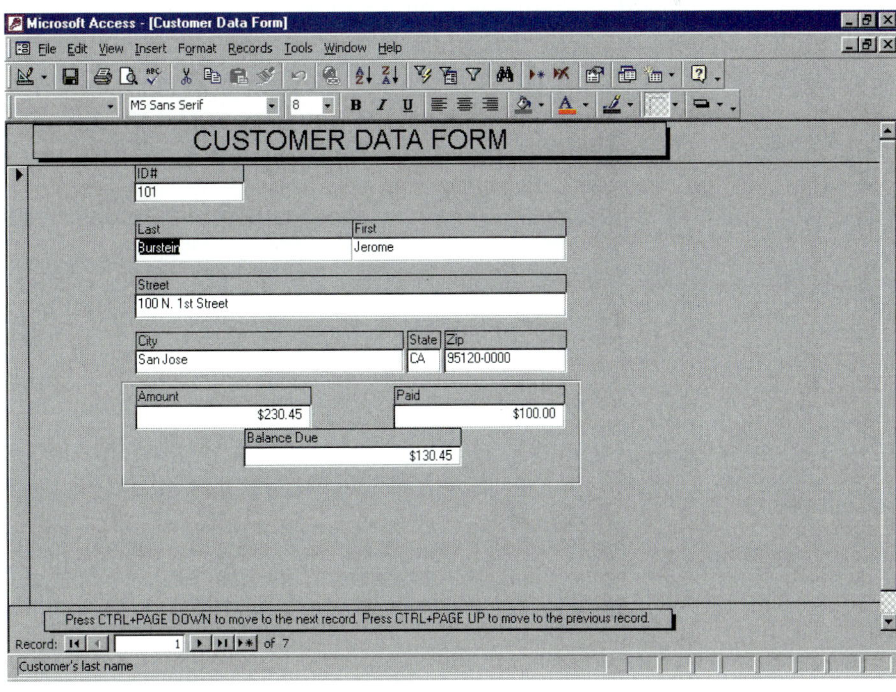

MODIFYING A FORM

Modifying a form involves making changes to its design. In the exercise to follow, you create a title in the Form Header band, place instructions in the Form Footer band, and insert new objects and rearrange and resize the existing objects in the Detail band. Your final form will resemble Figure DB3-11.

ADDING A HEADER. If you add a title to the Form Header, it will appear at the top of every form in Form view; however, it will appear at the top of only the first page in a printed copy of your form. If you add a title to the Page Header, it will appear at the top of every form in Form view and on every printed page. Remember that when you work with forms, each form displays a single record.

Before inserting a label object with the title "Customer Data Form" in the Form Header band, you need to resize the band. To do so:

1 Point to the top of the Detail band title row until the pointer changes to a resizing pointer, as shown in Figure DB3-12a

2 Drag it down until the space between the Form Header band and the Detail band matches the space in Figure DB3-12b, and drop it

3 Point to the right grid vertical wall, and drag and drop it to the 6 1/2-inch horizontal mark

4 Move the Field List window and the Toolbox so that the entire form is visible

Now, you are ready to insert a label object. Use Figure DB3-13a as a guide when performing the next two steps.

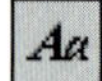

5 Click the *Label* toolbox button

6 Point the Label pointer to the top of the Form Header band, just after the 0-inch horizontal mark, and then drag and drop it at the 6-inch mark

Your label object should resemble Figure DB3-13a.

FIGURE DB3-12 ■ RESIZING A BAND

(a) Pointing to the top of a band's title changes the pointer to a resizing pointer. (b) Dragging the resizing pointer and band title row down resizes the band above it.

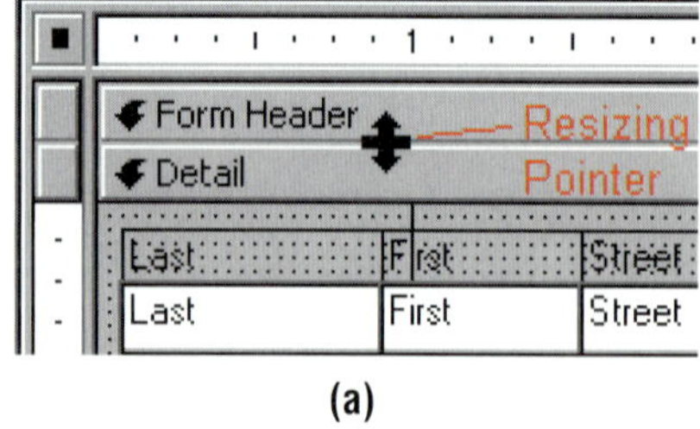

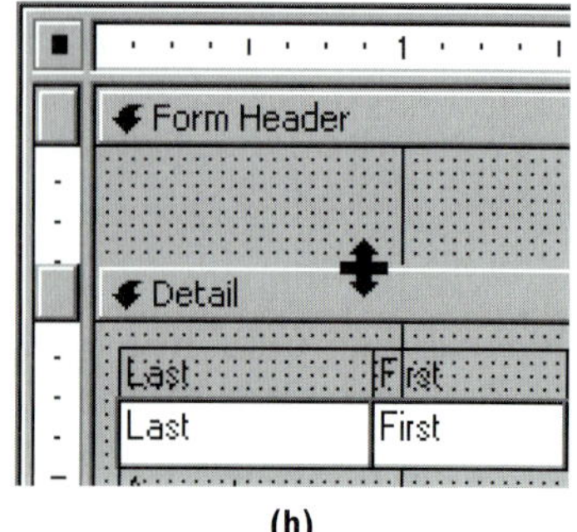

FIGURE DB3-13 ■ CREATING A LABEL OBJECT IN THE HEADER BAND

(a) Clicking the Label Tool-Box button and dragging diagonally will create a label object.
(b) The completed Form Title label object.

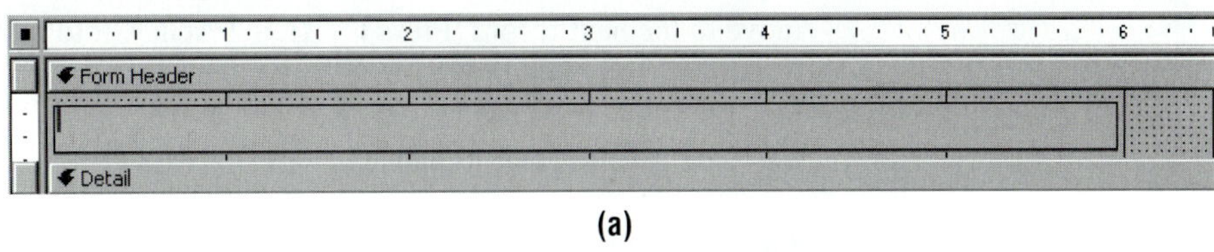

(a)

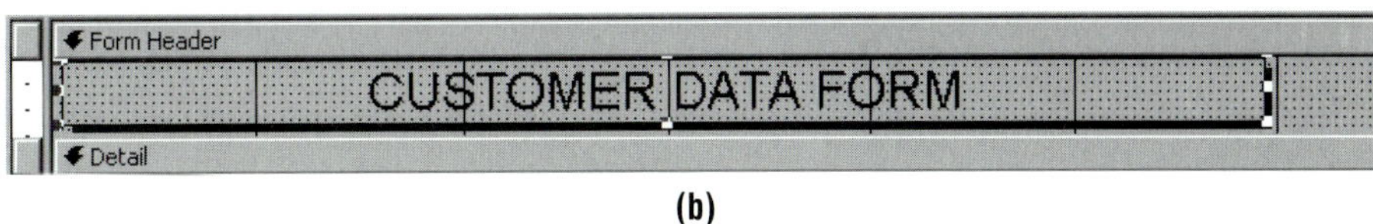

(b)

7 Type **CUSTOMER DATA FORM** and press ↵

Note that selection handles (small square boxes) appear on the borders of the label object. At this point, you can move the object (drag and drop) or resize it (drag a selection handle). You can also change the object's properties. For example, to add a shadow to the object's borders and change the font style to Arial and font size to 18:

8 Click *View, Properties,* and if needed, click the *All* tab

9 Scroll (move) down to the *Special Effect* box and then click it

10 Click the ▼ button of the *Special Effect* box, and then click *Shadowed*

Note that you can adjust a variety of other items using this tab. For now, though:

11 Scroll down to the *Font Name* box and then click it

12 Click the ▼ button of the *Font Name* box, use the scroll bar to locate *Arial,* click it and then press ↵

13 Scroll down to the *Font Size* box, type **18** , and press ↵

Tip: Instead of Steps 12 and 13, you can use the Formatting toolbar buttons.

14 Click the *Close* button of the Properties box

15 Click the *Center-align* toolbar button

16 If needed, resize and move the label object to match Figure DB3-13b

17 Click outside the label object to deselect it

18 Click *File, Save* to resave the form   **Ctrl** + **S**

Tip: To add a Page Header/Footer, click _View_, _Page Header/Footer_.

ADDING A FOOTER.   To add the instructions "Press CTRL + PAGE DOWN to move to the next record. Press CTRL + PAGE UP to move to the previous record." in the Form Footer band:

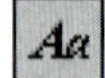

1 Click the _Label_ toolbox button

2 Point the Label pointer to the top left corner of the Form Footer band, and then drag and drop it at about the 6-inch mark, as in Figure DB3-14a

3 Type Press CTRL + PAGE DOWN to move to the next record. Press CTRL + PAGE UP to move to the previous record.

4 Press ↵

Tip: Note that the label has resizing selection handles on its border. Dragging a handle resizes the object.

Although you can use the Properties box to center and place a border around this label, it is more efficient to use toolbar buttons. Try this:

5 Click the _Center-align_ toolbar button to center the text

6 Click the ▼ button of the _Special Effect_ toolbar button's drop-down box

7 Click the _Special Effect: Shadowed_ toolbar button (bottom center button)

8 Click outside the object to deselect it

9 Resave the form

Your footer should resemble Figure DB3-14b.

FIGURE DB3-14 ■ CREATING A LABEL OBJECT IN THE FORM FOOTER BAND

(a) Clicking the _Label_ Tool-Box button and dragging diagonally will create this label object.

(b) The completed Form Footer label object.

The objects in the Detail band have been moved to these positions.

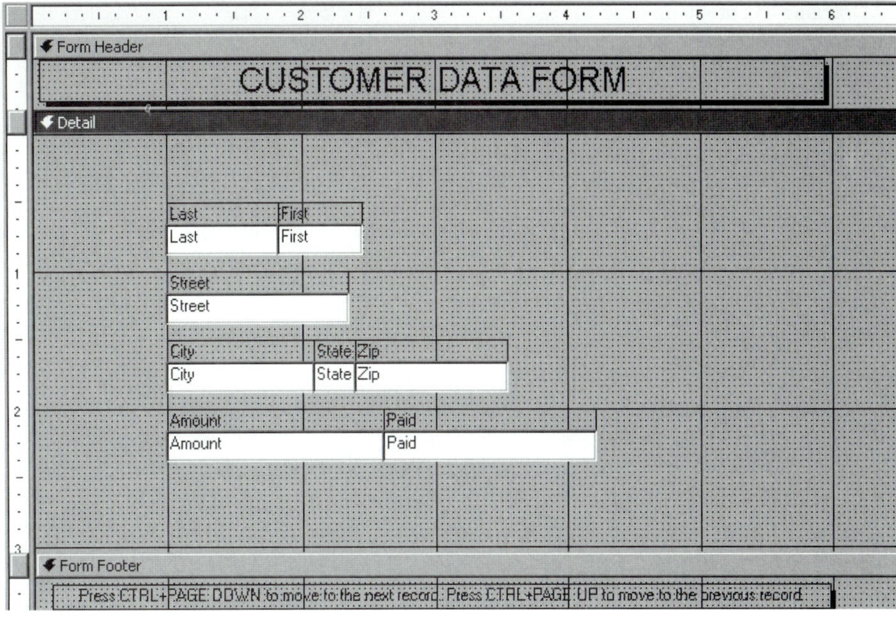

MOVING OBJECTS.   To move the objects as in Figure DB15:

1 To make room for new objects, drag and drop the Form Footer band title row so that the Detail band is 3 inches high, as in Figure DB3-16

Your screen will resemble Figure DB3-16 after you make this adjustment.

2 If necessary, move the Field List window and Toolbox away from the Form grid area, as in Figure DB3-16B

3 Click the *Amount* label object, and then **Shift** -click the *Amount* field object, the *Paid* label object, and the *Paid* field object to select them

As you perform the next steps, do not worry if the screen repositions itself as you drag and drop. Simply use the scroll bars to adjust your view. Also, if you make a mistake in positioning the objects, press *Ctrl + Z* (or click *Edit, Undo*) to undo your last actions. As you perform Step 4, note that the mouse pointer changes to a small hand when performing this drag-and-drop operation.

4 Drag and drop the selection at the 1-inch horizontal mark, just below the vertical 2-inch grid line, as in Figure DB3-17a

5 Click outside the selections to deselect them

DB

FIGURE DB3-16 ■ RESIZING THE DETAIL BAND

(a) Dragging and dropping the Form Footer band's title row will resize the Detail band.

(b) Repositioned view of the form in Design view.

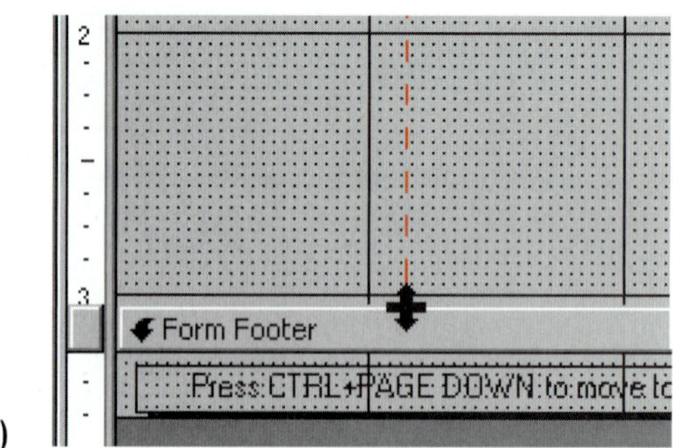

(a)

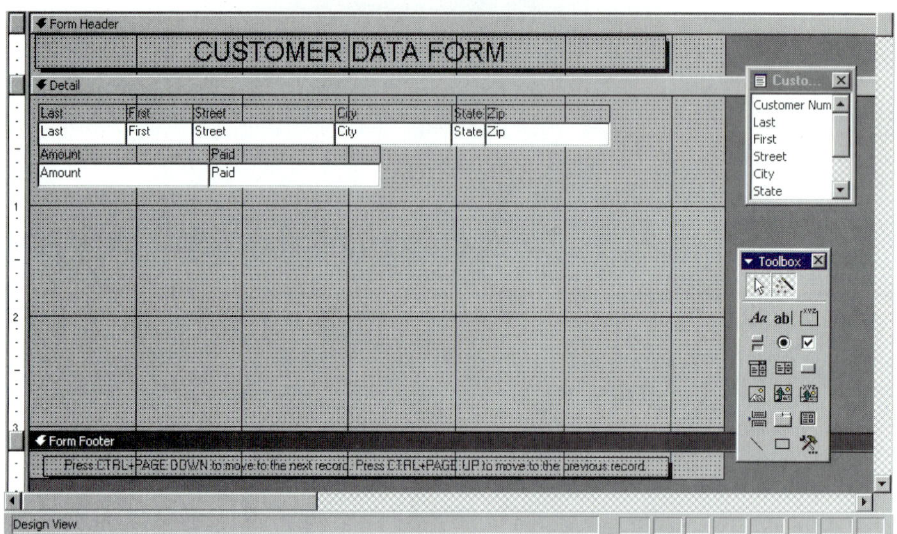

(b)

6 Select the following label and field objects: *City*, *State*, and *Zip*

(Remember, click the first object and then *Shift*-click each additional object.)

7 Drag and drop the selection at the 1-inch horizontal mark, just below the 1 1/2-inch vertical mark, as in Figure DB3-17b

8 Click outside the selection to deselect

9 Using the same techniques, move the other objects to reposition them, as in Figure DB3-15

10 Click *File, Save*   **Ctrl** + **S**

Before resizing these objects, you will practice adding objects to the form.

FIGURE DB3-17 ■ MOVING OBJECTS

(a) The selected *Amount* and *Paid* label and field objects have been moved to this position.
(b) The *City, State,* and *Zip* labels and field objects have been moved to this position.

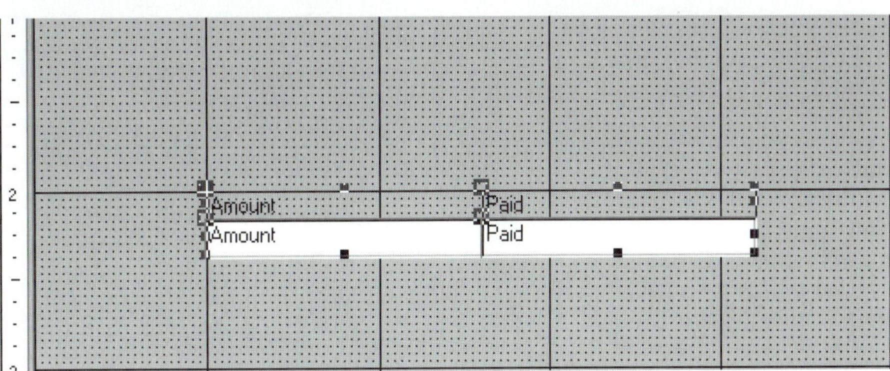

(a)

(b)

ADDING NEW FIELD OBJECTS. The procedure to add a new field object to a form is the same as adding one to a report. For example, if you now wanted to include the *Customer Number* field that you did not select when creating the form:

 **1** Click the *Text Box* toolbox button

2 Point the *Text Box* mouse pointer at the 1-inch horizontal mark, just below the 1/4-inch vertical mark in the Detail band, and click

3 Click outside the selection to deselect

4 Click the *Text#* label object to select it

5 Point to the top left handle on the selected *Text#* box until the pointer changes to a small hand pointing its index finger, as in Figure DB3-18a

6 Drag and drop the text box until it is above the *Unbound* box, as in Figure DB3-18b

 **7** Click *View, Properties,* and the *All* tab

8 Click the *Caption* box, delete its contents, and type **ID#**

FIGURE DB3-18   ■   ADDING A NEW FIELD OBJECT

(a) The *Text Box* Toolbox button is used to create a new field object.
(b) Dragging the top left corner selection handle moves the Label object without moving its related field object.

(a)

(b)

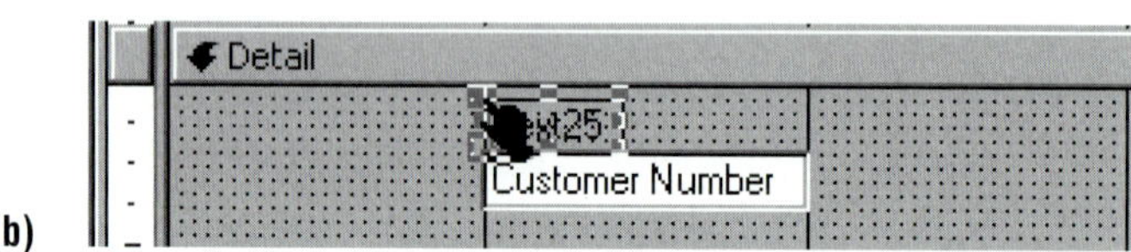

9 Scroll to the *Border Style* box, click it, click the ▼ button, and then click *Solid* to place a solid line on the border

10 Keep the Properties dialog box open, and, if needed, drag its title bar to move it

11 Click outside the *ID#* label object to deselect it

12 Click the *Unbound* field object to select it (your Properties dialog box should now display the properties for this object)

13 Click the *All* tab of the Properties dialog box

14 Scroll to the *Name* box, click it, delete its contents, type **ID#** , and press ↵

15 Click the ▼ button of the *Control Source* box, and then click *Customer Number*

16 Click the *Close* button of the Properties dialog box

17 Deselect the *ID#* field object, and resave the form

> **Tip: Another method to insert a field object is to use the Field List window (View menu).**

ADDING A CALCULATED FIELD OBJECT.   To add a field object that calculates the balance due below the *Amount* and *Paid* objects as in Figure DB3-19, do the following:

1 If necessary, use the scroll bars to reposition the screen so that the Detail band area under the *Amount* and *Paid* objects is visible

2 Click the *Text Box* toolbox button

A Calculated field object has been added to calculate the balance due.

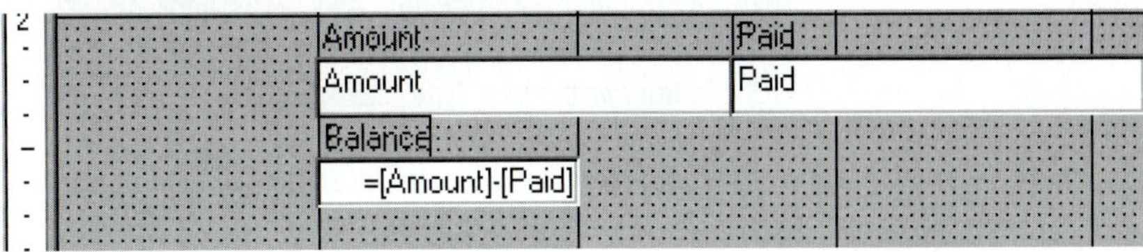

3 Point the *Text Box* mouse pointer at the 1-inch horizontal mark and the 2 1/2-inch vertical mark, and click to place the objects, as in Figure DB3-20a

4 Use the techniques in the previous exercise to move the *Text#* label object above the *Unbound* field object, as in Figure DB3-20b

5 If needed, click outside the selected objects and then click only the *Text#* object

6 Click *View*, *Properties*, and then the *All* tab

7 Scroll (move) to the *Caption* box, click it, and type Balance Due

8 Move to the *Border Style* box, click the ▼ button, and then click *Solid* to place a solid line on the border

9 Deselect the object but leave the Properties dialog box open

10 Select the *Unbound* field object

11 Click the *All* tab of the Properties dialog box

(a) The *Text Box* Toolbox button can also be used to create a Calculated field object.
(b) The repositioned label object.

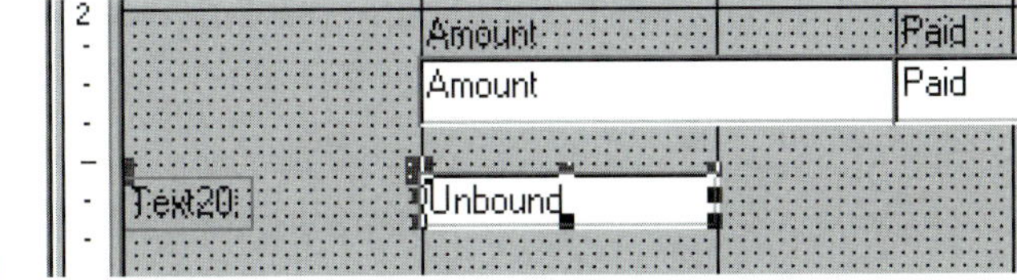

(a)

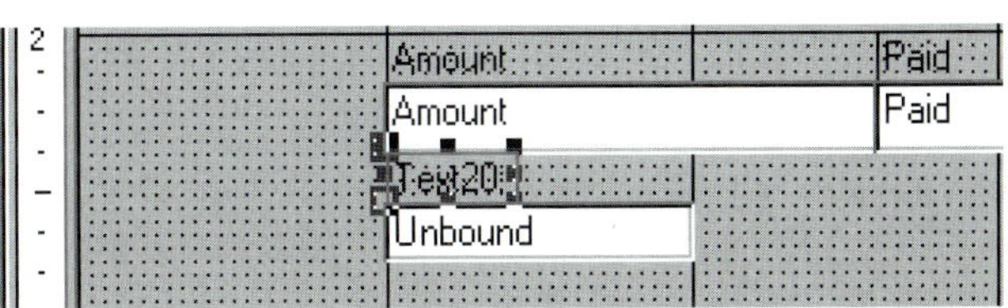

(b)

12 Scroll (move) to the *Name* box, click it, delete its contents, type **Balance Due** , and press ↵

13 In the *Control Source* box, type **=[Amount]-[Paid]** and press ↵

14 In the *Format* box, type **Currency**

15 Scroll (move) down to the *Text Align* box, click it, click the ▼ button, *Right,* and press ↵

16 Click the *Close* button of the Properties dialog box

17 Deselect the field object, and resave the form

Your new objects should resemble those in Figure DB3-19. Note that only the word "Balance" appears in the label object. You will correct this shortly.

RESIZING OBJECTS.   The techniques applied next are the same as those for resizing objects in a report. Remember, you can use the Size submenu (in the Format menu) for a variety of resizing procedures. You can also use drag-and-drop techniques. You will practice both techniques next.

When you are finished, your screen should resemble Figure DB3-21. Items marked with a 1 in the figure indicate that you should resize them. Items marked with a 2 indicate that you should move them.

1 Click the *ID#* label object and then Shift-click the *Customer Number* field object to select them

FIGURE DB3-21 ■ THE COMPLETED RESIZED OBJECTS

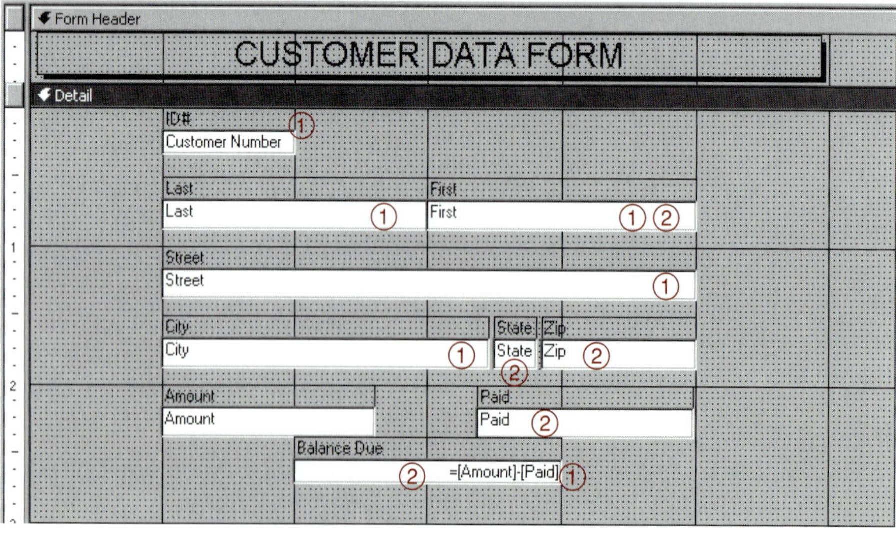

2 Click *Format*, *Size*, To *Widest*

3 Click outside the objects to unselect

4 If necessary, use the scroll bars to reposition your screen to view the *Last* and *First* fields

5 Select the *First* label and field objects, and then drag and drop them at the 3-inch horizontal mark

6 Drag and drop the center right selection handle of the label object to the 5-inch mark

7 Deselect the objects

8 Use the same techniques to rearrange and resize the other objects to agree with Figure DB3-21

9 Resave your form

ADDING GRAPHICS.   You can add lines and rectangles to a form or report to enhance its appearance. You can also add other objects such as *ClipArt* (a collection of graphic, sound, and video files) or a picture (such as a logo or photograph) from a file. Only adding a rectangle to your form is demonstrated next. See the appendix for instructions on inserting ClipArt or a picture file.

To add a rectangle around the *Amount, Paid,* and *Balance Due* objects as in Figure DB3-11:

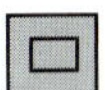

1 Click the *Rectangle* toolbox button

2 Point to about the 7/8-inch horizontal and a little above the 2-inch vertical marks

3 Drag diagonally down and to the right to about the 5 1/8-inch horizontal and 2 7/8-inch vertical marks

4 If needed, drag a selection handle (small square) on the border of the selected rectangle to resize it

The rectangle should surround the other controls. If it does not, delete it and redraw it.

5 Deselect the rectangle

6 Resave your form

7 Click *View*, *Form View*

Your form should look like Figure DB3-11. The form is now ready for use.

8 Close the Form View window

USING A CUSTOM FORM

As demonstrated earlier, you can use forms to view, enter, or edit data in a table. The next exercise uses the Customer Data form you created to refine your skills in its operations.

1 Launch Access, open the CUSTOMER.mdb database file, and click the *Forms* object type button if necessary

2 Double-click the *Customer Data Form* icon to open the form

3 Maximize the window

Your form should again resemble Figure DB3-11.

VIEWING DATA.   For a list of shortcut keys for quickly scrolling through fields and records, see Table DB1-7. Refer to Figure DB1-16 for mouse techniques to scroll through records. Techniques to adjust *tab order* and to hide or display toolbars are discussed next.

After you modify an existing form or create a custom form, the **tab order** in which you scroll to each field may not be in a logical order. This might occur because you added, removed, or moved field objects in the form's design. Note that the selection highlight is currently in the *Last* field of the Customer Data Form, and not the *ID#* field. As you perform Step 1, notice the tab order of the fields:

1 Slowly press `Tab` nine times

After you moved to the *Paid* field, you jumped to the *ID#* field and then to the *Balance Due* field. To adjust the tab order so that you begin with the *ID#* field and end with the *Balance Due* field:

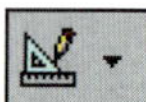

2 Click *View*, *Design*

3 Click *View* (If necessary, the *More* button), *Tab Order*

The Tab Order dialog box appears. To change the tab order to begin with the *ID#* field:

4 Click the *ID#* row indicator to select the row, as in Figure DB3-22a

5 Drag the selection to the top of the list, as in Figure DB3-22b

6 Click *OK*

7 Resave the form

> **Tip:** Click the *Auto Order* button of the Tab Order dialog box to instruct Access to set the tab order from top to bottom or left to right.

8 Click *View*, *Form View*

9 Press `Tab` ten times, and notice the new tab order

(a) The Tab Order dialog box can be used to change the tab order of objects in a form or table.
(b) The ID# has been moved by dragging and dropping its row.

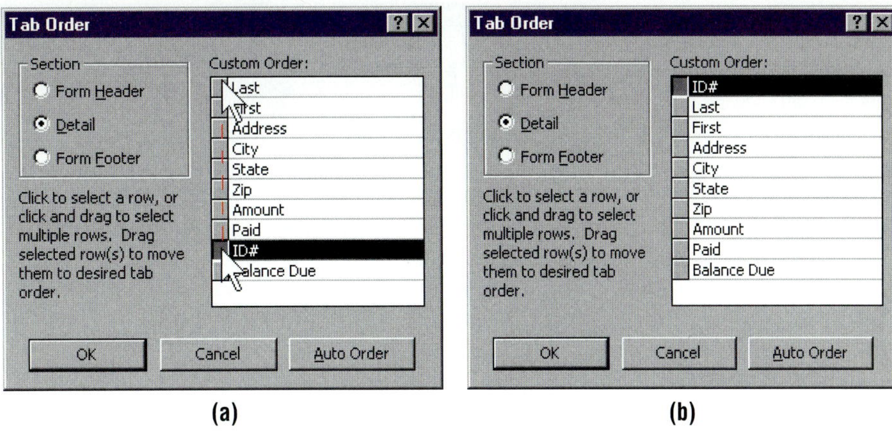

(a)   (b)

---

10 Press **Ctrl** + **Home** to move to the first cell of the first record

To prevent (or at least reduce) unauthorized modification of a form, you can hide the toolbars. Try this to hide the Form View toolbar and the menu bar, as in Figure DB3-23:

1 Click *View* (if necessary, the *More* button), *Toolbars, Customize*

2 Click the *Toolbars* tab, scroll to view, click the *Menu Bar* check box, click the *Properties* button, the *Allow Show/Hiding* check box to place a check in it, and then the *Close* button

3 Click the *Menu Bar* check box to remove its check mark

4 Click the *Form View* check box and then the *Formatting (Form/Report)* check box to remove their check marks

All toolbar check boxes should be empty.

5 Click the *Close* button of the Toolbar dialog box

Your screen should resemble Figure DB3-23. Now, to display the menu bar and Form toolbar again:

6 Press **Alt** + **-** (minus), **N** to minimize the current Customer Data Form window

The Database window should appear. If you have other windows open, they may also appear. First, you will reset the menu bar to display; then, you'll switch back to the Customer Data Form window and reset the Form View toolbar to display.

7 Right-click the current toolbar for its shortcut menu, and click *Customize*

FIGURE DB3-23 ■ **FORM SECURITY**

The menu bar and toolbar have been hidden to prevent unauthorized reprogramming.

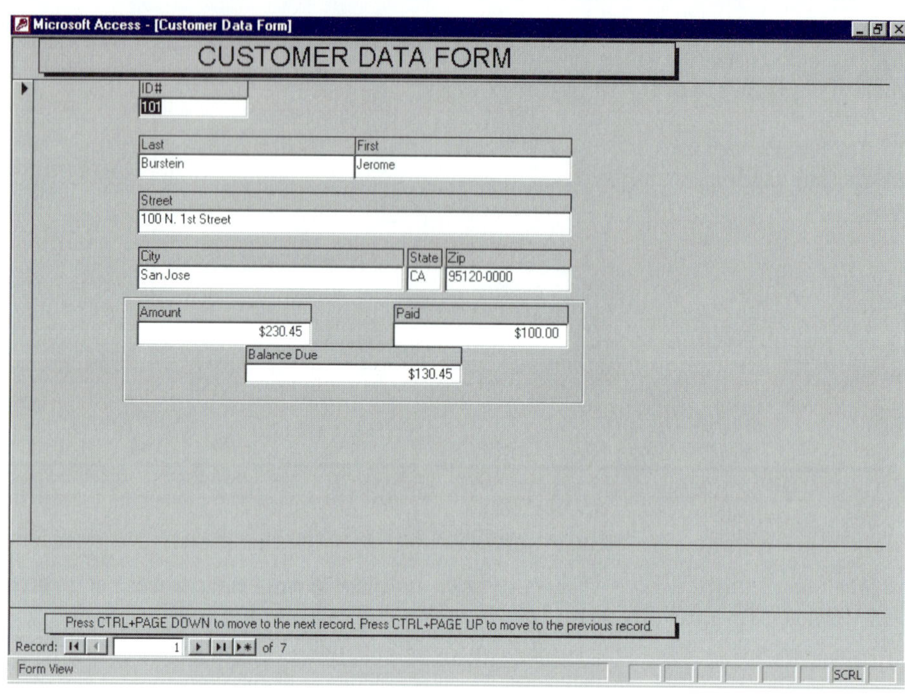

8   Click the *Menu Bar* check box to place a check mark there

9   Click the *Properties* button, the *Restore Defaults* button, *Yes*, and then the *Close* button

10   Click the *Close* button of the Toolbar dialog box

11   Maximize the Customer Data Form window

12   Click *View*, *Toolbars*, and *Form View*

13   Click *View*, *Toolbars*, and *Formatting (Form/Report)*

Your screen returns to its original display.

DATA ENTRY.   To see the effect of the new screen format, try the following data entry exercise:

1   Open the Customer Data Form if necessary

2   Click *Insert, New Record*

3 Enter the following customer data (remember, press **Tab** , **Enter** , or the **↑** or **→** key to move to the next field; press **Shift** + **Tab** or the **↓** or **←** key to move to the previous field)

ID#	450
Last	Laudon
First	Kenneth
Street	501 Fifth Avenue
City	New York City
State	NY
Zip	10003-0000 (Remember, if you did not use the Mask feature, you will need to type the hyphen "-".)
Amount	455.62
Paid	400.00

Notice that the balance due of $55.62 automatically appears in its field box. This field cannot be edited because it contains a formula.

EDITING.   Use the Customer Data: Form window to change the last four digits of each zip code to those displayed in Table DB3-3. To make this procedure easier, first sort the records in alphabetical order by the *Last* field.

1 If needed, open the CUSTOMER.mdb database window and then the Customer Data Form window

2 Press **Ctrl** + **Home**

3 Move to the *Last* field

4 Click *Records*, *Sort*, *Sort Ascending*

5 Use the zip code data in Table DB3-3 to update your database

Remember, pressing *F2* toggles between a selection highlight and an insertion point. Pressing *Ctrl + Pg Dn* moves to the same field in the next record. Pressing *Ctrl + Pg Up* moves to the same field in the previous record.

TABLE DB3-3 ■ ZIP CODE DATA

Last	Zip
Burstein	95120-1234
Hill	60605-0078
Kee	10003-3390
Laudon	10003-1101
Martin	10001-2220
Parker	87051-9283
West	60601-1666
Williams	60601-5577

6 **Close all windows in the Access work area**

7 **If desired, exit Access**

☑ CHECKPOINT

Perform these tasks.

1. Create a customized form displaying all fields from the Student table (DCHECK UNIT3 database file). Name the form Student Data Form, adjusting any objects as needed to view its data.
2. Draw a rectangle frame around the STUDENT NAME field.
3. Using the form, add two more names and sets of test scores to the Student table.
4. Put a calculated field—AVERAGE—on the form between the Test3 and Class fields to average exam scores. Format as fixed with zero decimal places.
5. Place a rectangle frame around the average.

MASTERY SET 3-4: RELATIONAL DATABASES— USING MULTIPLE TABLES

Until now, you have been using only one table at a time. However, Access is a true relational database. This means that you can work with more than one table at a time, sharing data as if the tables were each part of one large table.

At times, you will want to use data from more than one table to create lists or reports, or you may even want to develop forms that display data from a number of sources. Access will do this for you by creating separate forms for each table and then linking the forms together using a common data field called the **key field.**

In Access, the form for the main table you are using is called the **main form,** whereas each form to which it refers is called a **subform.** Access can *embed* (place) many subforms in a main form. There is one basic rule for linking tables: One field must be common to both the master table and the detail (linked) table—it must have the same data type and size in both tables. This field serves as the connection between two separate tables. Forms from different tables can be linked in the same database file or between database files. Only linking forms within the same database file is discussed here. Refer to the appendix and your online help to link to an external database file.

The following exercises demonstrate two types of links that are available in Access: a *one-to-many* link and a *many-to-one* link. (Although Access can also create other links, they are not discussed here.)

These exercises use tables from the MAGICAL database file. This file may be found in the Access subdirectory at Harcourt Brace's Web site, on a separate diskette, or on your LAN. Check with your instructor as to the location of this file. If you do not have the MAGICAL file or want to create it from scratch, you can use the information in Table DB3-4 to help you.

1 **If needed, obtain (copy) the MAGICAL database file from the appropriate source**

2 **If you need or want to create the MAGICAL database file, create a new database file with that name, use the information in Table DB3-4 to create the MAGIC INVENTORY and MAGIC VENDORS tables in the MAGICAL file, and then save the file**

TABLE DB3-4 ■ STRUCTURE AND DATA FOR THE MAGIC INVENTORY AND MAGIC VENDOR TABLES

(a) Magic Inventory table structure.
(b) Magic Inventory table data.
(c) Magic Vendors table structure.
(d) Magic Vendors table data.

(a)

Field Name	Data Type	Description	Field Size
ID	Text	Item identification number	3
ITEM	Text	Item name	20
COST	Currency	Cost per unit	Auto
PRICE	Currency	Sales price per unit	Auto
VENDOR	Text	Vendor selling item	3
STOCK	Number	Count of item/units on hand	Auto

(b)

ID	ITEM	COST	PRICE	VENDOR	STOCK
B68	BALLOONS	$6.80	$9.95	TRI	8
C45	CARD ON CEILING	$4.50	$6.95	TRI	8
E11	CHANGING PICTURE	$1.10	$1.95	TMH	22
E68	CHINESE STICKS	$16.80	$24.95	MRU	13
M98	CIGAR THRU QUARTER	$19.80	$29.95	TMH	38
E60	CLOSEUP PAD	$6.00	$8.95	TMH	28
E67	COLOR CHANGING	$0.90	$0.95	TRI	8
E30	INCREDIBLE PEN	$13.00	$18.95	TMH	36
E49	LOLLIPOP TRICK	$0.90	$0.95	TRI	8
D72	MAGIC DICE	$7.20	$10.95	TMH	28
E41	MULTIPLYING RABBITS	$4.10	$5.95	TRI	10
E68	NOISE BOX	$16.80	$24.95	TMH	36
E25	PAPER HAT TEAR	$2.50	$3.95	MRU	13
C17	PLAYING CARDS	$1.70	$2.95	TRI	7
R44	RAINBOW ROPES	$14.40	$21.95	MRU	13
R16	ROPE TO SILK	$21.50	$31.95	MRU	14
E29	SLIP OFF SPOTS	$2.90	$3.95	MRU	13
S34	SPONGE BALLS 1"	$0.90	$1.20	TMH	18
S13	SPONGE BALLS 2"	$1.30	$1.95	TMH	22
C12	THREE CARD ROUTINE	$1.20	$1.95	TRI	9
E26	TOP HAT	$12.60	$18.95	MRU	13
M50	VANISHING QUARTER	$5.00	$7.95	TRI	9
E81	WATCH WINDER	$8.10	$11.95	MRU	15
E34	WISH BOTTLE	$3.40	$4.95	TRI	9
E22	ZIPPER BANANA	$2.20	$2.95	MRU	15

(c)

FIELD NAME	DATA TYPE	DESCRIPTION	FIELD SIZE
VENDOR	Text	Vendor identification code	3
COMPANY	Text	Vendor name	20
ADDRESS	Text	Vendor address	25
CITY	Text	Vendor city	20
STATE	Text	Vendor state	2
ZIP	Text	Vendor zip code	5

(d)

VENDOR	COMPANY	ADDRESS	CITY	STATE	ZIP
TRI	TRICKS, INC.	9876 Wand Way	Denver	CO	80110
TMH	THE MAGIC HOUSE	75 Rabbit Hutch Blvd.	Hollywood	CA	90021
MRU	MAGIC R US	1735 Showbiz Street	Brooklyn	NY	11201

3 **If needed, open the MAGICAL.mdb database file**

Now, you will develop forms for the MAGIC INVENTORY and MAGIC VENDORS tables and then embed one in the other, thus linking data from the two tables. The MAGIC INVENTORY table contains a sample product list for a small mail-order business. The MAGIC VENDORS table contains detailed listings for suppliers. Note that the VENDOR code field is identical in both, making it the common field that can link the two tables.

CREATING A ONE-TO-MANY LINK

In a **one-to-many link,** each record within the main form points to many records in a subform. In this exercise, you will embed a MAGIC INVENTORY subform ("Products") in a main MAGIC VENDORS form ("Vendor") so that the screen will show all the products associated with a given vendor. You'll perform the procedure mostly with the help of Access's wizards. You will then smooth out a couple of rough edges using techniques you have already learned in working with the Report Design view. Figure DB3-24 shows the final product. Take a minute to examine this form. Note that it displays the TRICKS, INC., record from the MAGIC VENDORS table. Beneath that record is a list of all the products that your store purchases from that vendor. One field (the key field) is common to both tables: The *VENDOR* field. This is the field on which the two tables are linked in this form. The use of a key field (the primary key of the Magic Vendors table) allows Access to quickly find and bring together data that are stored in separate tables.

Notice also the two sets of Record scroll buttons. One set permits you to scroll through the MAGIC VENDORS (Vendor) form, and the other lets you scroll through the MAGIC INVENTORY (Products) form. In the following exercise, you will create this form.

FIGURE DB3-24 ■ THE COMPLETED ONE-TO-MANY LINK

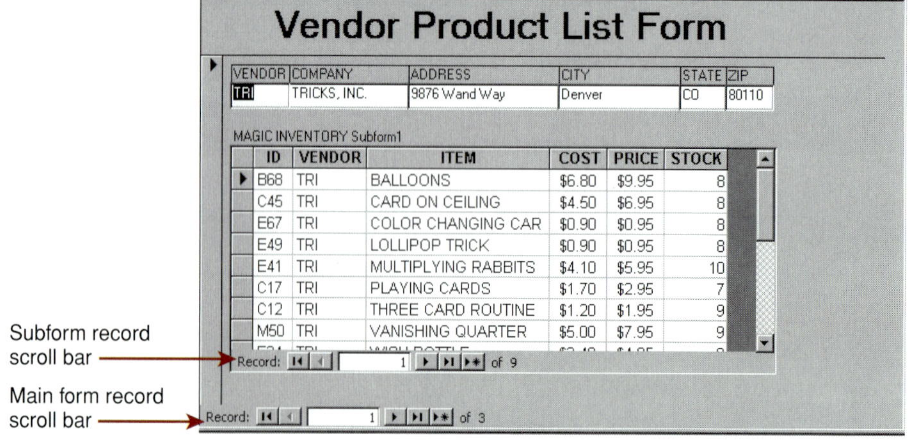

Subform record scroll bar

Main form record scroll bar

1 If needed, click the *Tables* object type button

You should see icons for the MAGIC INVENTORY and MAGIC VENDORS tables. You may wish to display them and compare them with the figures so that you can become familiar with their contents and structure. To begin the work of creating the form itself:

2 Click the *Forms* object type button

3 Double-click the *Create form by using wizard* icon

In the first Form Wizards dialog box, you select your source from Tables/Queries and then the fields you want displayed on the form. The main table in this exercise will be MAGIC VENDORS, which contains a list of the three vendors that sell merchandise to your retail store.
Select the MAGIC VENDORS table and then all of the fields:

4 Click the *Tables/Queries* drop-down box's ▼ button, *Tables: MAGIC VENDORS*, and then *OK*

5 Click the >> button to select all fields, and then click the *Next >* button

The next dialog box asks which type of layout is preferred. In this case, justified is the closest to the end product:

6 Click the *Justified* option, and then click the *Next >* button

The next dialog box asks you to designate a style. You can select the style you want, but the figures in this book use *Standard.*

7 Click *Standard,* and then click the *Next >* button

Next, indicate the title for the form:

8 Type Product List by Vendor Master Form , click the *Modify the form's design* option, and then click the *Finish* button

9 Click the Form Design View window's Maximize button

Access uses the information you have provided in these dialog boxes to create the form. Access displays the form in Design view, as seen in Figure DB3-25a. You could have designed this form without the Access Form Wizard, but using it saved several minutes of work.
Using Figure DB3-24 as a guide:

10 Point to the top of the Form Footer band title row until the pointer changes to a vertical re-sizing pointer similar to the one in Figure DB3-25b

11 Drag and drop it to just above the 3-inch vertical mark, as in Figure DB3-25c (your screen may reposition as you enlarge the Detail band)

12 Use the scroll bars to adjust the view to display the top of the form

FIGURE DB3-25 ■ PREPARING A FORM FOR A ONE-TO-MANY LINK

(a) The Product List by Vendor master form in Design view.
(b) Pointing to the top of the Form Footer band row changes the pointer to a resizing pointer.
(c) Drag down to resize the Detail band to the 3-inch vertical mark.

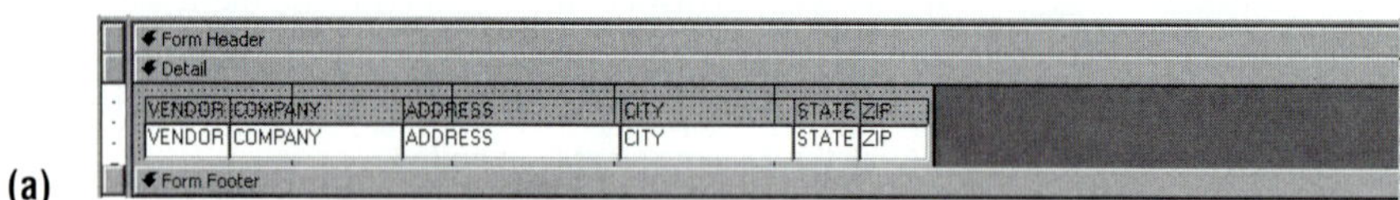

(a)

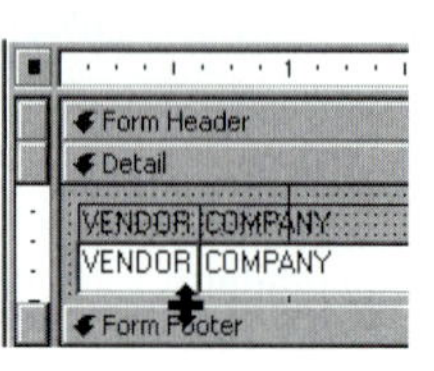

(b)

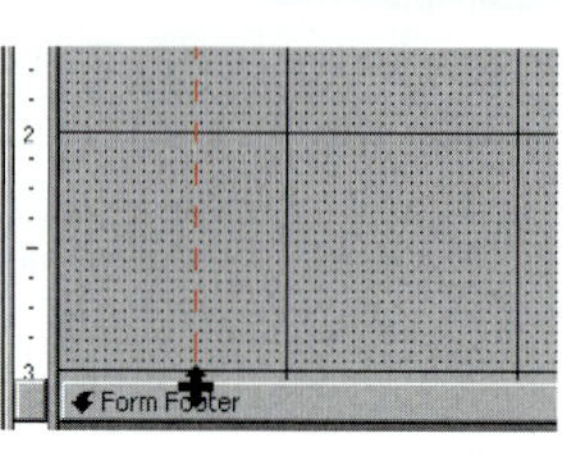

(c)

 **13** Click the *Subform/Subreport* toolbox button

14 Point to the 1/8-inch horizontal, 3/4-inch vertical mark, and drag diagonally to the 5-inch horizontal, 2 3/4-inch vertical marks to create the subform box for displaying all the products purchased (MAGIC INVENTORY) from the vendor display in the main form (MAGIC VENDORS)

> **Tip: You can easily reposition or resize the subform rectangle, so do not be concerned if you don't position it perfectly the first time.**

Not only does this procedure result in positioning the subform being indicated, but it also activates the Access Subform/Subreport Wizard. You will see a series of dialog boxes in which you can record your preferences for the subform.

The first dialog box (see Figure DB3-26a) asks whether you want to use an existing form or whether a new one needs to be designed from a table or query.

15 Click the *Table/Query* option and then the *Next >* button

Now Access wants to know which table and which fields from the table are desired.

16 Click the ▼ button of the *Tables and Queries* drop-down box, click *Table: MAGIC INVENTORY,* select the fields in the order shown in Figure DB3-26b, and then click the *Next >* button

Next, Access searches through the fields of the two tables (MAGIC VENDORS and MAGIC INVENTORY) for possible links (fields of the same type and size). As Figure DB3-26c shows, Access found only one: VENDOR. Because this field is present in both tables, it is the field you will use to link the data. In other words, the Wizard will designate VENDOR as the primary key in the MAGIC VENDORS table, where it is a unique identifier. The MAGIC INVENTORY table, which contains multiple records with identical vendor data, does not use it as a primary key.

17 Click *Show MAGIC INVENTORY for each record in MAGIC VENDORS using VENDOR,* and then click the *Next >* button

FIGURE DB3-26 ■ THE SUBFORM/SUBREPORT WIZARDS

(a) This dialog box is used to select an existing form or create a new one from tables and queries.
(b) This dialog box is used to select fields to be placed in the subform/subreport.
(c) This dialog box displays fields that are linked between the two tables.
(d) This dialog box is used to name the subform/subreport.

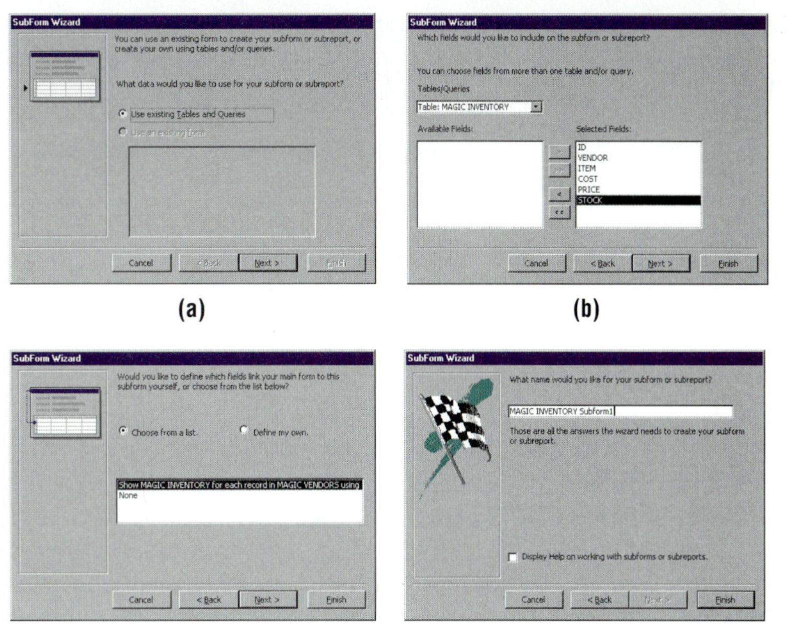

(a)

(b)

(c)

(d)

Finally, Access needs a name for the subform. As shown in figure DB3-26d:

18 Type **MAGIC INVENTORY Subform1** , and click the *Finish* button

The Subform/Subreport Wizard inserts the subform into the rectangle you drew and displays the final product in Design view.

19 Drag and drop the Subform object's selection handles to resize its base to the 2 3/4-inch vertical mark and its width to the 5-inch horizontal mark

Now, add the title "Vendor Product List Form" to the Form Header band:

20 To expand the height of the Form Header band, drag and drop the top of the Detail band title row down to the 1/2-inch vertical mark

21 Click the *Label* toolbox button

22 Point to the 1/8-inch horizontal mark, just below the Form Header title row, and drag and drop diagonally to the 5-inch horizontal, 1/2-inch vertical mark, as in Figure DB3-27a

23 Type **Vendor Product List Form** and press ↵

24 Click the ▼ button of the *Font Size* toolbar drop-down box and then *24*

(a) Click the *Label* Toolbox button, and then drag and drop to create this label object.
(b) The completed form title.

(a)

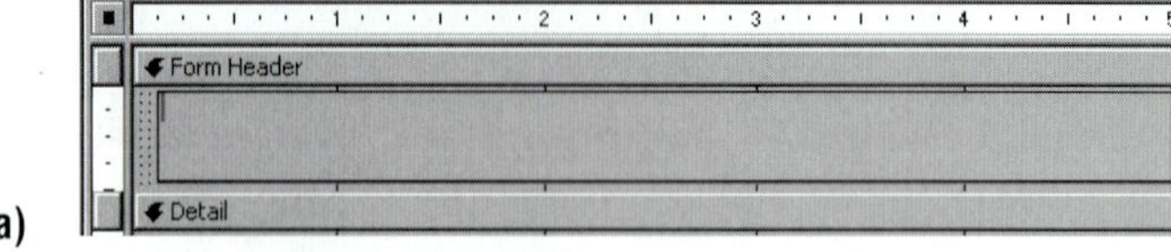

(b)

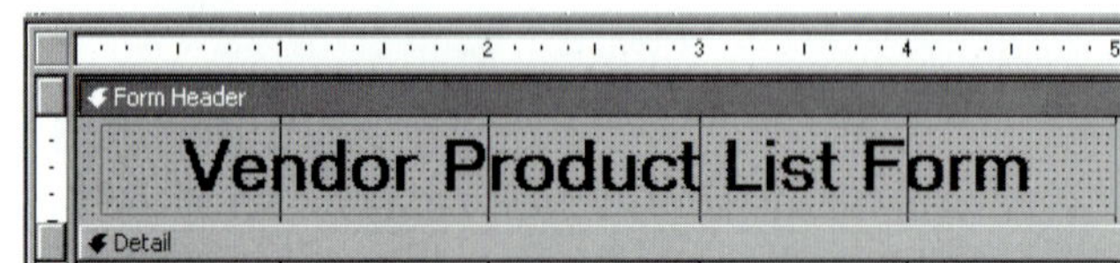

25 **Click the *Bold* toolbar button**

26 **Click the *Center-align* toolbar button**

The Form Header band should resemble Figure DB3-27b.

27 **Click *View, Form View***

Now, to adjust the column widths of the MAGIC INVENTORY subform:

28 **Select all columns in the MAGIC INVENTORY subform**

(Remember, click the first column indicator [*ID#*], and then *Shift*-click the last column indicator [*STOCK*].)

29 **Click *Format, Column Width* and then the *Best Fit* button**

30 **Click any cell in the subform to deselect**

31 **Click *File, Save As;* name the form Vendor Product List Form, and then click *OK***

32 **Verify that your work is comparable to Figure DB3-24**

USING THE LINKED FORMS. Once a subform is embedded in the main form and the forms are linked through a common field—whether you or the Form Wizard designed the form—you need only view the completed main form to display the desired fields. The following exercise demonstrates the uses of the one-to-many link.

1 **If needed, open the MAGICAL database and then the Vendor Product List Form**

The form displays the first vendor in the MAGIC VENDORS table with an embedded detail list of products from the MAGIC INVENTORY table that relate to this vendor. You can edit values in either table directly in this form. You can also append new records and delete existing records.

Note the following features:

- A set of scroll buttons for the main table data is at the bottom of the window.
- A set of scroll buttons for the detail table data is at the base of the subform.
- A vertical scroll bar for the detail table is in the subform.

Recognize that the vendor code for all the products corresponds with the vendor code of each vendor. Normally, you would not need to display the VENDOR field in the subform, but it was done in this exercise so that you can verify that the two files are linked on this field. If you use the scroll buttons to change vendors, all the detail records change to correspond to that vendor. First, if needed, save the form, and then take some time to explore its features.

2 Press **Ctrl** + **Pg Dn** to move to the TMH vendor

Note that the MAGIC INVENTORY subform automatically displays the products purchased from THE MAGIC HOUSE. To scroll through the subform:

3 Click the first cell of the subform

4 Use the *Tab, Enter,* arrow keys, or scroll buttons to scroll through the subform's content

5 Click the first cell in the Main form (upper pane) and if necessary drag over its contents to select it

6 Press **Ctrl** + **Home** to return to the first field in the first record

7 Close all windows in the Access work area

CREATING A MANY-TO-ONE LINK

In a **many-to-one link,** multiple records within the main form point to one record in the subform. In effect, it is a reverse one-to-many link. In this exercise, a MAGIC VENDORS subform ("Vendor") will be embedded into a main MAGIC INVENTORY form ("Product") so that the form will show the specific single vendor information associated with each product. The procedure is mostly an inversion of the process you used in designing the previous form. Figure DB3-28 shows the final product of this exercise. In this case, however, you are first going to design the subform and then the main form. Finally, you will insert the subform into the main form. Naturally, you can get Access Wizards to do most of the work for you.

1 Open the MAGICAL database window if necessary

2 Use Steps 2 through 9 in "Creating a One-to-Many Link" to create another justified layout form from the MAGIC VENDOR table; however, this time, name the form MAGIC VENDOR Subform1

FIGURE DB3-29 ■ CREATING A MANY-TO-ONE LINK

(a) The MAGIC VENDORS Subform1 in Design view.
(b) The objects have been repositioned to these locations.
(c) The MAGIC VENDORS Subform1 has been selected as the subform.

(a)

(b)

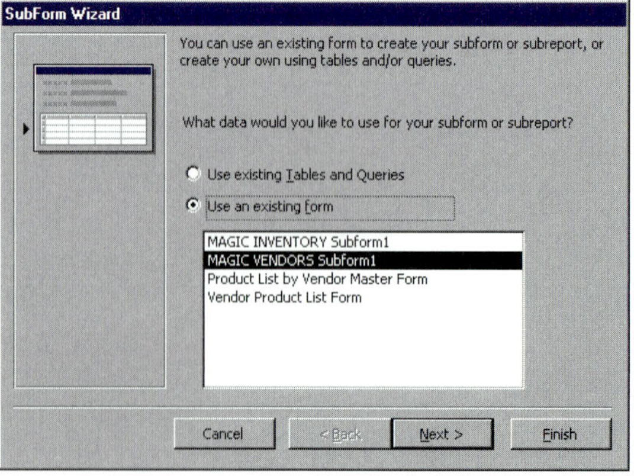

(c)

Your form should resemble Figure DB3-29a.

3   **Close the MAGIC VENDORS Subform1 window**

The subform is now ready to be inserted into the main form. To create a main form:

4   **Click the *Forms* object type button, the *New* button, *AutoForm: Columnar*, the ▾ button of the *Choose the table or query. . .* drop-down box, *MAGIC INVENTORY*, and then *OK***

5   **Click *View*, *Design View***

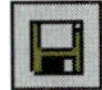

6   **If needed, maximize the Form Design window**

7   **Select the label and field objects for *PRICE*, *VENDOR*, and *STOCK***

(Click the first object and then *Shift*-click each additional object.)

8   **Drag and drop the selection to the 3-inch horizontal mark to the right of the *ID*, *ITEM*, and *COST* objects, as shown in Figure DB3-29b**

9   **Click outside the selection to deselect**

10   **Drag and drop the Form Footer band title row to just above the 3-inch vertical mark to enlarge the Detail band**

11   **Click *File*, *Save***   `Ctrl` + `S`

12   **Type** Magic Product Information Master Form **and click *OK***

Now, both forms have been designed. It is time to insert the subform (MAGIC VENDORS Subform1) into the main form (Magic Product Information). At this point, you should see Magic Product Information on your screen in Design view.

13   **Open the toolbox if necessary (*View*, *Toolbox*)**

14   **Click the *Subform/Subreport* toolbox button**

15   **In the Detail band, point to the 1/8-inch horizontal, 1-inch vertical mark, and then click**

(Do not worry about the subform's size. If needed, you will adjust this later.)

Access activates the Subform/Subreport Wizard. Again, you see a series of dialog boxes, but in this case, the subform already exists. Using Figure DB3-29c as a guide:

16   **Click the *MAGIC VENDORS Subform1*, and then click the *Next >* button**

In the next dialog box, Access recognizes that VENDOR is the only possible link between these two tables. The dialog box should display "Show MAGIC VENDORS for each record in MAGIC INVENTORY using VENDOR." All you have to do is this:

17   **Click the *Next >* button**

Finally, Access asks what name should be assigned to the subform. The default name is fine:

18 **Click the *Finish* button**

Access displays the finished product in Design view.

19 **Select the object label *MAGIC VENDORS Subform1,* and at the top left of the *Subform* field object, press** `Delete`

Now, add the title to the Form Header:

20 **Use the techniques of Steps 20 through 26 in the "one-to-many" exercise to place the title "Magic Product Information Form" in the Form Header (make the label 1/2 inch in height by 5 1/2 inches in width, give it a font size of 24, and make it boldfaced and centered)**

21 **Click *View, Form View***

22 **Alternate between Design view and Form view, making adjustments as necessary until your screen matches the one in Figure DB3-28**

When you finish, take some time to look at the form in Form view. Note again that the vendor code for the product corresponds with that of the vendor. If you use the scroll buttons to change products, the detail record changes to correspond to that product. Save the form, and then take some time to explore its features.

23 **Click *File, Save***   `Ctrl` + `S`

24 **Close the Form window and exit Access**

Tables are linked only when you use a form or report that has been designed using a many-to-one or one-to-many relationship. You can use tables separately by selecting other forms or by using no forms at all.

☑ CHECKPOINT

Perform these tasks.
1. In the DCHECK UNIT3 database file, using the Student table, create a query called Student Social Security# that includes only the *SOCIAL SECURITY* and *STUDENT NAME* fields. Save this query as Student Social Security # query.
2. Copy the Student table as Student Tests and then delete only the *SOCIAL SECURITY* field and its data in the new table. (*Note:* There is a one-to-one relationship between the Student Tests table and the Social Security # query.)
3. Create a form called Master Student Form that will link the Student Social Security # query and Student Tests table data together using the *NAME* field as the key field. The form should display "STUDENT NAME," "SOCIAL SECURITY," "TEST1," and "TEST2" on one form screen. The data in the *STUDENT NAME* field must be the same in both tables. Print the form.
4. Move the subform to another part of the screen, and print the form.
5. Describe the difference between a one-to-many link and a many-to-one link.

MASTERY SET 3-5: CREATING BASIC CHARTS

Most people understand information more readily when it is presented as a **chart**—a pictorial representation of data. Access's chart feature gives you the power to quickly develop a basic chart from table data. The following exercises demonstrate how to generate, view, and print charts.

1 **Launch Access, and open the CUSTOMER.mdb database file**

2 **Click the *Forms* object type button**

> **Tip:** The Chart Wizard is available when either the *Forms* or the *Reports* object type buttons are selected.

CREATING A CHART

The following exercises create the column chart shown in Figure DB3-30. Charts can appear on an Access form or report. A **column chart** displays numeric data as a set of evenly spaced vertical bars whose relative heights indicate values in the range being charted.

> **Tip:** In Access, a column chart is a chart that displays bars vertically. A bar chart displays bars horizontally.

1 **Click the *New* button, *Chart Wizard*, the ▼ button of the *Choose the table or query...* drop-down box, *Customer List,* and then *OK***

DB

FIGURE DB3-30 ■ CREATING A CHART

This chart was created using the Chart Wizard.

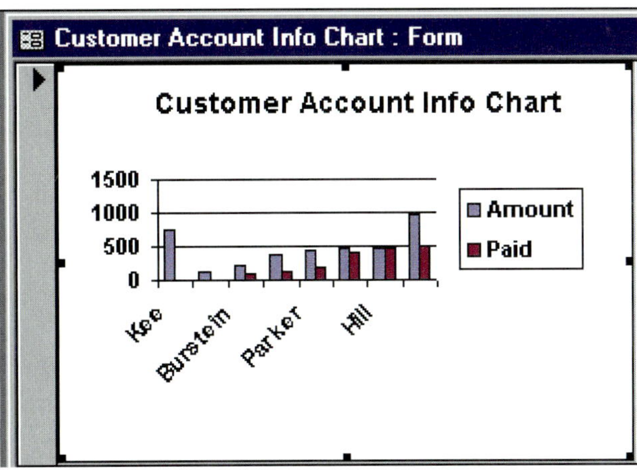

FIGURE DB3-31   ■   THE CHART WIZARD

(a) This dialog box is used to select the fields that will appear in the chart.
(b) This dialog box is used to select the type of chart to be created.
(c) This dialog box is used to define how the chart will summarize or group data.
(d) This dialog box is used to title the chart.

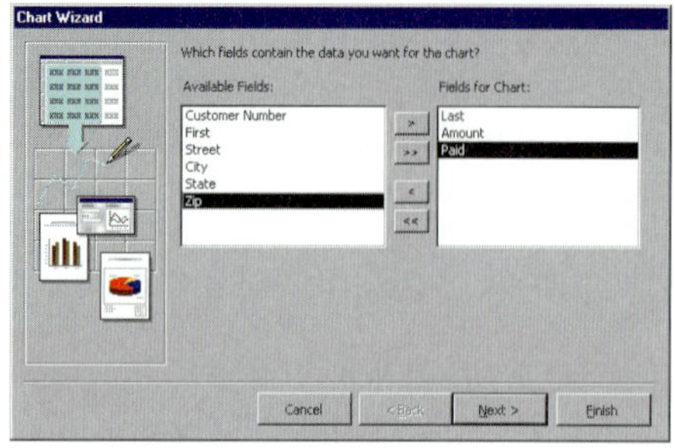

(a)

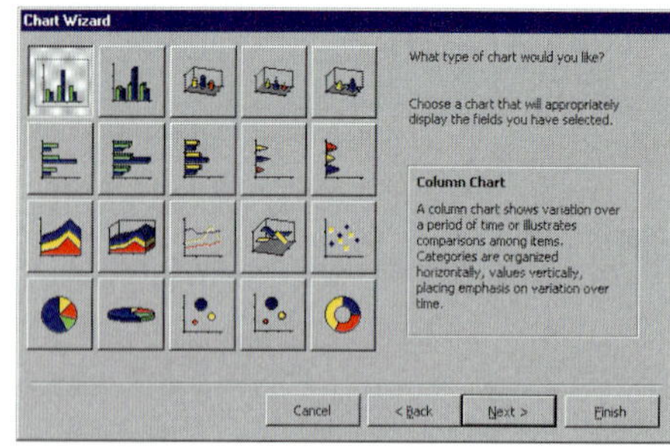

(b)

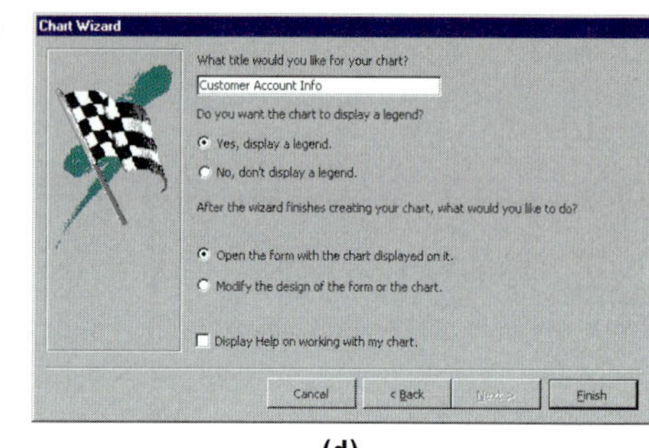

(c)

(d)

You now see the first in a series of four dialog boxes that will help you construct a chart. These dialog boxes are reproduced in Figure DB3-31. Use this figure to guide you in the completion of these dialogs.

2 Select the fields *LAST, AMOUNT,* and *PAID,* as in Figure DB3-31a (double-click each or click the > button for each field), and click the *Next* > button

The second dialog box appears, presenting a variety of chart types.

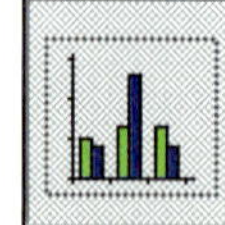

3 Click *Column Chart* as in Figure DB3-31b and then the *Next* > button

A third dialog box for layout appears. Here you can add or remove data from the chart. The items listed in the list box on the chart control the data that will appear. First, remove the sums, as follows:

4 Double-click the *SumOfAmount* label for the Summarize dialog box, click *None,* and then click *OK*

Now, to add Paid data to the chart:

5 Drag the *Paid* label from the right list to the left, and drop it just below the *Amount* label at the top left of the chart

Next, to remove the Paid Sum from the chart:

6 Double-click the *SumOfPaid* label for the Summarize dialog box, click *None,* and then click *OK*

Your dialog box should correspond to Figure DB3-31c.

7 You can click the *Preview Chart* button in the dialog box to verify that the chart is approximately correct, and then click the *Close* button

8 Click the *Next >* button to advance to the last dialog box

9 Type Customer Account Info as the chart title, as in Figure DB3-31d, and then click the *Finish* button

Access will need a moment for calculations, but then the chart will appear, similar to Figure DB3-30. The chart will probably need some additional attention, though. Your results may vary, depending on the default settings that you or your system's manager provided. Some basic chart editing techniques are demonstrated next.

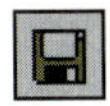

10 Click *File, Save,* type Customer Account Info Chart , and click *OK*

11 Close the Form window

> Tip: The process for inserting a chart on a report is identical to that for placing it on a form.

EDITING A CHART

Editing a chart is a little different from working with other kinds of objects in Access because you need to work with Microsoft Graph—the program that created the chart. Microsoft Graph is shared by most programs in Microsoft Office. This manual does not provide detailed instructions for using Microsoft Graph. However, some basic chart editing procedures are demonstrated next.

1 Open the Customer Account Info Chart in Design view

2 Maximize the Form Design window

RESIZING A CHART.   Resizing a chart requires that you first resize it in Microsoft Graph and then in Form Design view. To launch Microsoft Graph:

1 Click the *Chart* once to select it

2 Drag the right-center selection handle to the 6-inch horizontal mark

Note that only the Chart's frame, not its content has been resized. To resize the Chart:

3 Double-click the chart in Design view

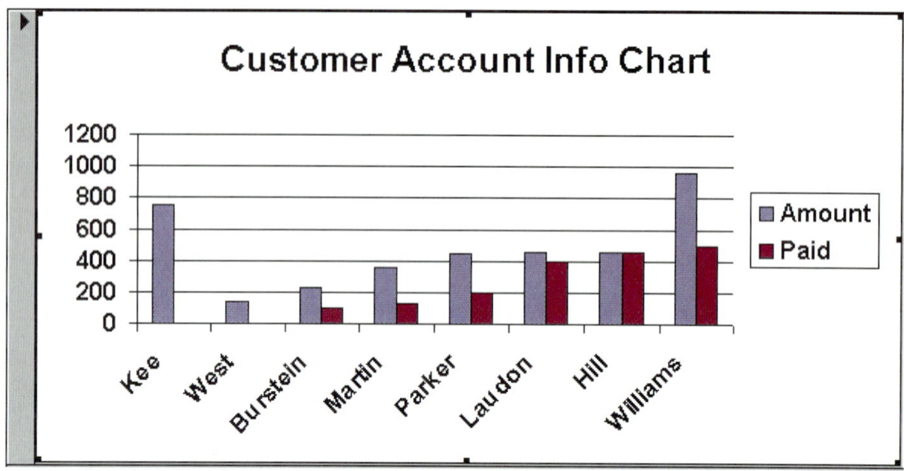

This step accesses Microsoft Graph's features to edit your chart. Note that a spreadsheet window with the chart's data also appears. At this point you can use the spreadsheet to edit its data. For now:

4 In Microsoft Graph, drag and drop the borders of the interior chart window to resize it to almost fill the exterior Chart frame (3 inches high by 6 inches wide)

5 Double-click outside the Chart and spreadsheet window to deselect the chart

 **6** Resave the chart

 **7** Click *View*, *Form View*

Your chart should resemble Figure DB3-32.

CHANGING CHART TYPE. Access offers 14 standard charts and 20 custom charts. Each standard chart has a variety of subcharts. Shortly, you will briefly examine all of these. To activate Microsoft Chart:

1 In Form View, double-click the chart object to launch Microsoft Graph

2 In the menu bar, click *Chart*, *Chart Type* to display the Chart Type dialog box, as in Figure DB3-33

Note that the current chart type, *Column*, and its related subchart are selected. A brief description of the chart also appears in the bottom right of the dialog box. As you change your chart type, the description changes.

Try this to view a few standard chart types:

(a) The Chart Type dialog
box is used to change a
chart's type.
(b) A 3-D column chart.
(c) A 3-D pie chart.

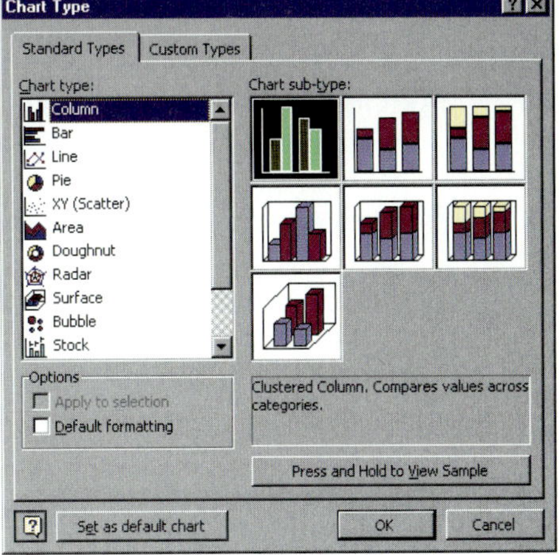

(a)

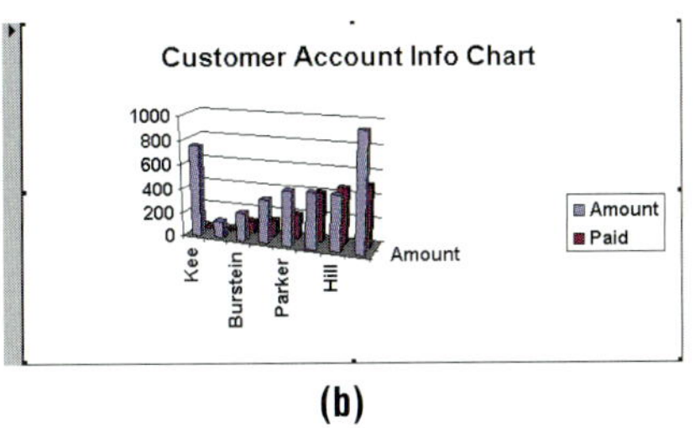

(b)

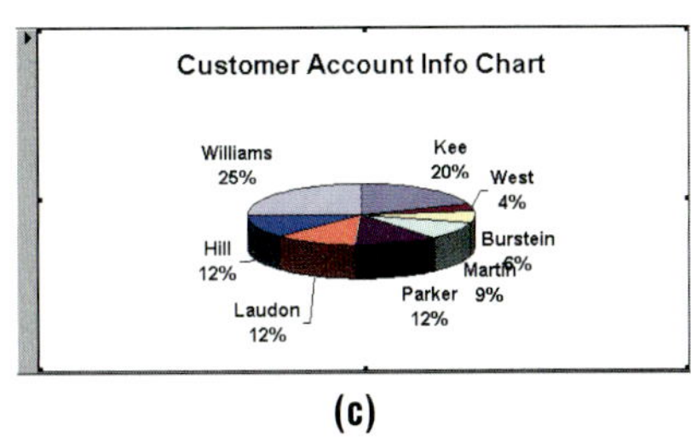

(c)

3 Press ↓ to move to the next chart type, point to the *Press and hold to view sample* button, press and hold your left mouse button to view a sample, and then release your mouse when finished

4 If you wish, repeat Step 3 to examine a few more chart types

Tip: Click the *Custom Types* tab, click a few chart types to view them, and then click the *Standard Types* tab to return.

To practice changing chart type, make the following changes:

5 Click *Column,* the *3-D column* subtype button (bottom left button), and then *OK*

6 Click outside the Chart to close Microsoft Graph and to switch back to Form view in Access

The 3D-column chart is displayed as in Figure DB3-33b. A *3D-column chart* displays values across categories and across series. Now, try another chart change:

7 Double-click the Chart object to launch Microsoft Graph again

8   Click *Chart*, *Chart Type*

9   Click the *Standard Types* tab if needed

10   Click *Pie*, the *3-D Pie* subtype button (top center button), and then *OK*

11   Click *Chart*, *Chart Options*, the *Legend* tab, and the *Show Legend* check box to remove checkmark

12   Click the *Data Labels* tab, the *Show label and percent* option, and *OK*

13   Click outside the Chart to close Microsoft Graph, and switch back to Form view in Access

A 3D-pie chart appears, as in Figure DB3-33c. A **pie chart** displays each value as a slice of a circle. It can only display a single series of values.

14   If you wish using the techniques above, try a few more chart changes

15   When you are done, click *File*, *Close*, to close the Chart Form without saving it again

16   If you desire, exit Access

> **Tip: You can always save a modified chart form under a different name if you don't want to lose an existing form. (Use the Save As command.)**

MODIFYING OTHER CHART SETTINGS.   Your chart can be modified in two environments: Access and Microsoft Graph. In Access, when viewing the chart on a form or report in Design view, you can use all the techniques you have used before on other Access objects to change the size and position of the object. You can display the Properties menu for the object and change the border, background color, and so forth, as you have done before.

In Microsoft Graph, you have much more control over the chart. You can add grid lines, change colors, annotate the chart with text boxes, change the orientation of 3-D charts, insert drawings, and so on. It will require a little exploration on your part to master those features of Chart that are important to your applications. Use the Help screens.

☑ CHECKPOINT

Perform these tasks and answer these questions.

1.   Using the Student table of the DCHECK UNIT3 database, create a standard stacked column chart that presents all test scores for students in the table and name it Student Chart.
2.   Describe the steps to change a chart's type.
3.   Change the chart to a 3-D area chart. Save the chart and then print it.
4.   What is the procedure to launch Microsoft Graph to edit a chart and then exit it and return to Access?
5.   What dialog box allows you to edit components of a chart when in Microsoft Graph?

MASTERY SET: 3-6: SHARING FILES

Earlier you learned how to copy, move, and link information between tables within a single database file. Here you explore several techniques to share information between Access database files and files of other programs. These techniques include linking, embedding, importing, and exporting. You also learn how to prepare database files for the World Wide Web and download database files from it.

LINKING DATA FROM OTHER APPLICATIONS

Typically, Access is used in conjunction with other Microsoft Office programs, such as Word, Excel, or PowerPoint. Office is known as a suite program—a set of separate programs that work together as one large program. Some suite programs provide additional menus or toolbar buttons that let you easily transfer information to other programs.

If you have other Office programs and a mouse, you can use *linking and embedding* techniques to combine information from different programs.

> **Tip:** Linking and embedding techniques will also work, for the most part, between any Windows programs that support them.

In linking and embedding, an **object** is a set of information. The file with the original information is called the **source file.** The file receiving the information is called the **container file** or **compound document.**

The term **OLE** (short for "Object Linking and Embedding") refers to transferring information from one program to another as an object. When you OLE an object, it retains its source file's display format in the container file. For example, if you OLE an Access table into a Word document, it will appear there in an Access table format. This is demonstrated shortly.

Objects may also be linked or embedded into a container file in formats that may differ from their source. Only OLE (objects linked or embedded as objects) operations are demonstrated here. You may want to try the other format options on your own.

Linking establishes an ongoing connection between the source file that provides the object and the container file that receives it. The object remains stored in the source file. The copy of the object in the container file is automatically updated when the source file's object is changed. For example, if an Access table is linked with a Word document, changes in the Access table will appear in the Word document.

Embedding inserts an object from the source file into a container file. The object then becomes part of the container file. Any changes made in the source file do not appear in the embedded object.

You can, of course, change information in the embedded object. Normally, an embedded object is edited using its source program but without changing the source file. However, embedded Access tables in Word documents are edited in Word. You might, for example, embed information from a Word document into an Access table and then change only the information in the container file (Access).

It is assumed that you have access to other Office programs to accomplish the next exercises.

LINKING AN OBJECT.   In the following exercise, you link the Customer List table from the Access CUSTOMER database file to a Word document. Although the procedure assumes you have experience with Word, you can perform the steps as outlined.

1 Launch Access, and open the CUSTOMER.mdb database file

2 Use the Simple Query Wizard to create a simple query from the Customer List table with only the *Customer Number, Last, First, Amount,* and *Paid* fields; name and save the query as Customer OLE Query

Leave the query table open for now.

3 Launch Microsoft Word and, if needed, open a new document

Note that a button appears for each program on the task bar. You will use these task bar buttons later to switch between programs.

4 Click *View, Toolbars, Database* to display the Database toolbar

 **5** Click the *Insert Database* toolbar button to display the Database dialog box

6 Click the *Get Data* button

In the Open Data Source dialog box, you identify the Access database file CUS-TOMER. Be sure to select the drive and folder appropriate for you. This dialog box operates like the Open dialog box:

7 If needed, click the ▼ button of the *Look in* drop-down box, and click *3 1/2 Floppy (A:)*

8 Click the ▼ button of the *Files of type* drop-down box and then *Microsoft Access Databases*

9 Click *CUSTOMER.mdb,* and then click the *Open* button

At this point, you can select any table or query from the CUSTOMER file to OLE into your Word document. To select the Customer OLE Query, as in Figure DB3-34a:

10 Click the *Queries* tab, *Customer OLE Query,* and *OK*

11 Click the *Insert Data* button

12 Click the *Insert Data as Field* check box

This check box instructs Word to link the data as fields with the Access file. Your dialog box should look like the one in Figure DB3-34b.

13 Click *OK*

The Access query table *Customer OLE Query* now appears in your Word document, as in Figure DB3-34c. Now, to see the dynamics of the OLE connection, try this:

FIGURE DB3-34 ■ OBJECT LINKING

(a) This dialog box is used to select the object to be OLEd.
(b) Selecting the *Insert data as field* check box will link the object.
(c) The completed linked object in Microsoft Word.

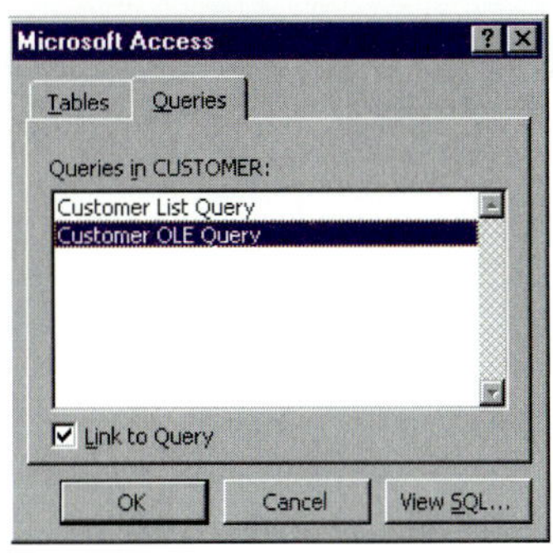

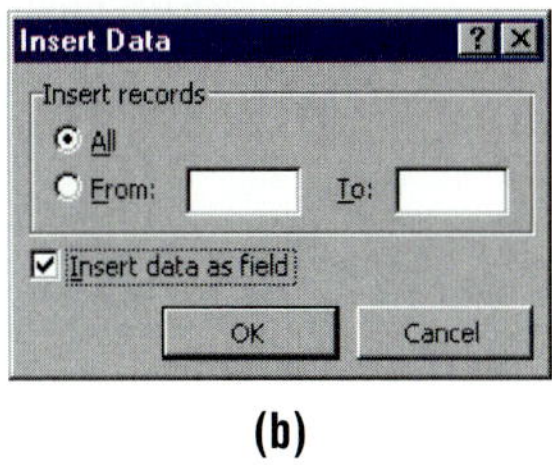

(b)

(a)

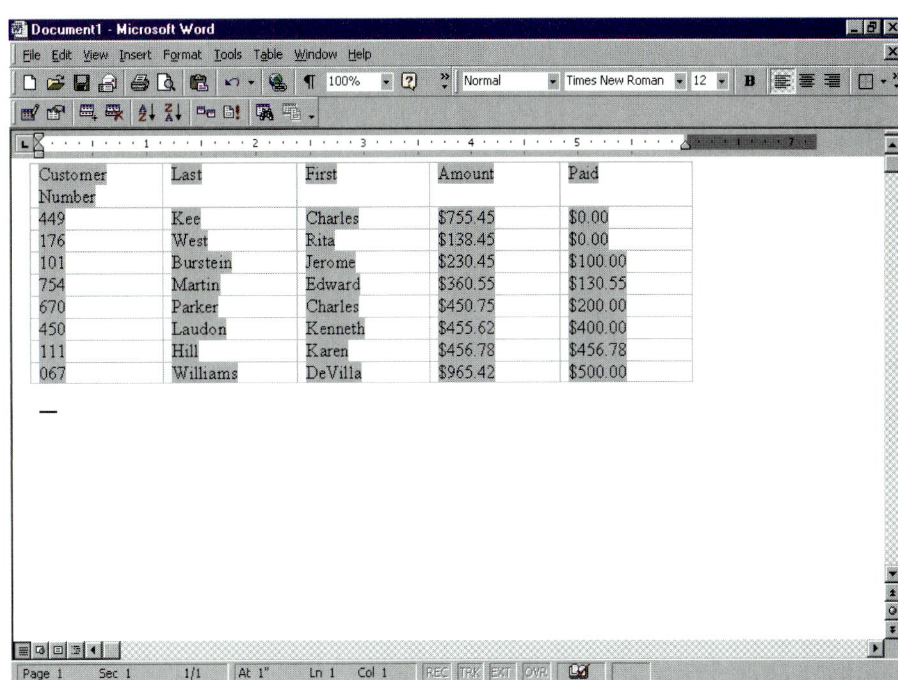

(c)

14 Click the *Microsoft Access* task bar button to switch to it

15 Change the *Paid* field value in Kee's record to 500 and in West's record to 100

16 Click the *Microsoft Word* taskbar button

17 If needed, press **F9** to update

The changes you made in your Access query table are also reflected in your linked Word document.

18 Click *File, Close, No* to close without saving — **Ctrl** + **F4** , **N**

19 Exit Word

20 Change Kee's and West's *Paid* field values back to 0 (zero)

21 Close the Customer OLE Query window

22 Exit Access

If you had saved the Word document and later made changes to the Customer List table while the Word document was not opened, the changes would appear the next time you opened it. Of course, this can happen only if both source and container files and programs are available in the same system.

EMBEDDING AN OBJECT.   Embedding an object simply inserts it into the container file. Changes made in the container or source file are independent of each other. The steps to embed an Access table instead of link it are almost identical except that you *do not* select the *Insert Data as Field* check box (Step 12 on page DB180).

> **Tip: In practice, an Access object would probably be embedded in a Word document or be hyperlinked to a Word document.**

PREPARING ACCESS OBJECTS FOR THE WORLD WIDE WEB

In addition to sharing data within your own computer applications or among fellow users in a local area network, Access provides the means to share your work with the entire world on the *Internet* through its *Web Page* features.

The **Internet** is a global interconnection of thousands of computer networks that enables millions of computers to communicate directly with one another. This giant network provides vast amounts of data—in text, graphic, and audio form—that can be shared by anyone with access to the Net. One important facet of the Internet is the *World Wide Web,* which lets users create or access multimedia documents easily. Most "Web" documents published (shared) on the World Wide Web are written in **HTML—** HyperText Markup Language.

Access can create three types of Web pages: Static HTML pages, Data access pages, and Server-generated HTML pages. **Static HTML pages** are Web pages whose data do not change. **Data access pages** allow you to edit and work with data from either an Access database, Microsoft Explorer (version 5 or later), or a Microsoft SQL Server database. **Server generated pages** allow you to view only data from certain data sources. Only Static HTML and Data access pages are discussed next. See your online help for Server generated page operations.

To access the Internet's World Wide Web and actually publish your Access object, you need the following:

- A computer that is configured for a TCP/IP (Transmission Control Protocol/Internet Protocol) network.
- A modem or other network connection.
- Access to a Web server—usually through an account with an Internet service provider (or your school).

■ Web browser software, which allows you to locate and view documents on the World Wide Web.

Even if your computer does not meet these requirements or you choose not to publish your document worldwide, you can still practice creating an HTML document. The following exercises demonstrate the techniques for converting an existing object.

EXPORTING AN ACCESS OBJECT TO A STATIC HTML FILE. Static HTML files display tables, queries and forms in a datasheet display when viewed through a Web browser. Reports are displayed in Report View format. Data in a Static HTML file are read-only. To export the Customer Report-By-City of the CUSTOMER database file to a Static HTML document, do the following:

1 Launch Access, and open the CUSTOMER.mdb database file

2 Click the *Reports* object type button, and then the *Customer Report-By-City* icon

3 Click *File* and then *Export*

4 If necessary, click the ▼ button of the *Save in* box and then the *3 1/2 Floppy* or the appropriate folder or drive

5 Click the *File name* box, delete its contents, and then type Customer Report-By-City Web Page

6 Click the ▼ button of the *Save as type* box, and then *HTML Documents (*.html;*.htm)*

7 Click the *Autostart* checkbox to instruct Access to view the HTML file in your browser

Your Export dialog box should resemble Figure DB3-35a.

8 Click the *Save* button

The HTML Output Options dialog box appears, as in Figure DB3-35b. This dialog box can be used to assign an HTML Template file. An *HTML template* is a file used to improve the appearance, consistency, and navigation of a Static HTML or Server-Generated HTML file. If you leave the HTML Template box empty, Access will use its default scheme. To accept the default scheme:

9 If needed, delete the content of the *HTML Template* box

10 Click the *OK* button

For a few moments, a dialog box will appear displaying "Now outputing…" and then the static HTML file will appear in your browser similar to Figure DB3-35c

11 Use the scroll bars to examine the content of your Web page and note that it is a read-only document

12 Click the *Close* button of your browser

FIGURE DB3-35 ■ EXPORTING TO A STATIC HTML FILE

(a) The Export dialog box can be used to export an Access object.
(b) The HTML Output Options dialog box.
(c) The Customer By City Report HTML file viewed in Microsoft Explorer.

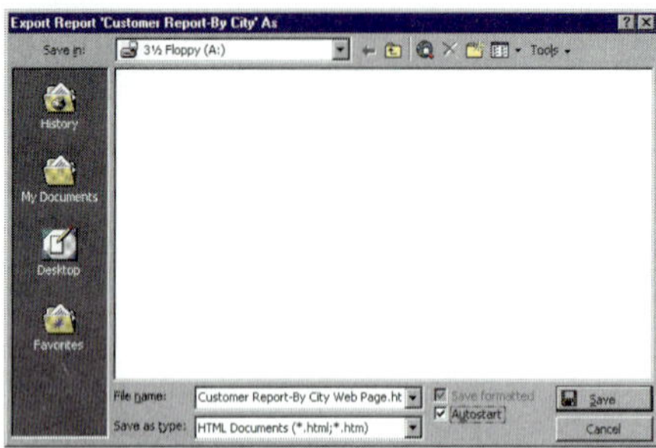

(a)

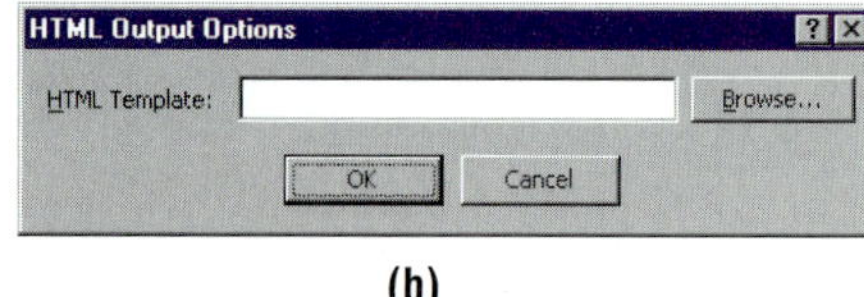

(b)

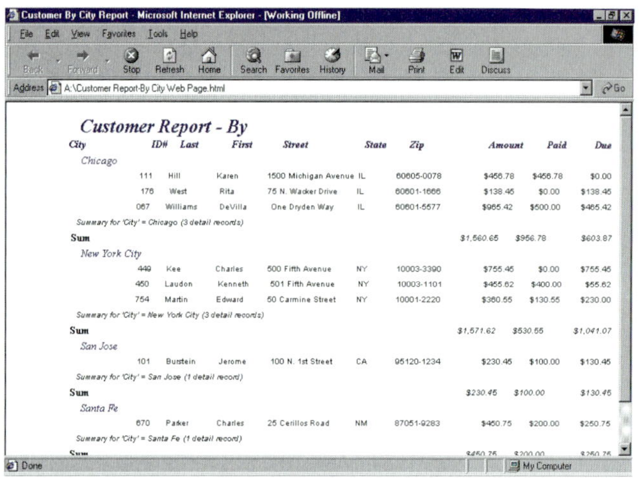

(c)

CREATING A DATA ACCESS PAGE.   Data access pages allow you to edit and work with live data on the Internet. In the next exercise you will create a Data Access Page from the Customer List Table.

1   If necessary, open the CUSTOMER.mdb Database file

2   Click the *Pages* object type button

3   Double-click *Create data access page by using wizard*

4   Click the ▼ button of the *Tables/Queries* drop-down box

5   Click *Customer List Table*

6   Click the >> button to select all fields, as in Figure DB3-36a

The next dialog box allows you to add grouping levels.

(a) This dialog box is used to select the Tables/Queries (source) and fields to be used in the Web Page.
(b) This dialog box can be used to add grouping levels to the Web Page.
(c) This dialog box is used to set sorting preferences.
(d) This dialog box is used to title the Web Page.

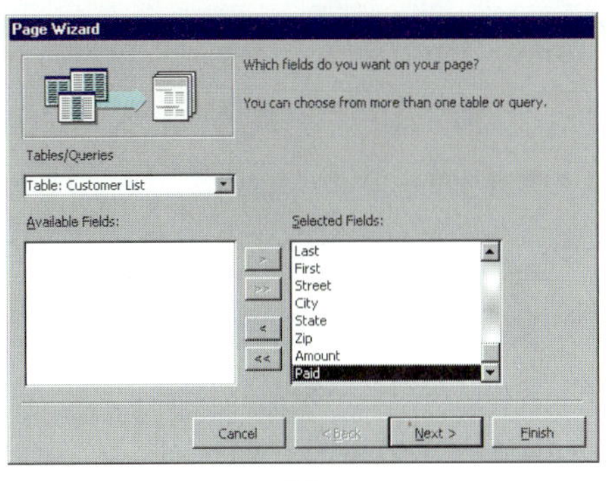

(a)

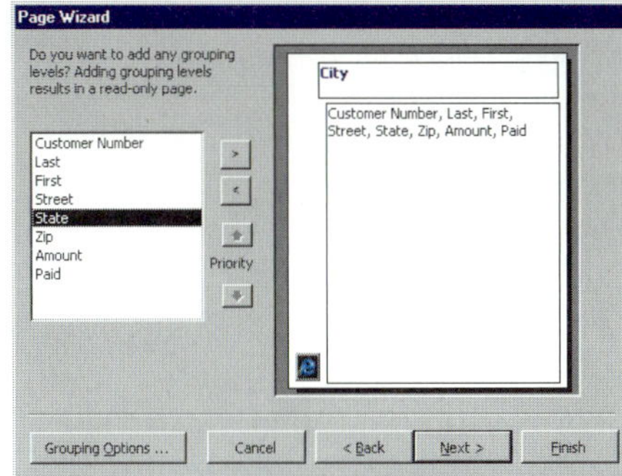

(b)

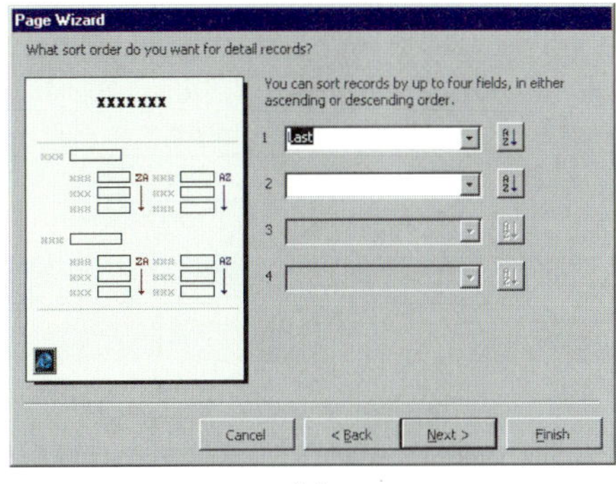

(c)

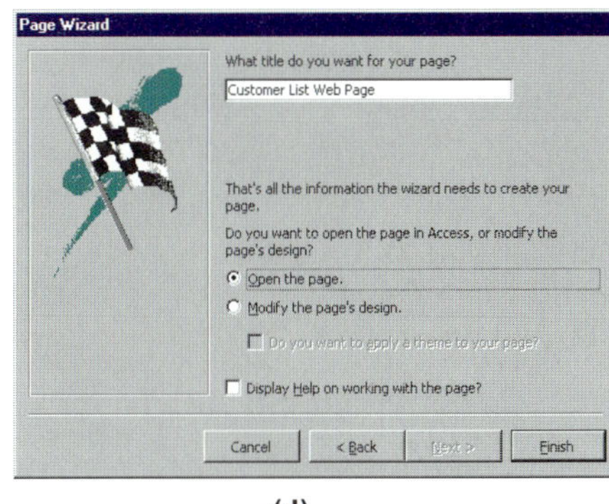

(d)

7 Click the *Next* > button

8 Click *City* and then the > button to group by city, as in Figure DB3-36b

9 Click the *Next* > button

10 Click the ▼ button of the *1* box and then *Last* to sort by the *Last* field, as in Figure DB3-36c

At this point, you sort by as many as four keys in ascending or descending order.

11 Click the *Next* > button and then type Customer List Web Page

12 Click the *Open the page* option

As displayed in Figure DB3-36d, you can select either *Open the page* or *Modify the page's design* (default). The *Open the page* option will display the page similar to the way it would appear on the Internet. The page design view allows you to edit the objects in the page.

13 Click the *Finish* button to open the page

FIGURE DB3-37 ■ **THE COMPLETED DATA ACCESS PAGE ADDRESS**

(a) The Completed Data Access Page contracted in Page View.
(b)The Completed Data Access Page expanded in Page View.

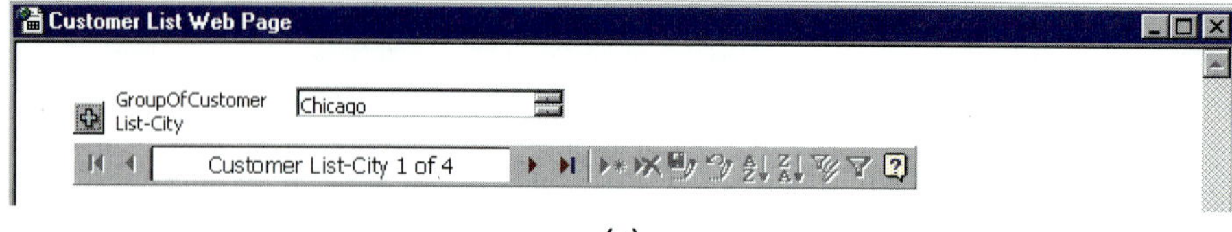

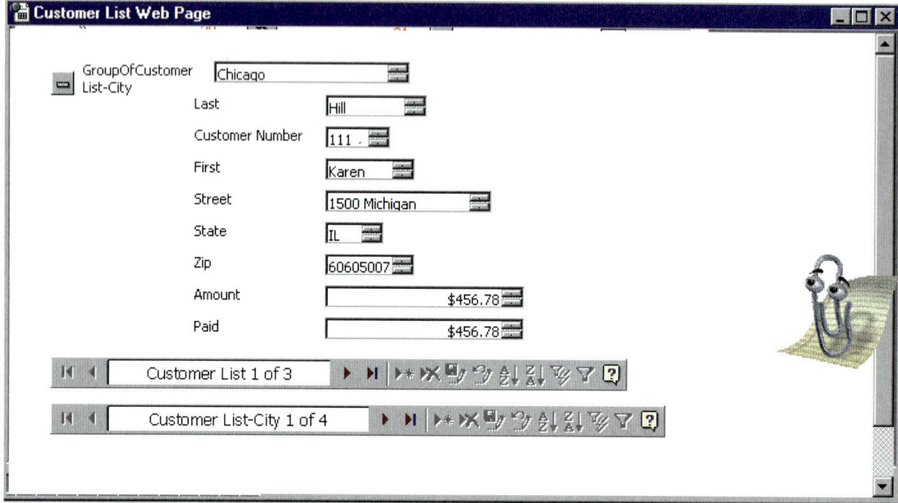

The Data access Customer List Web Page should first appear as in Figure DB3-37a. Now, to save the Web page:

14   Click *File, Save*   **Ctrl** + **S**

15   Type **Customer List Web Page** in the *File name* box and then click the *Save* button

16   Click the *Expand* icon to display an entire record, as in Figure DB3-37b

Note that only one record is displayed at a time in the data access page similar to Form View. In addition, all data are editable.

17   Use the scroll bar buttons to examine the records of the Web page

18   Click the *Close* button of the Customer List Web Page window

Note that the *Customer List Web Page* icon has been added to the list box. It can be used to view or edit the Web page.

Click *View, Toolbar,* and then *Web* to turn on the Web toolbar.

PUBLISHING WEB PAGES.   Once you have created a Web page, to publish it, you must save it in a *Web Folder.* A Web Folder is a shortcut to a *Web Server* (a computer directly connected to the Internet). Web pages are therefore saved on the Web Server, not your computer. For Access Web pages to function, the Web Server that you use must have Microsoft FrontPage server extensions installed. To create a Web folder, you can use the *Add Web Folder Wizard,* which is accessible through Web Folders in Windows Explorer. You can also create a Web Folder from Access's Open dialog box. See your online help for procedures to create and save to a Web Folder.

DOWNLOADING FROM THE WORLD WIDE WEB

If you have access to the Internet, you can also import HTML documents that you find on the World Wide Web into an Access database file. Once imported, you can save these objects for later use or printing as you desire. Try this:

1 **Launch Access, and open a new, blank database file named WEB**

You will use this database file to receive an imported HTML document.

2 **Click *View, Toolbars, Web* to open the Web toolbar**

The *Web* toolbar appears below the database toolbar, as in Figure DB3-38. You could now indicate the address of the document (Web page) you want to open. Each Web page in the World Wide Web is identified by a unique address, known as a **Uniform Resource Locator,** or **"URL"** for short. Each URL is divided into three parts: a *protocol,* a *domain* (the computer where the page is located), and a path (folder and filename) as shown in the sample URL in Figure DB3-39.

If you have access to the Internet, try importing the HTML document called "Customer Report Web Page.HTML" located on The Dryden Press's Web site as follows (if you do not have access to the Internet, just read through the following steps for future reference):

3 Click the address entry line on the Web toolbar

4 Type http://www.dryden.com/infosys/mts/Customer-Report-Web-Page.html

5 Press ↵ to access the file

6 If needed, connect to your Internet provider using your system's or lab's normal procedures

After a short wait, the document should open in your Web browser software. If so:

7 Save the document on your diskette (or in your folder) as Customer-Report-Web-Page.HTML

8 Close the Web browser software window

9 If needed, click Access's toolbar button to switch to it

Now you are ready to import an HTML file into an Access Web database file.

10 Click *File, Open* and then use the *Look in* drop-down box to switch to your 3 1/2-inch floppy drive (or the drive or folder appropriate for your system) that you saved the HTML file in Step 7

11 Click the ▼ button of the *Files of type* drop-down box, and then click *Web Pages (*.html;*.htm)*

12 Click the *Customer-Report-Web-Page.HTML* and then the *Open* button

13 If a Data Link Properties dialog box appears, click the *Cancel* button

After a few moments, the Web page will appear in Design View, as in Figure DB3-40a. At this point, you can edit the data objects. To view the page's data as in Figure DB3-40b:

14 Click *View, Page View*

15 Close the Customer By City Report window

16 Click *View, Toolbars, Web* to turn off the Web toolbar

17 If desired, exit Access

EXPORTING AND IMPORTING

Export and import commands facilitate data transfer by converting data into formats that other software packages can read. **Exporting** saves data in another format; **importing** opens data that have been saved in another format.

(a) When you use the Open command to open an HTML file it first appears in Design View.
(b) The HTML file in Page View.

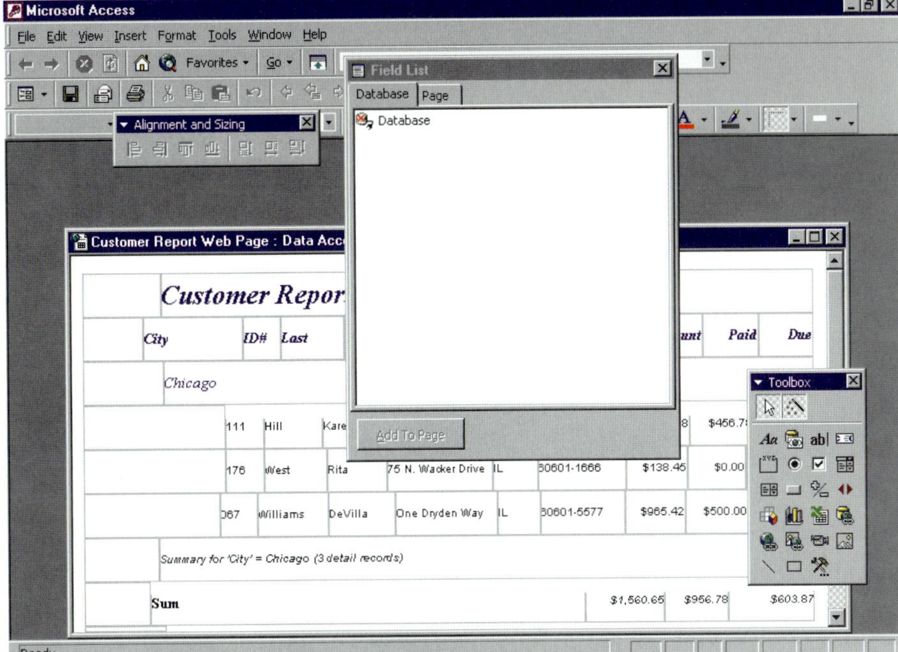

(a)

(b)

DB

DIRECT CONVERSION.   The easiest way to share data is to translate them into a form that another program can readily understand. For example, a spreadsheet can be converted directly into a database table, or vice versa. You might have to make some slight adjustments, but these are usually minimal. Access 2000 offers direct conversions for most popular software packages through its Export or Open (importing) dialog boxes.

ASCII—A COMMON DENOMINATOR.   When direct conversion is not available, ASCII conversion may still allow data transfer. **ASCII** (pronounced "ask-key") stands for the American Standard Code for Information Interchange. It is one of a few standard formats adopted by the computer industry for representing typed characters. ASCII eliminates the symbols unique to each software package, providing a common style for sharing data. In Access, ASCII files are called text files and are identified with the extension "TXT."

EXPORTING DATA FROM ACCESS.   Use the Export dialog box to export an object from an Access file, other popular database applications, spreadsheet packages, and popular word processors. Access 2000 offers direct conversion into the file types (formats) listed in Table DB3-5.

To save in any of these formats, use the *Save as type* drop-down box of the Save As/Export dialog box. For example, to save the Customer List table from the CUSTOMER database file in a dBASE IV format:

1 Launch Access, open the CUSTOMER.mdb database file, click the *Tables* object type button, and then click *Customer List*

2 Click *File, Export*   **F12**

3 Click the ▼ button of the *Save as type* drop-down box to see its list

4 If needed, use the list's scroll bar to locate *dBASE IV (*.dbf),* and then click it

Compare your *File name* and *Save as type* information with Figure DB3-41.

TABLE DB3-5 ■ EXPORT FILE TYPES

1	Text Files (ASCII)
2	Microsoft Excel 3 through 7, 97 and 2000
3	HTML Documents
4	dBase III, IV, and 5
5	Microsoft FoxPro 2.0, 2.5, 2.6, 3.0
6	Microsoft Word Merge
7	Rich Text Format
8	Microsoft IIS 1-2
9	Microsoft Active Server Pages
10	ODBC Databases
11	Lotus 1-2-3 WJ2

The Export command is used to export an object to another file type.

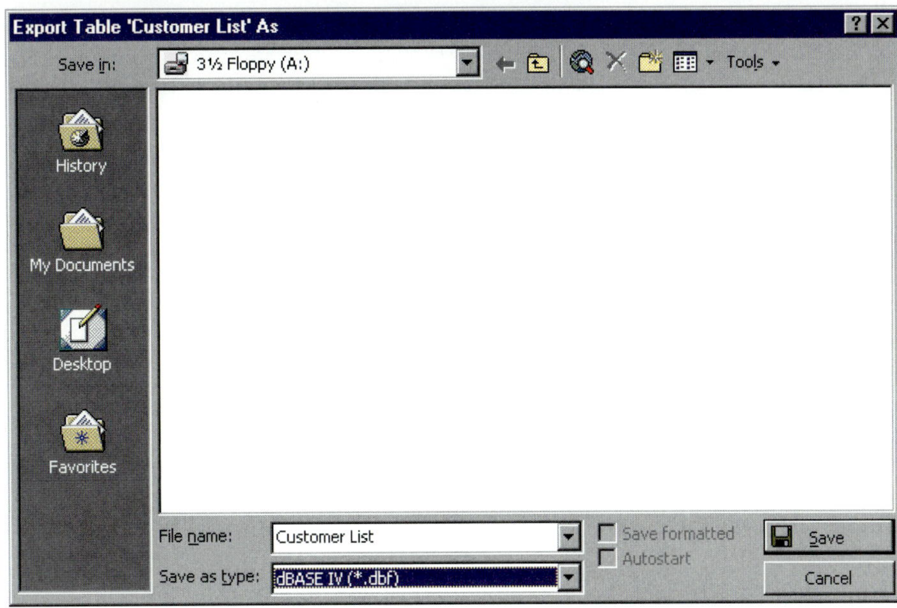

5 Click the *Save* button

IMPORTING DATA INTO ACCESS. To import any of the file types listed in Table DB3-6, create a new Access database file (or open a desired database file) to receive the imported file, click the *File, Get External Data, Import* or *Tables* object type button, the *New* button, *Import Table,* and then *OK* to start the Import Table Wizard. Follow the Import Table Wizard steps to import the data.

☑ CHECKPOINT

Answer these questions and perform these tasks.
1. What is object linking and embedding?
2. How do you activate a linked object for editing?
3. Describe the difference between exporting and importing a file.
4. Describe the different types of Web pages that can be created from Access's objects.
5. Describe the components of a URL address.

SUMMARY

■ Database management is an important part of data control. It includes techniques to duplicate, rename, and delete files and objects.

TABLE DB3-6 ■   IMPORT FILE TYPES

1	Text Files (ASCII)
2	Microsoft Excel
3	HTML Documents
4	dBase
5	Microsoft FoxPro
6	ODBC Databases
7	Exchange
8	Lotus 1-2-3/DOS
9	Paradox
10	Outlook

■ All records or a selection of records can be copied from one table to another using the Copy and Paste commands.

■ Label reports can be designed using the Label Wizard. The resulting form/report can be modified like any other report.

■ Customized forms can be created using the Form Wizard. These forms can be used for editing, viewing, and adding records. The order in which you tab to fields in a table or form, called tab order, can be reordered. Toolbars (including the menu bar) can be hidden to prevent unauthorized modification.

■ A calculated field manipulates data from other table fields to display a value not normally contained in the data.

■ The relational database feature of Access allows tables to be linked together through a main form and subforms. A common data field is used as the link called the key field. Multiple table use requires that a few conditions be met: one field of the same type and size must be common to both tables.

■ In a one-to-many link, each record within the main form points to many records in a subform; in a many-to-one link, multiple records within the main form point to one record in the subform.

■ A chart is a pictorial representation of data. Access uses Microsoft Graph to create and edit its charts.

■ The term *OLE,* or "Object Linking and Embedding," refers to transferring information from one program to another as an object. An object is a set of information. The source file is the document with the original information, and the container file or compound document is the document receiving the information.

■ An Access object (table, query, form, or report) can be converted into one of three types of HTML files for publication on the World Wide Web: Static HTML pages—"read-only" data which do not change, Data access pages—provide "live" editable data, and Server generated pages—provide "read-only" live data from certain data sources. HTML files can also be downloaded from the Web using the Web toolbar and Web browser software.

■ The Import Table Wizard and Export dialog box facilitate data transfer among programs.

■   ASCII is one of a few standard formats adopted by the computer industry for representing typed characters.

KEY TERMS

Shown in parentheses are the page numbers on which key terms are boldfaced.

ASCII (DB190)
Chart (DB173)
Column chart (DB173)
Container file (compound document) (DB179)
Data access pages (DB182)
Embedding (DB179)
Exporting (DB188)
HTML (DB182)
Importing (DB188)

Internet (DB182)
Key field (DB162)
Linking (DB179)
Main form (DB162)
Many-to-one link (DB170)
Object (DB179)
OLE (DB179)
One-to-many link (DB164)
Pie chart (DB178)

Server generated pages (DB182)
Shortcut icon (DB128)
Source file (DB179)
Static HTML pages (DB182)
Subform (DB162)
Tab order (DB158)
Uniform Resource Locator (URL) (DB187)

UNIT REVIEW

TRUE/FALSE

____   1. The database window is used to duplicate, rename, or delete database files.
____   2. Tab order refers to the order in which objects are arranged in a form or report.
____   3. Pressing *Delete* when an object is selected will delete that object.
____   4. Two tables with no common fields can be linked.
____   5. Subforms can be embedded into a main form.
____   6. In a many-to-one link, each main form is linked to a group of subforms.
____   7. In Design view, the *Text Box* toolbox button can be used to create a field object.
____   8. Calculated fields must be included in the table structure in order to be used in a form or report.
____   9. Access objects can be exported only to Microsoft Office products.
____ 10. A Data access page can be interactive with its user.

MULTIPLE CHOICE

____ 11. Forms can be used to _______ records.
    a. Add
    b. Edit
    c. View
    d. All of the above
____ 12. Which command can be used to adjust the order of the next field you move to by keyboard?
    a. Field Order
    b. Object Order
    c. Tab Order
    d. Sequence Order

_____ 13. Which commands are used to duplicate an object?
     a. Duplicate and Paste
     b. Save As
     c. Copy and Paste
     d. Cut and Paste

_____ 14. Which view is used to modify a form or report?
     a. Modify view
     b. Edit view
     c. Datasheet view
     d. Design view

_____ 15. What type of link is the link in which each record within a group of records from a main form is linked to one subform record?
     a. One-to-many
     b. HyperLink
     c. Embed
     d. Many-to-one

_____ 16. A main form record that is linked to one group of subform records creates a _______ link.
     a. One-to-many
     b. Many-to-one
     c. One-to-group
     d. One-to-one

_____ 17. Which of these statements about linked tables is true?
     a. A master form can be embedded into a subform.
     b. A subform can be embedded into a main form.
     c. The main form must contain no records.
     d. The subform must contain more records than the main form.

_____ 18. Which chart type can display only one series?
     a. Radar
     b. Area
     c. Pie
     d. Doughnut

_____ 19. What does Access use to create and edit charts?
     a. Chart editor
     b. Chart Designer
     c. Microsoft Graph
     d. Chart toolbar

_____ 20. Which command saves data in another software package's format?
     a. Save As
     b. Save
     c. Import
     d. Export

MATCHING

Select the term that corresponds to the feature indicated in Figure DB3-A.

_____ 21. Used to create a label object
_____ 22. Use to resize an object
_____ 23. A many-to-one link
_____ 24. A one-to-many link
_____ 25. A label object

FIGURE DB3-A ■ MATCHING FIGURE

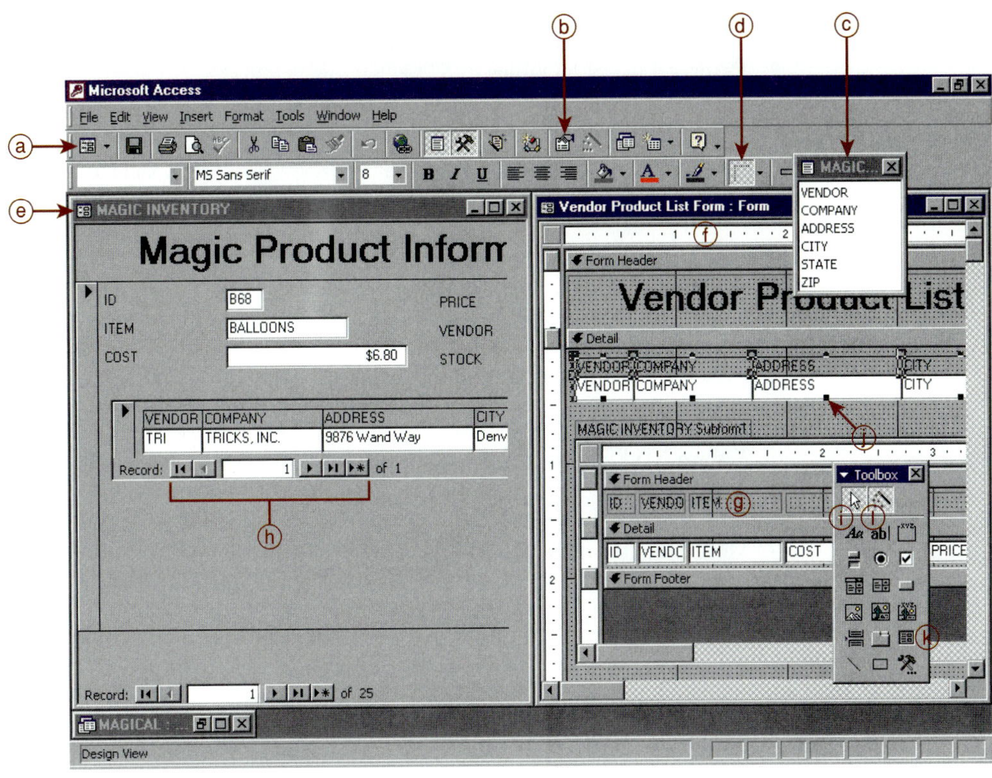

_____ 26. Use to scroll a subform's records
_____ 27. Can be used to switch to a different view
_____ 28. The Field List box
_____ 29. Use to create rectangles around objects
_____ 30. Displays a selection's characteristics

ANSWERS

True/False: 1. F; 2. F; 3. T; 4. F; 5. T; 6. F; 7. T; 8. F; 9. F; 10. T
Multiple Choice: 11. d; 12. c; 13. c; 14. d; 15. d; 16. a; 17. b; 18. c; 19. c; 20. d
Matching: 21. i; 22. j; 23. e; 24. f; 25. g; 26. h; 27. a; 28. c; 29. d; 30. b

EXERCISES

I. OPERATIONS

Provide the Access actions required to perform each of the following operations. For each operation, assume that Access has been installed on Drive C and that a data disk is in Drive A. Assume that the STOCK database file is on your data disk and that it contains tables named STOCK1, STOCK2, STOCK5, and PARTS. STOCK1 contains text fields named ITEM and CATALOG, a currency field named COST, and a numeric field named QUANTITY. A text file named STOCK5.TXT is also on the data disk.

1. Open the STOCK database file.

2. Display a list of all tables in STOCK.

3. Copy the STOCK1 table to STOCK3.

4. Add to STOCK3 those records in STOCK1 whose QUANTITY is greater than 99.

5. Rename STOCK2 as STOCK4.

6. Create a label form for STOCK1 that lists ITEM and CATALOG on the first line separated by a dash, QUANTITY on the second line, and COST on the third line of the label.

7. Create a customized form that displays all four STOCK1 fields near the center of the screen.

8. View a STOCK1 record using the form created in Exercise 7.

9. Create a form for STOCK1 using the AutoForm procedure.

10. Modify the form created in Exercise 9 by repositioning its data fields 1 inch to the right.

11. Create a form that links the STOCK1 and STOCK4 tables by a common ITEM field, using STOCK1 as the detail subform. Use any appropriate data fields.

12. Create a column chart displaying COST and QUANTITY fields for each item in the STOCK table.

13. Modify the chart created in Exercise 12 to a bar chart, and print it.

14. Import the ASCII delimited file named STOCK5.TXT.

15. Export STOCK1 to an Excel spreadsheet named STOCK6.

II. COMMANDS

Describe what is accomplished in Access by the following procedures. Assume that each part of the exercise is independent of all other parts.

1. Opening the database window for a database file

2. Right-clicking a database file icon in the Open dialog box

3. Clicking the *Table* object type button in the Database window

4. Clicking *Edit, Copy* when a table name is selected in the Database window

5. Pressing the *Delete* key when an object is selected on the Report or Form design screens

6. Pressing the *Delete* key when a table name is selected in the Database window

7. Opening a form in the Design view

8. Clicking and dragging the Subform/Subreport toolbox button

9. Clicking *View, Properties* when a field object is selected

10. Dragging a band's title row in Form Design view

11. Changing field data in a linked source database file

12. Dragging and dropping an item from the *Field List* box to a Form design view window

13. Clicking *File, Export,* the file type *Text Files,* and then the *Export* button

14. Clicking *View, Tab Order*

15 Clicking the *Tables* object type button, the *New* button, *Import Table,* and *OK*

III. APPLICATIONS

Perform the following operations using your computer. You need a hard disk or network that contains Windows and Access. In addition, you need your disk for file retrieval and for storing these exercises. Briefly tell how you accomplished each operation, and describe its results. *Note:* Of the three application exercises, each one relates to school, home, and business, respectively.

APPLICATION 1: ANALYZING DEGREE PROGRESS

1. Launch Access, and copy the DEGREE database file you updated for Unit 2 in the same folder.

2. Rename the COPY OF DEGREE as DEGREE 2.

3. Open the DEGREE database.

4. Copy the *structure only* of the DEGREE PLAN table as ACTUAL DEGREE RESULTS.

5. Add the following records to the ACTUAL DEGREE RESULTS:

Rec	Course	Number	Grade	Completed	Points
1	ART	3521	B	Yes	3
2	PSY	3414	A	Yes	4
3	POL	3601	I	No	

6. Append the records in the ACTUAL DEGREE RESULTS table to the DEGREE PLAN table.

7. Create Labels for your books using the DEGREE PLAN table. Include the *Course Name* and *Number* fields. Save the labels as Course Labels.

8. Create a custom form using the DEGREE PLAN table. Include all fields and save it as DEGREE PLAN FORM

9. Create a new table named CREDITS with the following structure without a primary key:

Field Name	Field Type	Width
Course	Text	5
Credits	Text	1

10. Enter the following data into the CREDITS table:

Rec	Course	Credits
1	CIS	4
2	ENG	4
3	MATH	4
4	SPAN	4
5	ACCT	3
6	PE	2
7	HIST	3
8	MUSIC	3
9	ART	3
10	PSY	3
11	POL	3

11. Create a one-to-many link using the CREDITS table as the main form (justified layout/standard style) and the DEGREE PLAN table as the subform. Save the linked form as COMPLETED DEGREE CREDITS. Be sure to add a title to the form using the same name.

12. Create a line chart using the *Course* and *Points* fields of the DEGREE PLAN table. Resize as needed and then resave the chart as GRADE POINTS CHART and print it.

13. Using Microsoft Word, create a letter addressed to your parent(s) indicating that the following table is a list of the courses you've taken and the grades you've received. (*Hint:* Create a query with only the *Course* and *Grade* fields and only completed courses. Link the query into the Microsoft Word letter.) Save the Word document as GRADES and then print it.

14. Convert the DEGREE PLAN table into a Data access page grouped by Course and sorted by Grade named PLAN DEGREE.HTML.

15. Exit Access.

APPLICATION 2: VIDEO COLLECTION

1. Launch Access, and copy the VIDEO database you updated for Unit 2 in the same folder.

2. Rename the COPY OF VIDEO as VIDEO 2.

3. Open the VIDEO database.

4. Copy the *structure only* of the VIDEO LIST table as GOLD VIDEO LIST.

5. Add the following records to the GOLD VIDEO LIST:

Rec	Video#	Volume	Start	Subject	Type	Time
1	1017	106	0000	Space Frontiers	SF	126
2	1018	107	2589	The Inevitable Terminus	C	90
3	1019	103	1170	Who are you?	C	152

6. Append the records in the GOLD VIDEO LIST to the VIDEO LIST.

7. Create labels for the VIDEO LIST table to be used to tab each video. Include the *Volume, Subject,* and *Time* fields. Sort by *Subject* and save under its default name.

8. Create a custom form (justified layout/standard style) named VIDEO LIST FORM using the VIDEO LIST table. Include all fields.

9. Create a new table named TYPE with the following structure and without a primary key:

Field Name	Field Type	Width
Type	Text	2
Defined	Text	25

10. Enter the following data into the TYPE table:

Rec	Type	Defined
1	C	Classic
2	M	Magic
3	SF	Science Fiction
4	A	Action
5	I	Instructional

11. Create a many-to-one link using the VIDEO LIST table as the main form (justified layout/standard style) and the TYPE table as the subform (all fields). Save the linked form as VIDEO TYPES FORM. Be sure to add a title to the form using the same name.

12. Create a line chart using the *Subjects* and *Time* fields of the VIDEO LIST table. Save the chart as VIDEO TIME CHART and print it.

13. Using Microsoft Word, create a letter indicating that the following table is a list of the classic videos you own. (*Hint:* Create a query named CLASSIC VIDEOS showing only the Subjects where the *Type* field equals C.) Link the query into the letter. Save the Word document as CLASSIC VIDEO COLLECTION and then print it.

14. Convert the VIDEO LIST table into a Static HTML file named LIST OF VIDEOS.HTML.

15. Exit Access.

APPLICATION 3: ADVANCED PAYROLL

1. Launch Access, and copy the PAYROLL database you updated for Unit 2 in the same folder.

2. Rename the COPY OF PAYROLL as BACKUP PAYROLL.

3. Open the PAYROLL database.

4. Copy the *structure only* of the PAYROLL LIST table as EXECUTIVE PAYROLL LIST.

5. Add the following records to the EXECUTIVE PAYROLL LIST:

Rec	Social Security	Last	First	Dept	Hours	Rate
1	010-10-1010	RED	PAULA	EXECUTIVE	50	40.00
2	121-21-2121	ORANGE	JANE	EXECUTIVE	60	60.00
3	131-31-3131	PINK	BOB	EXECUTIVE	80	50.00

6. Append the records in the EXECUTIVE PAY LIST to the PAYROLL LIST.

7. Create labels for the PAYROLL LIST table to be used as name tags. Include the *First, Last,* and *Dept* fields. Sort by the *Last* field and save as NAME TAGS.

8. Create a custom form using the PAYROLL LIST. Include all fields with a summary statistic for the *Hours* column.

9. Create a new table named VACATION with the following structure and without a primary key:

Field Name	Field Type	Width
Dept	Text	20
Vacation	Weeks	Number

10. Enter the following data into the VACATION table:

Rec	Dept	Vacation Weeks
1	Sales	3
2	Accounting	3
3	Human Resources	2
4	Executive	4

11. Create a one-to-many link using the VACATION table as the main form (justified layout/standard style) and the PAYROLL LIST table as the subform. Resize objects as needed and then save the linked form as VACATION FORM. Be sure to add a title to the form using the same name.

12. Create a 3-D column chart using the *Dept,* sum of *Hours,* and average of *Rate* fields of the PAYROLL LIST table. Save the chart as PAYROLL CHART, and print it.

13. Using Microsoft Word, create a letter indicating that the following table is a list of the employees who worked overtime. (*Hint:* Create a query named OVERTIME to list employees whose hours were greater than 40. Link the query into a letter.) Save the Word document as EMPLOYEE EXCEEDING 40 HOURS and then print it.

14. Convert the PAYROLL LIST table into a Data access page named PERSONNEL.HTML. Group fields by department and sort by the *LAST* field.

15 Exit Access.

MASTERY CASES

The following mastery cases allow you to demonstrate how much you have learned about this software. Each case extends a fictitious problem from Unit 1 and can be solved using some of the skills you may have learned in this unit. If you do not have the file referred to in a case, create it by following the instructions in Units 1 and 2. Design your responses in ways that display your mastery of the software.

These mastery cases allow you to display your ability to:

- Manage database files.
- Copy and append tables.
- Create labels.
- Design a customized form.
- Use multiple tables.
- Convert an Access object to an HTML document.

CASE 1: DESIGNING A CUSTOMIZED ENTRY FORM

Using the file and data you modified in Unit 2's course record, design a form that will display the title "GRADUATION PROGRESS" centered at the top and that will also effectively display each record's data for review or editing. When completed, print a screen copy of one record using the new design. Convert the table to an HTML file.

CASE 2: USING MULTIPLE TABLES

Using the file and data you modified in Unit 2's music catalog, create a new file that includes data for album title, year of release, and record company. Then, design main and subforms to create a one-to-many link that will display the selection titles and play lengths for all records that match each album name in the new file. Print a sample screen from one album.

CASE 3: CREATING LABELS

Using the file you modified in Unit 2, design a label that can be used to mail a special sale announcement to each client in the database. Include in the label the date of the client's next appointment. When done, print the labels for those clients whose birthdays are coming up next month.

ACCESS 2000 REFERENCE APPENDIX

This brief appendix extends your abilities by listing commands and features not included in the Access mastery sets. A list of commonly used Windows keys and Access keys is first. Next is a Quick Command Reference, followed by instructions for accessing the MouseKeys feature so that you can use the numeric keypad to invoke mouse actions. Next is a Toolbar Reference, and finally, selected Access features arranged in alphabetical order for easy reference.

Unless otherwise indicated, this appendix refers to all windows in Access's work area as database (document) windows. Objects include any item within a database window, including tables, queries, forms, reports, macros, and modules. A cell is the intersection of a column and a row of a table.

COMMON WINDOWS KEYS

Common Windows keys concern basic menu and dialog box operations, file management, window manipulation, and editing commands. They also include a variety of shortcut keys.

Keys	Function
Alt + F4	Exits Access (or any Windows program) or any dialog box.
Alt + Spacebar	Opens the Access window's (or any program window's) control menu.
Alt + – (minus)	Opens the control menu of a database (or document) window.
Alt + Tab	Switches to the last program used when operating multiple programs.
Alt + Esc	Switches to the next running program when operating multiple applications. A program can be running as a window or as a task bar button.
Alt + Print Screen	Copies an image of the active program window (or dialog box) to the Clipboard for future pasting.
Arrow keys	Move the selection highlight one cell at a time in the direction of the arrow.
	Move the insertion point one character at a time in the direction of the arrow when editing data within a cell, text box, or drop-down box.
	Move the selection highlight in the direction of the arrow to each item on a menu or list (in a list box or drop-down box).
	Can also be used in conjunction with other keys to perform such tasks as resizing a window, moving a selection (data, chart, table, or object), or moving a drawing or editing tool.
Ctrl + Alt + Delete	Exits the current program if it stops responding to the system.
Ctrl + B	Turns the boldface feature on and off in Form or Report view.
Ctrl + C	Copies a selection (data, chart, table, or object) to the Windows Clipboard for future pasting.
Ctrl + Esc	Opens the Start menu.
Ctrl + F	Starts the Find feature.

Keys	Function
Ctrl + *F4* or *Ctrl* + *W*	Closes the active database (document) window.
Ctrl + *F6*	Moves the highlight to another database (document) window or icon.
Ctrl + *Shift* + *F6*	Switches to the previous database window.
Ctrl + *H*	Starts the Replace feature.
Ctrl + *I*	Turns the italic feature on and off in Form or Report view.
Ctrl + *N*	Creates a new database.
Ctrl + *O*	Opens a database.
Ctrl + *P*	Prints the current object or selection.
Ctrl + *S*	Saves the current database object to the database file.
Ctrl + *U*	Turns the underline feature on and off.
Ctrl + *V*	Pastes the contents of the Windows Clipboard to a desired location.
Ctrl + *X*	Cuts (moves) a selection to the Windows Clipboard for future pasting.
Ctrl + *Y*	Repeats close.
Ctrl + *Z*	Undoes the last action.
Shift + Arrow key	Selects a block (group) of cells in the direction of the arrow in Datasheet view.
Shift + *Tab*	Moves the dotted selection rectangle to the previous option in a dialog box or Form or Datasheet view.

ACCESS KEYS

Unique Access keys are for invoking commands that relate only to Access features. Function keys used alone and in conjunction with the *Shift, Ctrl,* and *Alt* keys are listed first.

Keys	Function
F1	Invokes the Access Help feature.
Shift + *F1*	Invokes context-sensitive Help.
F2 (Edit)	Switches between navigation mode (selection highlight) and edit mode (insertion point).
F3	Renames a selected object.
F4	Opens a combo box.
Ctrl + *F4*	Closes the active database window.
Alt + *F4*	Exits Microsoft Access.
F5	Switches from Form Design to Form View. In Form view, highlights record number box.
F6	Moves between the upper and lower panes of a window.
Alt + *F6*	Activates the Office Assistant balloon.
Ctrl + *F6*	Moves to the next database window.
F7	Invokes the spell-checker program.
F8	Turns on Extend (selection) mode files listed in the Open or Save As dialog box.
F9	Updates the contents of a Lookup field list box or combo box or recalculates fields in window.
Ctrl + *F9*	Minimizes the window in Access's work area.
F10 or *Alt* (Menu)	Activates the selection highlight on the menu bar.
Ctrl + *F10*	Maximizes a window in Access's work area.
F11	Moves the Database window to the front.
F12	Invokes the Save As command (File menu).
Shift + *F12*	Invokes the Save command (File menu).
Ctrl + *F12*	Invokes the Open command (File menu).
Ctrl + ; (semicolon)	Inserts the current system date.
Ctrl + : (colon)	Inserts the current system time.
Ctrl + ' (apostrophe)	Repeats the value from the same field in the previous record.
Ctrl + + (plus)	Adds a new record.

Keys	Function
Ctrl + – (minus)	Deletes the current record.
Ctrl + R	Selects a form or report.
Ctrl + A	Selects all objects.
Ctrl + End	Moves the selection highlight to the last cell in your table (lower right corner).
Ctrl + Home	Moves the selection highlight to the beginning of the table.
Ctrl + Shift + End	Expands a selection to the last cell in a table (lower right corner).
Ctrl + Shift + Home	Expands a selection to the beginning of a table.
Pg Up	Moves the selection highlight one screen up.
Pg Dn	Moves the selection highlight one screen down.
Scroll Lock	Turns the scroll lock on or off.
Shift + Arrow key	Expands a selection by one cell.
Shift + Enter	Adds a control to a form or report in Design View.
Shift + Pg Up	Expands a selection one screen up.
Shift + Pg Dn	Expands a selection one screen down.
Shift + Spacebar	Selects the entire row.
Shift + Tab	Enters a cell entry and moves to the previous cell in the row.
Tab	Enters a cell entry and moves to the next cell in the row or range.

QUICK COMMAND REFERENCE

Following is a chart summarizing some of Access's most popular features. When invoking menu commands by mouse, simply click the item(s) (or point to it if the item opens a submenu). With the keyboard, press the *Alt* key and the underlined letter of the menu bar item and then the underlined letter of the menu item. Otherwise, perform the actions as indicated.

Note that certain commands are only available depending on the object you are working on.

Feature	Commands	Shortcut Keys
Bold	Bold toolbar button	*Ctrl + B*
Canceling		
Pull-down menu (menu bar)	Click outside of menu	*Alt* once or *Esc* twice
Back one menu level		
Undo Last Command	Click other menu item	*Esc*
	Edit, Undo	*Ctrl + Z*
Change Directories		
Default	*Tools, Options, General* tab, type the identity of the new directory (e.g., A:\), *OK*	
Current Session	*File, Open,* ▼ button of the *Look in* box, select desired drive/directory, Close button	*Ctrl + O* or *Alt + F, A, Alt + I,* select drive/ directory, *Alt + F4*
Charts		
Create a Chart	*Forms* or *Reports* object type button, *New* button, *Chart Wizard*	
Edit a Chart	Double-click *Chart* in Design View	
Columns		
Width	*Format, Column Width*	
Freezing	*Format, Freeze Columns*	
Unfreezing	*Format, Unfreeze All Columns*	

Feature	Commands	Shortcut Keys
Copy a Selection		
Copy to Clipboard	*Edit*, *Copy*	*Ctrl* + *C*
Paste to New Location	*Edit*, *Paste*	*Ctrl* + *V*
Edit Cell Data	Double-click cell	*F2*
Embedding a Selection (Object)	Select source range, *Edit*, *Copy*, move to destination, *Edit*, *Paste*	*Special*, *Paste*, *OK*
Enter Data into a Cell	Click desired cell, type data	Arrow keys to desired cell, type data, press ↵ to accept or *Esc* to cancel
Exit Access		
By menu bar	*File*, *Exit*	
By title bar	Close button	*Alt* + *F4*
By Access Program icon	Double-click Access program icon	
By control menu	Right-click title bar, *Close*	*Alt* + Spacebar
Forms		
Create	*Forms* object type button, *New*	
Edit	*View*, *Design View* or *Forms* object type button, the *Design* button	
Freezing/Unfreezing Columns	*Format*, *Freeze Columns* or *Unfreeze Columns*	
Italic	*Italic* toolbar button	*Ctrl* + *I*
Help		
Office Assistant	*Help*, Microsoft Access Help	*F1*
Access	*Contents and Index*	
Dialog box	? button on right end of title bar	
Launch Access	In Windows, *Start* button, *Programs*, *Microsoft Access* (or *Microsoft Office*, *Microsoft Access*)	
Move a Selection		
Move to Clipboard	*Edit*, *Cut*	*Ctrl* + *X*
Paste to New Location	*Edit*, *Paste*	*Ctrl* + *V*
Open File(s)	*File*, *Open*, type filename or select it from the list, *Open* button	*Ctrl* + *O*, type filename, ↵
Print		
Preview	*File*, or *View*, *Print Preview*	
To Paper	*File*, *Print*, select "Print what" options, "Page Range" options, and "Copies" options, *OK*	*Ctrl* + *P*, select "Print what" options, "Page Range" options, and "Copies" options, ↵
Print Options	*File*, *Page Setup*, *Margins* tab, or *Page* tab, or *Columns* tab	
Queries		
Create	*Queries* object type button, *New*	
Edit	*View*, *Design View*, or *Queries* object type button, the *Design* button	
Run Query	*Query*, *Run*	
Crosstab Query	*Query*, *Cross tab Query*	
Update Query	*Query*, *Update Query*	
Make Table Query	*Query*, *Make Table Query*	
Append Query	*Query*, *Append Query*	
Delete Query	*Query*, *Delete Query*	

Feature	Commands	Shortcut Keys
Save		
Database object	*File*, *Save* or *Save As*	*Ctrl* + *S* or *F12*
Spell Check	*Tools*, *Spelling*	*F7*
Select		
Cells	Drag across cells	
Chart or Graphic	Click the item	
Object		
Shortcut menu	Right-click the item	
Tables		
Create	*Tables* object type button, *New*	
Edit	*View*, *Design View*, or *Tables* object type button, *Design* view	
Underline	*Underline* toolbar button	*Ctrl* + *U*
Undo	*Edit*, *Undo*	*Ctrl* + *Z*

MOUSEKEYS

MouseKeys is a feature of the Accessibility Options that you can access through the Control Panel. It enables you to use the numeric keypad to invoke mouse actions such as clicking, right-clicking, double-clicking, and dragging and dropping. To use an Accessibility Option, the program must first be installed on your system. You can check this through the Windows Add/Remove Programs feature.

CHECKING FOR THE ACCESSIBILITY OPTIONS FEATURE

If the *Accessibility Options* icon appears in the Control Panel, then it has been installed on your system and is ready for use. To check:

1   **Click the *Start* button**   `Ctrl` + `Esc`
2   **Point to *Settings***
3   **Click *Control Panel***
4   **Examine the Control Panel window for the *Accessibility Options* icon**

   If the *Accessibility Options* icon does not appear and you have the Windows 95 CD-ROM (you must also have a CD-ROM drive) or setup disks, go to the "Installing Accessibility Options" section for installation procedures. If you want to turn on the *MouseKey* option, see the "Turning MouseKeys On and Off" section. To exit the Control Panel:

5   **Click the Control Panel's *Close* button**

INSTALLING ACCESSIBILITY OPTIONS

Install the Accessibility Options using the Add/Remove Programs dialog box.

1   **Click the *Start* button**   `Ctrl` + `Esc`
2   **Point to *Settings***
3   **Click *Control Panel***
4   **Double-click the *Add/Remove Programs* icon**

5   Click the *Windows Setup* tab
6   Click the *Accessibility Options* check box
7   Click the *Apply* button
8   Insert the Windows CD-ROM or appropriate disk as requested on the screen
9   Click the *OK* button

TURNING MOUSEKEYS ON AND OFF

The MouseKeys feature can be turned on or off using the Mouse tab of the Accessibility Properties dialog box. When the MouseKeys feature is on, you can use the numeric keypad to invoke mouse actions. To turn the MouseKeys feature on or off:

1   Click the *Start* button
2   Point to *Settings* for its submenu
3   Click *Control Panel* for its window
4   Double-click the *Accessibility Options* icon for its dialog box
5   Click the *Mouse* tab
6   Click the *Use MouseKeys* check box
7   Click the *OK* button to exit the dialog box
8   Click the *Close* button of the Control Panel window

Ctrl + **Esc**

When the MouseKeys feature is on, a mouse icon appears in the message area of the task bar. Double-clicking this icon will also open the Accessibility Properties dialog box.

FIGURE DBA-1 ■ MOUSEKEYS

(1) Pressing and holding the *Ctrl* key with these keys speeds up the pointer movement.

Pressing and holding *Shift* with these keys slows down the pointer movement.

(2) When on, pressing the *5* key invokes their action.

Mouse Icon Appearance	Operation	Numeric KeyPad Keys
	Horizontally, vertically (1)	←, →, ↑, ↓
	Diagonally (1)	*Home, End, Pg Up, Pg Dn*
	Click	*5*
	Double-click	*+*
	Switch to right-click (2)	*–, 5* or *+*
	Switch to both click (2)	**, 5* or *+*
	Switch back to normal (left) click	*/*
	Drag Turn on mouse button hold down	*Ins* (Do not hold)
	Drag Mouse (1)	←, →, ↑, ↓, *Home, End, Pg Up, Pg Dn*
	Turn off mouse button hold down	*Del* (Do not hold)

USING MOUSEKEYS

When the MouseKeys feature is on, the mouse pointer movements can be controlled by using the numeric keypad. See Figure DBA-1 for their operations.

TOOLBAR REFERENCE

Toolbar buttons provide quick access to Access's commands by mouse. Toolbar buttons are grouped in sets and may appear below the edit line of the Access window or in a floating toolbar window.

Some toolbars automatically appear when you invoke a related command. For example, the Forms toolbar appears when you are in Form Design View.

Access comes with a variety of preset toolbars, 21 of them are displayed in Figure DBA-2. These toolbars can be turned on or off using the Toolbars command of the View menu. You can also turn a toolbar on or off using its shortcut menu.

A toolbar can be moved by dragging its background or title bar. It can also be resized when not attached to the Access window. Toolbars in this state are called floating toolbars, and they have their own title bars and control boxes. To resize a floating toolbar, drag one of its walls or corners.

Existing toolbars can also be customized and new toolbars can be created. Use Access's online help to guide you through these operations.

The toolbar button numbers in the following table correspond to Figure DBA-2.

To use the numeric keypad for mouse actions, the MouseKeys feature and *Num Lock* must be on. When on, a Mouse icon appears in the message area of the taskbar. Double-clicking this icon opens the Accessibility Options Properties dialog box for adjusting or turning off the MouseKeys feature.

No.	Function	No.	Function
1	Align Left	24	Relationships
2	Align Right	25	New Object
3	Align Top	26	Microsoft Access Help
4	Align Bottom	27	Import
5	Size Height	28	Link Tables
6	Size Width	29	Database Window
7	Size Height/Width	30	View
8	More Buttons	31	Grid
9	New	32	Go To Field:
10	Open	33	Font
11	Save	34	Font Size
12	Print	35	Bold
13	Print Preview	36	Italic
14	Spelling	37	Underline
15	Cut	38	Fill/Back Color
16	Copy	39	Font/Fore Color
17	Paste	40	Line/Border Color
18	Format Painter	41	Special Effect
19	Can't Undo	42	Object
20	Office Links	43	Center
21	Analyze	44	Line/Border Width
22	Code	45	Style
23	Properties	46	Decrease Indent

No.	Function		No.	Function
47	Increase Indent		54	Multiple Pages
48	Numbering		55	Zoom:
49	Bullets		56	Close
50	Mail recipient		57	Query Type
51	Zoom		58	Top Values
52	One Page		59	Add Objects to SourceSafe
53	Two Pages		60	Get Latest Version

FIGURE DBA-2A ■ ACCESS TOOLBARS

Alignment and Sizing
1 2 3 4 5 6 7 8

Database
9 10 11 12 13 14 15 16 17 18 19 20 21 22 23 24 25 26 27 28 8

Fliter/Sort
12 13 14 15 16 17 18 19 29 25 26 8

Form Design
30 11 12 13 14 15 16 17 18 19 22 23 29 25 26 8

Form View
30 11 12 13 14 15 16 17 18 19 23 29 25 26 31 8

Formatting (Datasheet)
32 33 34 35 36 37 38 39 40 31 41 8

Formatting (Form/Report)
42 33 34 35 36 37 1 43 2 38 39 40 44 41 8

Formatting (Page)
45 33 34 35 36 37 1 43 2 46 47 48 49 38 39 40 44 41 8

Macro Design
11 12 13 14 15 16 17 18 19 29 25 26 8

Page Design
30 11 50 12 13 14 15 16 17 19 23 29 26 8

Page View
30 11 50 12 13 14 15 16 17 18 19 23 29 26 8

(continued)

FIGURE DBA-2B ■ ACCESS TOOLBARS, CONTINUED

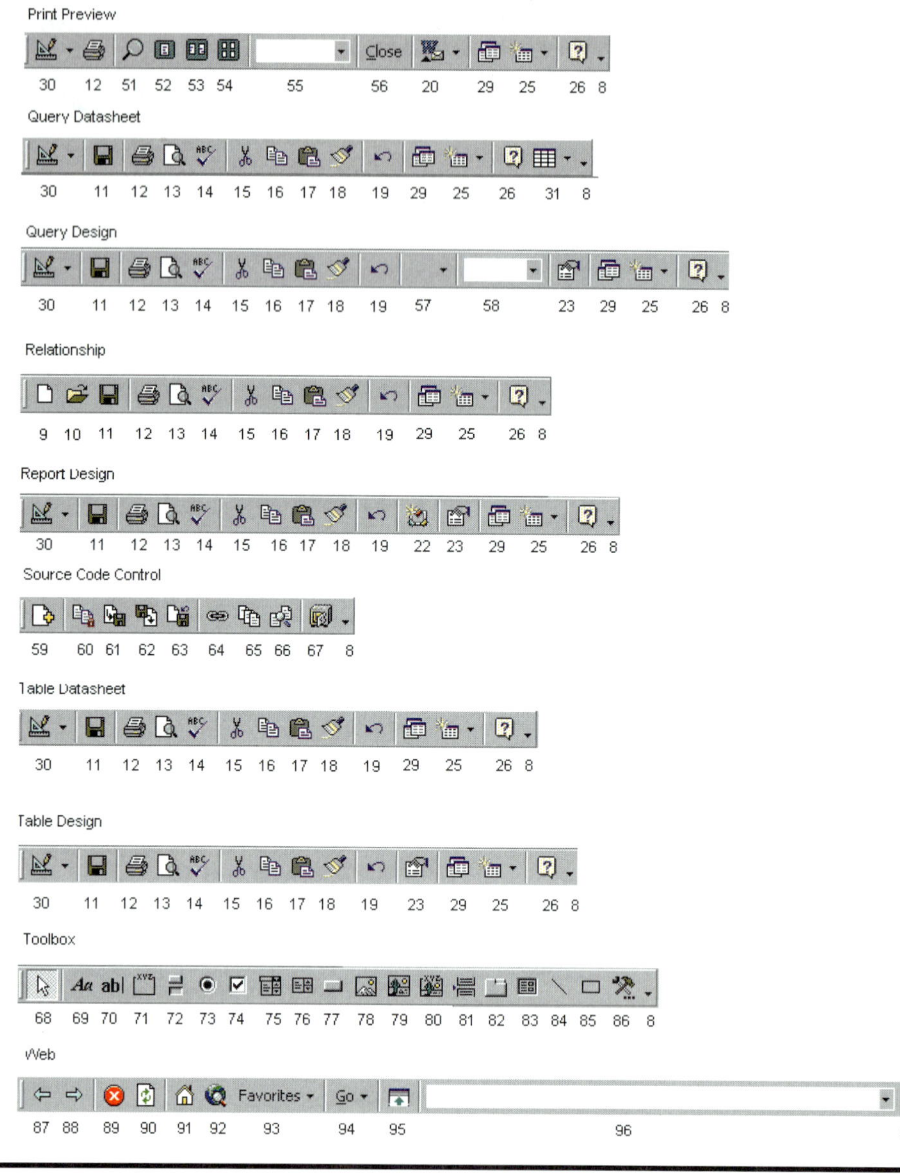

No.	Function	No.	Function
61	Check Out	69	Label
62	Check In	70	Text Box
63	Undo Check Out	71	Option Group
64	Share Objects	72	Toggle Button
65	Show History	73	Option Button
66	Show Differences	74	Check Box
67	Run SourceSafe	75	Combo List
68	Select Objects	76	List Box

No.	Function		No.	Function
77	Command Button		87	Back
78	Image		88	Forward
79	Unbound Object Frame		89	Stop Current Jump
80	Bound Object Frame		90	Refresh Current Page
81	Page Break		91	Start Page
82	Tab Control		92	Search the Web
83	Subform/Subreport		93	Favorites
84	Line		94	Go
85	Rectangle		95	Show Only Web Toolbar
86	More Controls		96	Address:

OTHER ACCESS FEATURES

The following features, listed in alphabetical order, are not covered in the Access mastery sets.

DATABASE UTILITIES

Compacting a database file defragments its contents to free disk space. Compacting should be done after tables have been deleted. To compact or repair a database:

1   **Click *Tools, Database Utilities, Compact and Repair Database***

An MDE file is one with all source codes removed. These codes are needed if you want to modify objects. MDE files also reduce a database file's size and, therefore, free disk space. To make an MDE file:

2   **Click *Tools, Database Utilities, Make MDE File***

OFFICE LINKS

To merge with Microsoft Word:

1   **Click *Tools, Office Links, Merge It with MS Word***

To publish it with Microsoft Word:

1   **Click *Tools, Office Links, Publish It with MS Word***

To analyze it with Microsoft Excel:

1   **Click *Tools, Office Links, Analyze It with MS Excel***

RELATIONSHIPS

To create relationships between objects:

1   **Click *Tools, Relationships***
2   **Click the desired tab, object, and then the *Add* button**
3   **Repeat Step 2 for each additional object**
4   **Click the *Close* button**

5   Drag and drop the desired fields to create relationships between common fields
6   Click the *Close* button of the dialog box

SECURITY

To assign a password to a database file:

1   Click *Tools, Security, Set Database Password*

To encrypt and decrypt a database:

1   Click *Tools, Security, Encrypt/Decrypt Database*

GLOSSARY

AND connector. An option for finding records that meet both of two specified conditions. (DB84)

ASCII. A standard format adopted by the computer industry for representing typed characters. ASCII is an acronym for American Standard Code for Information Interchange. (DB190)

Average command. The command that computes the arithmetic mean (average) of all numeric fields or expressions. (DB89)

Band. A section in a form or report. All objects in a section will print at the same time. (DB103)

Bound control. A control that displays field data such as a field object. (DB104)

Calculated control. A control that displays the result of a mathematical equation, for example, a summary statistic. (DB104)

Chart. An object that is a graphical representation of data. (DB173)

Close. To exit a window, file, or application program. (DB28)

Column chart. A chart that represents data in columns (bars) of differing heights or lengths to show the relationships among the data. (DB173)

Columnar Report. A report that lists fields vertically. (DB94)

Container file (compound document). The file receiving information in an OLE operation. (DB179)

Control. A graphical object in a report band, including text boxes, list boxes, check boxes, option buttons, command buttons, lines, and rectangles. (DB104)

Count command. An Access command that returns the total number of records or the total number of records that meet a specified condition. (DB89)

Criterion. A stated condition used in a query. (DB77)

Data. Essentially, facts; pieces of information. (DB2)

Data access pages. Web pages that allow you to edit and work with data from either an Access database, Microsoft Explorer (version 5 or later), or a Microsoft SQL Server database. (DB182)

Data Entry. An Access command that displays only a single record line in a table window for each new record entry. (DB36)

Data type. The attribute of a field or variable that determines what kind of data it can hold. (DB23)

Database. A collection of data or objects related to a particular topic or purpose. A database can contain tables, forms, reports, queries, and modules. (DB2)

Database management system (DBMS). A program that enables you to organize data so that they can be easily stored, accessed, modified, and maintained. (DB2)

Database window. The standard display of object names in a database file. (DB14)

Datasheet view. A column-and-row tabular display of a table. (DB30)

Default value option. The Access option that lets the program provide the value that will be used (as in a dialog box) if you do not change it. (DB27)

Design view. A window that shows the design of a query, form, report, or table. From Design view, you create new database objects or modify existing ones. (DB30)

Dynaset. A table-like data set produced by a query. Edits made to a dynaset are passed on to the underlying table. (DB76)

Embedding. The process of inserting an OLE object into another file. (DB179)

Exporting. An output technique that saves data in a format readable by other programs. (DB188)

Field. An individual element of data that contains one or more typewritten characters or images. (DB2)

Field name. A unique name of up to 64 characters assigned to identify a field. (DB23)

Field object. An object that displays field data. (DB104)

Field size. The maximum width in characters that a field can contain. (DB25)

Filtering. A feature that suppresses the display of all records except those you want to see. (DB73)

Find. The process of locating records that contain specified values. (DB43)

Form. An Access object that defines the way a record will be displayed on the screen. (DB15)

Freeze Columns. A feature that makes chosen columns appear along the left of a Datasheet view. (DB68)

Group. A band that prints every time the value in a specified field changes. (DB99)

HTML. HyperText Markup Language—the language in which most Web documents published (shared) on the World Wide Web are written. (DB182)

Importing. An input technique that retrieves data that has been saved in another format. (DB188)

Internet. A global interconnection of thousands of computer networks that enables millions of computers to communicate directly with one another. (DB182)

Key field. A field common to two tables and by which the tables are linked. (DB162)

Label object. An object that displays a title. (DB104)

Landscape. An option that prints an object horizontally across the paper. (DB99)

Linking. The process of connecting two or more tables by a common field. (DB179)

Literal string. A series of characters that always prints or displays without variation. (DB90)

Macros. Preprogrammed instructions used to automate an operation. (DB15)

Main form. The portion of a form that displays data from the master table of a set of linked tables. (DB162)

Many-to-one link. A technique for linking tables in which a group of main records are linked to one detail record. (DB170)

Mask. A pattern that controls the appearance of all data entered into a desired field. It is set in Table Design View. (DB63)

Module. A collection of instructions that are frequently used. A module may also be used to associate (connect) different objects. (DB15)

Natural order. The original order in which records were entered into a table. (DB72)

Object. Any collection of text, graphics, sound, or video that can be shared, via linking or embedding, with OLE; in Access, an object may be a table, form, report, or query. (DB14, DB179)

Office Assistant. An Access help resource that enables you to pose questions as sentences or keywords to obtain customized responses. (DB17)

OLE. An abbreviation for Object Linking and Embedding, a technique for transferring information from one program to another as an object. (DB179)

One-to-many link. A table-linking technique in which each main record is linked to a group of detail records. (DB164)

OR connector. An option for finding records that meet either of two specified conditions. (DB84)

Pie chart. A chart that displays data as parts of a whole circle, where each data "slice" corresponds to a percentage of the total. (DB178)

Portrait. An option that prints an object vertically on a piece of paper. (DB99)

Primary Key. A field (or set of fields) that uniquely identifies each record in a table. Assigning a primary key will rearrange records in that order. It also prevents you from entering records with duplicate primary key data. (DB24)

Print Preview. A feature that lets you see on the screen an object as it will appear when printed on paper. (DB47)

Properties. The features of an object that determine the way the object will behave in the Access environment. (DB22)

Query. A question that is asked of a table to select specific records or restrict field displays. (DB15, DB75)

Record. The portion of a table that contains information about an individual entity—a person, place, or thing. One record is represented in each horizontal row of a table or in each form. (DB2)

Replace. A command used to search for one string of data and replace it with a different string. (DB43)

Report. A display of data designed to be printed. (DB15, DB94)

Required. A field property that forces a user to enter data in that specific field in every record. (DB25)

Scrolling. Moving forward or backward in a table, from record to record. (DB39)

Selection handles. Small square boxes located along the border of a label, field, and calculated field object that enable you to change the size of the object. (DB104)

Server generated pages. Web pages that allows you to view only data from certain data sources. (DB182)

Shortcut icon. An icon that can be used to launch a program or open a file from a location different from its source. (DB128)

Shortcut keys. Keystrokes in combination with other keystrokes (usually *Ctrl, Alt,* or *Shift*) that perform a menu action. (DB6)

Shortcut menus. Context-sensitive menus that are available by pointing to a certain area of the Access screen and right-clicking. (DB9)

Sorting. Rearranging table records in a particular order, alphabetically or by some other criteria. (DB72)

Source file. The file in an OLE operation that holds the original information. (DB179)

Static HTML Pages. Web pages whose data do not change. (DB182)

Status bar. The horizontal bar at the bottom of the Access window that displays information about commands, tool bars, and other options. (DB9)

Subform. A form within a form that can display information from a different database on a main form. (DB162)

Sum command. An Access function that returns the numeric total of the selected numeric fields of all records or the numeric total of the selected numeric fields of records meeting a specified condition. (DB87)

Summary statistics. Totals for a desired column that are the result of a Sum, Average, and/or Count command. (DB87)

Tab order. The order in which you move to different fields within a table or form. (DB158)

Table. A two-dimensional representation of data in which rows represent records and columns represent fields. Also, a database document that stores data. (DB2)

Tabular Report. A report organized in the form of a column-and-row table. (DB94)

Text box. An object that can display a title (label object), field data (field object), or the result of a mathematical equation (calculated field object). (DB104)

Title bar. A window component, located at the top of the window, that identifies a program or document. (DB9)

Toolbar. A set of buttons that carry out common menu commands, usually found near the top of the Access window. (DB9)

Unbound control. A descriptive or decorative control, such as a label object, line, or rectangle. (DB104)

Undo. An Access command that reverses the last procedure you performed. (DB104)

Uniform (Universal) Resource Locator (URL). The unique address of each Web page in the World Wide Web. (DB187)

Validation rule. A field property that specifies a test that must be passed by data to be accepted in a specific field. (DB27)

Wildcard characters. Characters that can be used in both the Find and Replace dialog boxes to facilitate a search. Two common wildcard characters are the asterisk (*), which substitutes for any group of characters, and the question mark (?), which substitutes for any single character. (DB45)